How to Sell Anything on Yahoo!®...and Make a Fortune!

Build and Run a Successful Online Business with Yahoo!® Shopping

Skip McGrath
Dennis Prince

New York   Chicago   San Francisco   Lisbon
London   Madrid   Mexico City   Milan   New Delhi
San Juan   Seoul   Singapore   Sydney   Toronto

The McGraw·Hill Companies

McGraw-Hill books are available at special quantity discounts to use as premiums and sales promotions, or for use in corporate training programs. For more information, please write to the Director of Special Sales, Professional Publishing, McGraw-Hill, Two Penn Plaza, New York, NY 10121-2298. Or contact your local bookstore.

How to Sell Anything on Yahoo!® ... and Make a Fortune!
Build and Run a Successful Online Business with Yahoo!® Shopping

1234567890 DOC DOC 019876

ISBN-13:   978-0-07-226279-7
ISBN-10:   0-07-226279-6

Sponsoring Editor
Roger Stewart

Editorial Supervisor
Patty Mon

Project Manager
Vasundhara Sawhney

Acquisitions Coordinator
Agatha Kim

Copy Editor
Sally Engelfried

Proofreader
Raina Trivedi

Indexer
Perri Weinberg-Schenker

Production Supervisor
Jean Bodeaux

Composition
International Typesetting
and Composition

Illustration
International Typesetting
and Composition

Art Director, Cover
Jeff Weeks

Contents

Foreword

The way I see it, getting ahead isn't for everyone. In fact, in my journeys across the expanse of cyberspace, I've found plenty of folks who talk a lot about making big, fat fortunes but very few who actually do it.

"Idea people"—I've met thousands of them, online and off, and they're always ready to tell me the best way to get a deal, get ahead, and get into the fast lane. Funny thing, every time I loop the track, those "financial visionaries" are still idling in their same spot—*talking* treasure, standing still. It's too bad, really, since many of the ideas spouted are legitimate and much of the philosophy is well founded, so why don't they act upon it?

The Internet was made for visionaries and idea people, folks who have always been long on approach but short on self-funding. The Internet was actually *built* by this brand of innovator (not the government-funded types of 1969 but, rather, the inventors and investors of the late 1980s and early 1990s) and their efforts have been proven to be nothing short of revolutionary. Information sharing was their driving motivation, breaking down barriers of time and geographic boundary to deliver the "instantaneous experience" that rivaled the microwave oven (and *that* was fast cooking). The information was fast and freely flowing and, very soon thereafter, so was the cash.

In a veritable flash, the time-honored trading medium—the classified ad—was useful only for training a puppy, lining a birdcage, or wrapping fish. Trade journals likewise became nothing more than periodical fly swatters or ad-hoc craft mats. The Internet connected people—buyers and sellers—in a way never before imagined and never so quickly assimilated. From the very first "for sale" listing posted to the Usenet, early adopters found themselves set loose in a proverbial "brave new world."

You say you want a revolution?

As e-commerce became the newest buzzword among financial analysts and profit per-capita pundits, fledgling portals began to spring up like tender sprouts amid a freshly tilled landscape. With quirky names like *Amazon*, *AuctionWeb at eBay*, and *Webvan* (groceries online-really?), online pioneers hung their virtual shingles on the cyber-signposts and declared themselves "open for business." Although the Great Browser Wars threatened to hamstring the financial harvest that was prophesied to come, the masses made their way through the maelstrom and began to buy, buy, buy! Even when the American economy stumbled, sputtered, and limped along through the tail end of the 20th century, the Internet and its ever-expanding citizenry effectively and efficiently guided the nation through the choppy waters of financial peril.

Deliverance from a threatening Digital Depression, believe it or not, was prompted by online offerings such as desirable domain names, high-powered consultants for hire, and even a spare kidney. Sure, the Internet played host to the more eccentric among us, some who figured the whole venture was but a lark and fun should be had before this digital house of cards ultimately collapsed. But it didn't collapse—it stood strong and encouraged newcomers to build upon its undaunted foundation. It inspired inventiveness and the courage to offer the sorts of products or services that, at once, seemed far-fetched yet ultimately proved the economic truth that practically every offering has its motivated buyer—if only the two can meet. This is where you come in. The folks who built the modern-day Internet are folks just like you; people with vision, determination, and the stubborn drive to succeed. And how.

Just as you've seen folks strike it rich at eBay or harness the affiliate incomes offered at *Amazon*, *Google*, and elsewhere, so too have folks found opportunity to carve out their own fortunes in areas that were formerly known as merely information hubs. So when Yahoo climbed to the top of the information gathering and dispensing mountain and was practically on the tip of everyone's tongues, they determined they had the following that would propel them into a viable e-commerce contender. Though they had sought to unseat eBay's 300-pound auction gorilla (admirable attempt, but no), they later introduced a way for online entrepreneurs to *supplement* their eBay earnings by tapping the millions of regular Yahoo visitors, they who were becoming increasingly inclined to take a break from information mining in deference to stroll a virtual store or two (or more). Yahoo developed a platform whereby industrious folk could build their own online store and begin marketing their wares to the millions of passersby, they who frequented the Yahoo webspace. Today, we know this platform as Yahoo Merchant Solutions, a tool and a technology that, like the Internet itself, has been honed and refined to enable just about anyone to start up their own Web business. Anyone, that is, who's more than just a talker—someone who's a *doer* but not necessarily a rabid overachiever.

The beauty of Yahoo Merchant Solutions is they allow people like you and me the opportunity to experiment with merchandising, dabble in dealership, and explore the realm on online money making. So many of the "idea people" have proclaimed they have a great product to sell if only they could find a way to mass market it. They've found it and their earnings are bound only by their desire to learn and apply methods and techniques that now rest in your very hands.

And that's what this book is all about—applying knowledge, tools, and techniques that co-author Skip McGrath and I have acquired along the sometimes-winding road on online marketing and merchandising. We've pooled our collective experiences (over twenty years between us now) and wrote it all down here to straighten out some of the learning curves and provide you a straight path to success and fortune in the burgeoning realm of Yahoo Merchant Solutions.

Will you get rich quick? Probably not. Idea people blather on about "instant fortunes" and "buried treasures" ready to be tapped, but real-world riches are still made the old-fashioned way—through thoughtful design and well-applied principles. Skip and I have smoothed over the rough spots for you to provide you with more than just a "how to" schematic—this is an approach, practical, tactical, and ready to apply.

Here is your personal invitation to claim your fortune. Reach out and take it, unless you're satisfied listening to the endless litany of those idea people. No, I didn't think so.

—Dennis L. Prince

Acknowledgments

First of all, I would like to thank my agent, Marilyn Allen, who hooked me up with all the good folks at McGraw-Hill. They have all been a pleasure to work with. My editor Roger Stewart is patient and has a great sense of humor. Despite what some may think, writing a book can be stressful, and Roger has a way of helping an author relax while still working to a deadline.

Agatha Kim, who has since moved on to other things was a great help, and her able replacement, Carly Stapleton, has stepped in near the end to keep us all on track.

My project manager, Vasundhara Sawhney, at International Typesetting and Composition has worked diligently to catch my mistakes and improve the occasional tortured prose that slips into a manuscript when I'm not paying attention to what Brother Xavier taught me in 8th Grade English.

Patty Mon did a great job of managing the editorial flow, and Jeff Weeks was responsible for the exceptional cover design.

Finally, I want to thank my co-author Dennis Prince, who was a great collaborator, and is a respected author in his own right.

—Skip McGrath

Every new book is an adventure and, for me, the journey here has been invigorating and satisfying, to be sure. First, I thank my co-author Skip McGrath for the excellent collaboration and the expertise he readily brings to this topic. Not only does he possess a keen marketing mind but is also very well centered in his passion to help others become successful in their efforts. His impressive experience is well matched by his unfailing commitment to his readers.

Next, I want to thank Roger Stewart at McGraw-Hill. I've been fortunate to have delivered other titles to M-H, though this was my first opportunity to work with Roger. He is a consummate professional in his approach and style in guiding a project to completion. His attention to detail, complimented by his refreshingly affable demeanor, has made delivering this book a truly enjoyable experience. Thanks, Roger!

The other folks working at and with McGraw-Hill, including Agatha Kim, Carly Stapleton, Vasundhara Sawhney, and the rest are likewise a top-notch team who can faithfully deliver an excellent book.

Last, my thanks go to the online enthusiasts who have kept in continual contact with me in regards to the opportunities, challenges, and successes of taming the virtual marketplace. I appreciate your passion as well, I read every one of your letters, and I appreciate your enthusiasm that allows me to continue sharing my experiences in this way. There's so much more to achieve and I look forward to continually rubbing elbows with you all along the way.

—Dennis Prince

Introduction

Before you make a fortune, you have to start somewhere. That "somewhere" is typically located somewhere in between figuring out what product or service you have to sell and whether you sell it on Yahoo, eBay, your own web site, or at a retail store, a flea market—or any combination thereof. I have written this book for two categories of people—those who already own a business and would like to learn how to market it on the Internet and the average Jane or Joe who sees the potential of the Internet and would like to grab a piece of it.

If you are in the first group, you already have a product or service to sell and just need to figure out how to do it. But, you also have to determine if there is a market within the Internet for your particular product or service. As you will see that is not always an easy question to answer. The Internet graveyard is littered with the virtual bones of thousands of companies that had successful offline operations and failed when they attempted to take their successful business models online. Supermarket.com thought they could create a virtual supermarket online. After hundreds of millions of dollars in venture capital and $700 million raised in a public offering they went bankrupt. The problem wasn't their execution. They had is all, great web site, automated warehouses, delivery trucks and so on. The problem was that no one wanted to buy their groceries online. On the other hand in 1999, Tony Hsieh told his friends he was going to start selling shoes online. Everyone told him he was crazy. People have to try shoes on to buy. By the end of 1999 his sales were less than $50,000, but he thought he proved the concept. In 2005, his online shoe store, Zappos.com did over $370 million in sales and Tony is projecting over $600 million for the 2006 fiscal year. The point? You never really know if a new business model will be successful online, so it's better to test it on a small scale before committing a large amount of money.

If you are in the second group, you have the luxury of starting from scratch. Yes, this is truly a luxury; in fact it can be a significant advantage if you keep an open mind and throw out any preconceived ideas you might have of what will make a successful Internet-based business. You may already have a product and just need to test it or you may want to start an internet business and are trying to find something to sell. In this case you are going to have to do a fair amount of research to determine you product niche and then test it to see if it will succeed.

Whether you have a product to sell or even If you don't know yet what you are going to sell, we are going to cover research and market testing to show you how to make those choices and how to test your market without spending large sums of money.

Once you decide what you are going to sell online, you need a sales venue. It could be eBay, Overstock.com or one of the many other auction or shopping sites. Another way is to hire a webmaster and set up your own e-commerce web site. A third way to go—and one that is gaining in popularity with thousands of online entrepreneurs is using a template-based web site such as Yahoo Stores. Yahoo calls their offering Yahoo Small Business Merchant Solutions, but most people still call them Yahoo Stores and that is how I will refer to them in this book.

The great advantage of setting up a Yahoo Store is that you can set up and test your business ideas fairly inexpensively. You don't need to spend thousands of dollars on a web designer, and purchase shopping cart software and other utilities.

Yahoo Stores is an e-commerce enabled web site that uses template-based web site creation software to help you build your web store. What that means is that you don't need to know any special computer code (called HTML for Hyper Text Markup Language), or have any graphic design or programming skills. You don't need any special software to get started except for the SiteBuilder software download that Yahoo gives you for free when you sign up for their store.

When you set up a Yahoo Store, you start by picking from one of several hundred design and color combinations, create your text, set up an integrated shopping cart (you don't have to purchase separate shopping cart software), write your product descriptions and upload your product photos. Yes—there is a bit more too it than that, but it is not really that difficult and almost anyone with average computer user skills can figure it out. My neighbor's 16-year-old daughter set up a Yahoo Store to sell her handmade beaded jewelry. I know you think every 16-year-old is a computer genius, but this young lady really wasn't.

Yahoo Stores are used by thousands of web site entrepreneurs and even large businesses. The Kennedy Space Center uses Yahoo Stores to sell tour tickets and Service Merchandise uses a Yahoo Store to run their multi-million dollar a year Internet sales business. At the other end of the virtual mall are thousands of small mom and pop-sized operations that sell almost everything imaginable. Some of them are not so small any longer—literally many thousands of individuals have made fortunes on the Internet.

I don't know what you consider to be a fortune. If you are working as a retail store clerk making $20,000 a year and you find a way to make $50,000 a year on the Internet then that is probably a fortune to you. For others, they are looking for a way to make hundreds of thousands of dollars a year. It all depends on your point of view.

I have operated five different web sites and currently still run three of them. In my best year I sold almost $400,000 with online sales and my profit was almost half of that. Today one of my web stores grosses about $12,000 a month selling drop shipped products that I don't pay for until they are sold. The profits aren't that much—I average about 30%, but once I set up the store, I spend less than 2 hours a week on the business. It pretty much runs on autopilot. I have also started a couple of web businesses that failed. In a funny way I consider those failures my greatest successes. I learned so much from those failures; they practically guaranteed the success of my next ventures.

Lastly, before we get started I would like to tell you about an additional resource that comes with the purchase of this book. Whenever I read books about computers or the Internet they are always filled with dozens of links to various web sites related to the topics the author is covering. This book is no different. I find it is always a pain to be reading a book when maybe you are not next to your computer and have bookmark the page or write down the web address to check later. Also, webmasters are always changing their links. A link that works on the day I wrote about it may not be there a few months from now when you pick up this book. So I have created a special web page on my web site at www.skipmcgrath.com/yahoobook. If you go to this web page, I have listed live links to all of the resources listed in this book.

Creating a Successful Online Business

Setting up your Yahoo Store is the easy part. Creating a successful online business requires several crucial steps to succeed. First you need a product to sell for which there is a market on the web, a reliable source of supply where you can buy the product at a price where you can make a profit, a way to get visitors to your web site, and the ability to close the sale on your web site, collect the money, deliver the product and most importantly get the customer to come back to buy again.

Understanding this process and getting it right is critical to the success of your store. This section will cover these essential steps and the strategies for implementing them. Getting this part of the process right will save you time and headaches later and help insure your ultimate success…and pave the path to fortune.

Part I

Creating a Successful Web Business

By Skip McGrath

Chapter 1

Before Getting Started

Whenever I purchase a how-to book, I have a tendency to skip the first few chapters and get right into the meat of the subject and start working. If you currently own a successful offline business, or if you have previously owned an online business, some of this information may be redundant or about subjects you are already experienced in. Nevertheless, you may want to at least scan it anyway for some new ideas or things that you may have missed along the way. You could look at it as a sort of a business review—is there anything basic that you have overlooked that could help you succeed?

If this is your first attempt at setting up a business, I suggest you read this chapter very carefully. Lack of planning and ignoring the fundamentals has sunk thousands of what could have been successful businesses if they had just done the up-front planning and put systems in place to make them successful.

In the early days of the World Wide Web, people set up all kinds of websites and just started selling stuff to each other. It didn't take long, however, for big businesses to see what was going on and jump on the virtual bandwagon. The advent of large retailers changed the landscape forever. They created a presence with large amounts of money, supported by New York advertising agencies and the best web designers money could buy. They created a professional retail web experience that today's buyers expect and demand. Does this mean that you, the little guy or gal, cannot compete? No. It just means that you will have to create a standard of design, branding, and web experience that buyers have come to expect. Fortunately, the Yahoo Shops platform makes all of this very easy. By the same token, don't overlook how exasperated online surfers and shoppers have become with overworked and under-serving corporate sites. Sometimes, in this renewing cottage industry, the small guy can connect best with consumers, and readers should strive to strike a balance between the two camps.

Establishing Your Business

Once you figure out what business you are going to be in, you want to take the time to establish a licensed legitimate business and come up with a name that reflects your market or product category, inspires confidence, and lends itself to branding.

Naming Your Business

The best business names are those that reflect the industry you're in or the product category that you sell. If you sell designer sunglasses, business names such as Vision

Rays or The Sunglass Emporium are much more appropriate than, say, Internet Discount Sales or Stan's Online Marketplace.

You will also need to create a website URL for your business. When you are thinking up a name, give some thought to how it will look as a dot-com address. A shorter name makes for an easier-to-remember URL. VisionRays.com works much better than TheSunglassEmporium.com. It is shorter, easier to type correctly and, when you later append other pages to it, your URLs will not be excessively long. On the other hand, while the name VisionRays will be easy to associate with your product once someone visits your website, The Sunglass Emporium better describes what you sell if it comes up in the results when someone types "buy sunglasses online" into a search engine.

The best way to come up with a name for your business is with a combination of research and brainstorming. Start by performing web searches for websites that sell the same or similar product you plan to sell. These companies will most likely be your competitors anyway, so if you bookmark ("add to favorites" in your web browser application) these sites and put them in a folder named Competition, you can easily find them later when its time to research your competition. Once you have a list of names, sit down and write a list of at least 10 or 20 names that you can think of. Before you start narrowing down your choices, show both lists to your friends, family, or even better, other people who own businesses.

Now create a short list of the best names of your competitors and the best names on your list. The purpose of having the competitive names is not so much to think up something like theirs, but to give you an idea of what sort of names tend to resound with people. They are just there to help you with your brainstorming. Take the names on your list and type them into search engines and see what comes up. The first thing you want to be sure of is that no one else has the same or a closely similar name. Next, go to Yahoo's domain selection tool at **http://smallbusiness .yahoo.com** and type your business names into the search box shown in Figure 1-1. This will tell you if the name is already in use by another website or is available.

If, for example, you try the name VisionRays.com, you get a result that shows that the name is available (at the time I am writing this book). The results that come up will look like Figure 1-2.

Now, look at this checklist for each of the names on your list until you find a name that meets most or all of the following criteria:

- ◼ The name should describe or be easily associated with the type of products you plan to sell.

- ◼ The name should be easy to spell.

FIGURE 1-1   Yahoo Find a Domain search box

FIGURE 1-2   Yahoo domain search results for "VisionRays.com"

- In general, short names are better than long ones.

- The name is not already used by any companies in your industry and does not infringe on any trademarks (for example, if you are selling accessories for Nokia phones, you cannot call your company NokiaPlus.).

- The name is not easily confused with one of your competitors.

- The URL is available and not easily confused with others.

- A clever or "catchy" name is a plus, but only if it relates directly to your product or service.

By now you should have narrowed your choice down to less than three names, so it's just a matter of picking the one you like the best.

> **TIP** *Search engines respond better to hyphenated names if one of the words in your name is a product-related keyword. So Sunglass–Emporium.com is a more search engine–friendly than SunglassEmporium.com*

Business Licensing

There are two basic types of business licenses that are important to retail businesses: the local business license and a state business license (often called a state sales tax license) that allows you to purchase goods from wholesale suppliers without paying sales tax.

If you are starting a small online business out of the home, most communities do not require you to have a local business license unless your business involves customers coming to your location. If, however, you rent an office or warehouse space in a commercial area, then you will probably be required to get a local business license. In most communities, a general business license is very inexpensive, often as little as $25, but in some large cities, the cost can go as high as several hundred dollars.

The other type of license is your state business license or state sales tax number. If you are selling retail products on the Internet, you are required to collect sales tax on sales made to people in the state you are selling from or on goods shipped to your state. For example, I live in Washington state. When someone in Washington state buys something from my website, I have to charge and collect sales tax from them and pay the tax I collect to the state at the end of each quarter. But when I sell a product to someone outside Washington and ship the product there, then I neither collect nor pay sales tax.

The states have realized that they are losing millions of dollars in sales tax revenue to Internet businesses and are actively trying to get Congress to pass legislation to come up with a way to collect sales taxes on all Internet sales. So far all of the legislation and the pending bills exempt Internet businesses that gross less than $4 million a year; however, this could change. For the time being, err on the safe side and be sure to collect and remit sales taxes according to stated federal and local rules.

Another reason you need a sales tax number is that most wholesale companies will not sell to you without one and, if they do, they will charge you sales tax on the goods that you cannot recover from your customers if you don't have a sales tax license. Once you get a sales tax license, you will be assigned a sales tax number. You will have to furnish this number to any company you buy from to avoid paying the tax. A lot of companies simply print this number on their letterhead and or purchase order forms they use when buying product.

There is a third type of number you might need. It's not really a license, but I will cover it here anyway. If you hire an employee or if you incorporate or form a partnership, then you will need an Employer Identification Number (EIN) from the IRS. You use this number in place of your social security number when you file your business taxes, and you must furnish this number to companies that pay you money for any services you perform. For example, I sell advertising banner space on my website. The companies that pay me for that space need my EIN number in order to pay me and issue me an IRS 1099 form (Miscellaneous Income Form) at the end of the year. You can obtain an EIN immediately by calling the Business and Specialty Tax Line, 800-829-4933. The hours of operation are 7:00 A.M. to 10:00 P.M. Eastern Standard Time, Monday through Friday. An agent will take your information and assign the EIN right over the phone. You will then receive a hard copy by snail mail within a few weeks, but you can start using your EIN right away.

Business Types

If you already own a retail store and you are just now taking your business online, you have more than likely already completed the steps in this section. But if this is your first venture, you will want to decide what type of business formation you want to use. This decision affects how you file your taxes, how others in the business community see you, and how you treat your business liability.

The most basic form of business is called the sole proprietorship. This is where you or you and your spouse own your business outright and are completely responsible for all aspects of it. If you form a sole proprietorship, you simply keep separate records of your business income and expenses and file an IRS form called a Schedule C, Profit or Loss from Business, with your personal income taxes each year. Any profits from your business are added to your other taxable income and any losses may be deducted.

Sole proprietorship is the simplest form of business, but it is also the most risky. When you do business as a sole proprietor, you are completely at risk for all aspects of the business including liability. If you are sued as a result of your business activity, your automotive or homeowner's liability policy will most likely not cover you. This puts all of your personal assets (equity in your home, savings, future income, and so on) at risk.

The other two forms of doing business are the partnership and the corporation. Partnerships are most often used for professional service businesses such as doctors, law firms, and other professional services such as accounting firms and investment bankers. Most small businesses opt for a corporation. They are easy to set up and have many advantages. If you are truly always going to be a very small business—essentially a "hobby business," earning less than $1,500 a month—and you are not worried about the liability aspect, you are probably fine operating as a sole proprietorship. But if you are serious about growing a money-making online business you can live on, they you will want to consider incorporating.

"Oh, come on—I am just a small seller," you think. "Why would I want to incorporate? Doesn't that cost a lot of money and take a lot of work?" Let me try and answer those questions.

There are three reasons to incorporate:

- Image

- Liability

- Tax considerations

    - **Image**   Many large wholesale companies don't want to work with small resellers. If you are trying to get into wholesale trade shows and merchandise marts, being incorporated makes this much easier. Incorporating is actually very simple and inexpensive (I will cover that next), but many people don't realize this and tend to think of any company that is incorporated as a larger legitimate company.

    - **Liability**   We live in a country where lawsuit-hungry lawyers are out of control. One of the richest areas for lawsuits is product liability. If you sell a product that injures someone, you can be liable. You can buy product liability insurance, but you would probably have to take out a second mortgage on your home to afford it. Incorporating offers you protection from most forms of liability.

When you do business as a corporation you are considered a separate "person" under the law. If you sell a toy from your website and some child chokes on it, the victim's lawyer may try to sue you. If you are a sole proprietor and they win the lawsuit, they could attach your salary or other income, your investment accounts, and/or the equity in your home. But if a corporation sells the same item on the web, the victim/plaintiff can only sue the corporation. If they win, they can only attach the assets of the corporation. It is slightly more complicated than this, but the principal is sound, and it is one of the best reasons for incorporating.

■ **Tax considerations**   A corporation doesn't afford the ability to dodge taxes, but you can realize more tax breaks under the corporate umbrella than you can as a sole proprietor. I have been incorporated for the past four years, and each year I see many more tax savings than when I was a sole proprietor. If your online business is not your full-time job and you work or have another income, the corporation can even help reduce the taxes you pay on your other income in many cases.

If you incorporate you should hire a Certified Public Accountant (CPA) to advise you and prepare your corporate tax returns. Some people think hiring a CPA is expensive, but my view is that it can be far more expensive not to hire one. My CPA, who is a CPA, tax attorney, and former IRS district manager, charges $400 a year to do my corporate tax returns, but his skill combined with my corporate organization saves me several times that amount every year in taxes.

How about those other questions I asked at the beginning? Doesn't it cost a lot and take a lot of work? There are dozens of companies on the Internet offering online incorporation, some of them for as low as $99 plus the state filing fees. But you want to be careful. Take it from me and my personal experience: you don't want a catch-all boilerplate corporation. After some diligent searching, I found an excellent company that offers a combination of online and offline service. The company is Click & Inc. (**www.clickandinc.com**), and they sell an online package combined with personal, one-on-one service through e-mail and the telephone that will tailor a corporate package for your individual situation and for the state you live in, or the one you may wish to incorporate in. Their website contains a wealth of information, explaining the types of corporations, advantages and disadvantages of incorporating in different states, tax considerations, and much more. Some other well-known online incorporating sites include My Corporation (**www.mycorporation.com**) and The Company Corporation at **www.corporate.com**.

Establishing Your Company Image

Once you start your business, you will need to correspond and communicate with vendors, suppliers, customers, and others. If you want to be taken seriously, you will want to take the time to design a logo and print business cards, letterheads, and some standard business forms. As I mentioned before, you want vendors and suppliers to take you seriously and, depending upon what you sell, you may need to gain access to wholesale trade shows, merchandise marts, and design centers. These wholesale-to-the-trade-only venues are very strict about who they admit and go to great lengths to keep out the general public. Most of them will demand a business card and a copy of your business license or sales tax number as a minimum. In many cases they will also want to see copies of a checkbook in your commercial business name, printed purchase orders; once I was even asked to show them a photograph of my store (I talked my way past that one).

You can hire a designer to create a logo, business cards and letterhead, but there is an easier and less expensive way. One of the most well-known online logo design services is LogoYes at **www.logoyes.com** (see Figure 1-3). This website lets you design your own logo from a selection of hundreds of images, fonts, and type styles. You point, drag, and click until you get a logo you like, and you don't pay a dime until you do. Once you have the logo you want, you pay the $99 fee. This gets you a logo and 500 business cards to start you off.

If you want someone to do all the design work for you, you will pay a little more. There are several popular web-based services such as OnlineLogoDesign at **www.onlinelogodesign.com** and Logo Design Pros at **www.logodesignpros.com**. As of this writing, these firms charge in the $200 range for a complete logo design service, and they both offer a guarantee that they will keep working on your logo until you are happy. I have seen logo design firms offering services for as little as $50. You can find them if you do a Yahoo Search on the term *logo design*. But be careful, as this is one area where you get what you pay for.

Once you have a logo, take it to a quick-print shop such as Kinko's, and they will help you create letterhead, envelopes, and other forms in just a few minutes. To save money on forms such as invoices and purchase orders, you can buy the preprinted blank forms at an office supply store and have a rubber stamp made with your logo and name and address. Then you can just use the rubber stamp on the forms when you need them.

In Chapter 13 on designing your Yahoo Store, I am going to spend a lot of time talking about branding and the look and feel of your website. As you design your logo, give some thought to this and make sure your logo lends itself to a website design. Once again, the best way to find guidance is to look at other websites and

FIGURE 1-3   LogoYes website

note the ones your admire. Your logo should appear friendly and inviting if it is going to work on your site. Any images you incorporate into your logo should symbolize or suggest to a viewer the nature of your business.

Keeping Good Records

This may at first seem like another one of those obvious but boring subjects that is coming between you and getting started building your web store, but keeping good records—especially financial records—is crucial to the success of your business. This will become evident when we discuss business metrics.

I strongly suggest you invest in accounting and bookkeeping software. Although there are several programs available, QuickBooks has now become the industry standard for small-business bookkeeping software. Most of the merchant credit card companies, shopping cart programs, and other payment systems are set up to allow downloads into QuickBooks. The program is easy to learn, or even if you hire a bookkeeper, almost every small business CPA firm and bookkeeping service today is set up to work with QuickBooks. Spending a couple of hundred dollars on QuickBooks will actually save you money in several ways. First of all it will save you time—and time is money when you can spend it doing creative work that brings in sales and profits instead of manually keeping financial records. Second, you can link your business bank account, check writing, and even a debit card to QuickBooks so that every time you spend money it is a simple matter to allocate it to the correct expense account. The ability of QuickBooks to keep these records and print out reports will save you money when its time to do your quarterly and year-end taxes. The recordkeeping it provides will also help you out if the IRS ever audits you, saving you potentially dozens of hours reconstructing expenses and deductions. Also, remember that any money you spend on bookkeeping or any type of business or productivity software is a business expense that reduces your taxable income—and therefore your taxes.

TIP   *People new to starting and running a business often get confused over the terms "business expense" and "tax deduction." A business expense is money you spend to start and run your business other than the purchase of inventory. This includes expenses such as travel, advertising, monthly ISP fees, purchasing office supplies, software, postage, and so on. At the end of the year you calculate your gross income minus your expenses. This gives you your adjusted gross income, which is the amount you will put on your tax form as your business income. Deductions are amounts the IRS allows you to subtract from your adjusted gross income such as dependent deductions, home mortgage interest, and charitable contributions.*

Business Telephone and Fax

If you are running a business out of the home, you will want a separate business telephone that you can answer in the business name and use a businesslike voice mail recording. A lot of business owners today simply use a cell phone for their business rather than running a second line into their home. There is one problem with this, however, as some of the merchant credit card companies require you to have a hard-wired telephone number and list it in the directory.

If you don't want to actually run a second line into your home, an alternative is *distinctive-ring* telephone service. If you call your phone company, you can order a second telephone number that will actually ring on your home line, except it will ring with a completely different sound so you can recognize it as a business call. This way you can always answer in your business name when you hear the special ring, and you can train your children not to answer it. You can put voice mail on the line with a business message and you can list the number under your business name in your local directory. This service costs far less than installing a second telephone line. My phone company charges $29 month for a regular phone line, but a distinctive-ring line is only $6.99.

Finally, you will need a fax. Many wholesale companies will only send wholesale pricing out by fax, and many still require you to fax your sales tax certificate on letterhead before giving you wholesale prices. I still deal with two companies that require a signed purchase order form with each order, and faxing is much faster than mailing. And, while we're saving money to feather the fortune nest, why not mention PC-based fax software such as Symantec's WinFaxPro or eFax to eliminate the need for another piece of office equipment to clutter up the work area?

As I said at the beginning of this chapter, these steps may seem a little elementary, and you may be tempted to skip them and get right to designing your web store. But I assure you that taking the small amount of time it takes to accomplish each of these organizational tasks will pay huge dividends in the near future of your business. And, if you're already busily managing your retail store, why not take this as an opportunity to revisit your business setup and efficiency and see if there are ways to bring your business up to date?

Chapter 2

Elements of a Profitable Web-Based Business

Before you jump into designing your store, you need to understand the elements of a successful and profitable web-based business so you can implement them as you go through the various steps of setting up your business. I am going to cover each of these elements in great detail in later chapters, but you need to understand the chronological steps to set up your business before you start, so you can perform the necessary market research and take certain actions before actually setting up your store.

As I mentioned in the introduction, I have owned several offline retail businesses and five different web-based enterprises. I have experienced both failure and success. I assure you that understanding these concepts will greatly increase your chances of overall success and help you make money faster than if you stumble along using trial and error, as many Internet entrepreneurs do every day.

I call these steps my success formula. If I were starting a new web business today, I would go though every one of these, one at a time, even though I have done it before.

Finding Your Niche

You may already have a product to sell, but do you know if you can sell that product successfully on the Internet? If you want to sell a product that many others are already selling, such as baby clothes or digital cameras, it's easy to answer the question, "Can my product sell on the Internet?" But the bigger more important question is can *you* sell it on the Internet? Do you have the resources and capital to compete with these mega-sellers? Can you purchase your products in large enough quantity that you can still realize adequate margins in a highly competitive field? Or, have you discovered a chink in the armor of the big guys that you can exploit?

If you sell baby clothes, can you—or do you really want to—compete with Sears or Baby Gap? If you want to sell digital cameras, do you or could you compete with Best Buy or Ritz Camera? If you already own a large successful retail company, the answer could be yes, but if you bought this book because you are a small retailer who wants to expand to the Internet or someone like myself when I started—a guy looking for a way to make some money without having to invest thousands of dollars in a brick and mortar store—then you really need to asses what product you are going to sell and how you can approach it differently than many others are already doing. This is usually referred to as finding a market niche that you can exploit.

A market niche can be many things. It can be a totally new product, a product with a small but loyal following, a new way of marketing an existing product, or even selling products that everyone else is selling but selling them in large quantities or at extreme discounts. Sometimes a niche is nothing more than selling something everyone else is selling but convincing customers you offer something extra that others don't. For example, you could sell laptop computers but preload and test all of the software and offer each buyer one-hour of free telephone support with each sale. That is something the large discounters cannot afford to do, and it would allow you to charge a higher price.

The competition on the web is so extensive and fierce today that, unless you find a niche that you can exploit, you will have a very difficult time succeeding. Indeed, finding the right niche is not only crucial to your success, but is the key to making a large fortune on the Internet. The best news, though, is that finding a niche is well within your reach.

Getting Visitors to Your Site

Real estate people and retail store owners are fond of saying there are three secrets to success: Location, location, location. In brick and mortar retail, you have to locate your store where customers can find you. The web is totally different. Everyone is located in the same shopping center, but the shopping center is so huge that you need to help customers find your site. Unlike a shopping mall where people can walk along and browse in store windows and see many stores selling different products, the Internet has no real way to browse, traditionally speaking. Instead, people find you through one of four ways: searching, advertising, a referral, or they have been there before and remembered and bookmarked your site and come back.

I am going to cover all of these methods in subsequent chapters, and many of the techniques covered in various parts of this book will touch on the various ways to get visitors to your site. But, it is enough to remember for now, that unless you *get the eyeballs*, a marketing term that means exposing visitors to your site, you will never sell a thing. The chances of someone just stumbling into your Yahoo Store by accident are about as likely as your getting hit by a meteorite while you are having your morning coffee.

Making the Sale

Getting the eyeballs is crucial to your success, but you also have to make the sale once you get the visitor to your site. If you can't get the visitors to your site you will not have a chance to make the sale. Hundreds of companies raised millions of dollars in the public market during the late 1990s and spent the money on print and TV advertising to attract visitors to their websites. The problem was, once the visitors got there they couldn't make the sale. In some cases the market just wasn't interested in what they had to sell. In others the business model was so flawed, the more they advertised the more they sold, but they were losing money on each sale. I actually heard one Internet CEO interviewed on TV say, "We are losing money now on each sale, but we expect to make it up on volume."

That kind of thinking led to the infamous Internet stock bubble during which hundreds of thousands of investors lost their savings on companies like Pets.com, Drugstore.com, and others. One company, Musicmaker.com, went public when its annual revenues were only $75,000. Its market value after the public offering in 1999 was $700 million. One year later, its revenues were still under $1 million a year. Six months a later Musicmaker.com was bankrupt.

I am going to cover several methods of getting the visitors to your site as we go through the following chapters, but once you get them there you have to make the sale. To do this, you first need a product or a service that people want. Then you have to convince them that they should buy it from you, and they have to implicitly trust that you will deliver the product if they decide to buy. These sound like simple steps, but implementing them is harder than it sounds. Still, if you follow the flow and guidelines laid out here, you'll be able to attract more visitors and make more sales than if you took a less structured approach.

Getting Paid

In the early days of the Internet, an amazing number of companies sold products by asking customers to send in checks and money orders. Indeed, in its first two years, eBay, the web's most successful auction site, did almost 80 percent of its business by offline payment such as cash, check, or money order, and by the fourth year buyers and sellers were still doing over 25 percent of their business with these methods. However, as the Internet matured, buyers demanded the ability to pay by credit card. You will need the ability to accept credit cards, but there are now many ways to do that, each with their pros and cons. Also, the choice you make will impact the ability to execute the next strategy, up-selling and cross-selling.

Up-selling and Cross-Selling

Up-selling and *cross-selling* mean essentially the same thing. These terms refer to convincing a customer to increase the size of their order or add another product to their order at the time of the sale. You got the customer to the site, exposed them to a product they like or want, convinced them you are a trustworthy supplier, and they have already decided to purchase. This is the perfect time to increase the average selling price of your orders by adding to the sale. This is an extremely profitable strategy, yet I view dozens of websites every month that fail to take the simple steps to do this.

Delivering the Product

You've made the sale and now you have to deliver the product. Delivery is more than simply putting an item into a box and taking it to the post office or the UPS store. Shipping, handling, and insurance is a major cost center and a potential profit center for any online business. How you design and communicate your shipping policies, the choice of shipper and shipping options, and how you price your shipping all factor into closing the sale, preventing shopping cart abandonment rates, and controlling your costs. Getting this right can often be the difference between success and failure.

Customer Service

Unlike a retail store, when you sell on the web you never get to greet your customers face-to-face. Taking the time and effort to personalize your customer's buying experience and going the extra mile to follow up on your sales will reduce returns and charge-backs and pay long term dividends in referrals and repeat business.

Bringing Them Back for More

The initial advertising and promotional cost to capture a customer is a major cost center for any business, online or offline. The easiest way to reduce this cost is to provide such a great experience the first time that your customers come back time after time. It is much easier and less expensive to attract repeat customers than to find new ones. According to WebTrends, only 11 percent of Internet retail buyers return to the same website to make an additional purchase within 12 months of the initial sale. Learning the techniques to increase that percentage is a gourmet recipe for profits.

The following chapters in Part I will explore each of these topics in detail. As you design your store, you will have to make decisions based on this information. Once you have completed this section, I suggest you sit down and map out a plan for your web store before you jump into the design.

Chapter 3

How Competition, Supply, and Demand Affect Your Business

I remember studying supply and demand theory in Economics 101 at UCLA. When the teaching assistant took to the stage in the auditorium and put the supply and demand curve up on the board and explained it, I thought to myself: "It's a good thing I am going to school on the GI Bill. I would hate to be spending my own money for this."

To me the law of supply and demand was obvious. "The less the supply of something and the more demand for it, the higher the price someone would pay for it. When there was plenty of supply of a certain product, the prices tended to fall." I understood the law intuitively. It was so obvious, I didn't understand why they taught it in college.

I had learned the law of supply and demand by experience the previous summer. I was lying on the beach and realized I had forgotten my sunblock. Not wanting to get burned I walked over a mile from my spot on the beach to a stall on the boardwalk where I bought a tube of overpriced sunblock. It only took a moment to realize that other people lying on the beach might pay even more if they didn't have to walk a mile.

As a young college kid I didn't have any wholesale connections. So the next day I went to a discount drug store and bought 25 tubes of the cheapest sunblock I could find. I walked up and down the beach hawking my sunblock for three times the price I had paid. I sold all 25 tubes within two hours and made over $60.

I made over $3,000 that summer working a couple of hours a day hawking sunblock on the Santa Monica Beach.

This simple, easy-to-understand concept is easily evidenced on the Internet today. You can see it in action 24 hours a day. Goods sell at a price that reflects the available supply and the corresponding demand at a specific moment in time. Why is the "time" issue important? This has to do with the supply of a specific item at that very moment.

When a person types in a product name in a search engine such as Yahoo or Google, they are presented with hundreds or even thousands of pages along with sponsored search listing and advertisements. Many of these links are shopping services or comparison search engines. So if someone is searching for a specific model of digital camera, for example, the popular Nikon D-70, they will be presented with thousands of choices and often find a comparison site such as NextTag as shown in Figure 3-1. If you look at the results it states that NextTag found 13 matches. If you look at the matches, each one lists between 3 and 16 different sellers. Doing the math, that means there are somewhere between 100 and 200 different web sites selling this model of camera. If you look at the prices, you can also see quite a large price range. What do you think the chances

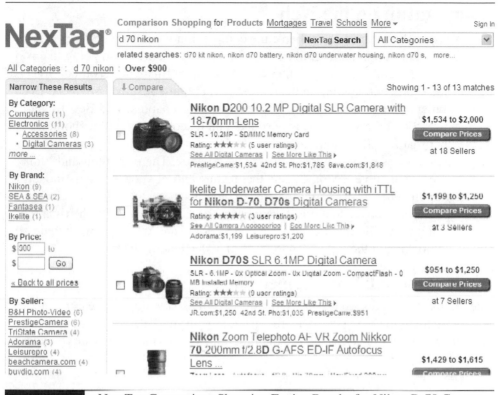

FIGURE 3-1 NextTag Comparison Shopping Engine Results for Nikon D 70 Camera

are of someone clicking on the results for those sites with the higher prices? Probably not that great.

The theory of supply and demand assumes that markets are perfectly competitive. This implies there are many buyers and sellers in the market and none of them have the capacity to influence the price of a product. In many real-life transactions, the assumption fails because some individual buyers or sellers or groups of buyers or sellers do have enough ability to influence prices. But the Internet is one of those "perfectively competitive" markets. In fact, the Internet is probably the single most efficient market in succeeding on the Internet. This does not mean you cannot succeed selling goods at higher prices –you can. The point here is that you need to be aware of the supply/demand situation and factor it into your planning.

Competition on the Web

The example above shows how fierce the competition is on the web for popular products such as a popular digital camera. In the next chapter I am going to cover the concept of niche marketing. Unless you have large financial resources you can pretty much forget competing in the market for popular consumer products. Even mega retailers such as Wal-Mart, Costco, Service Merchandise and Best Buy are selling directly on the web. This may sound a bit discouraging, but it shouldn't be. Remember that for all its iniquitousness, the Internet is still pretty young –about where aviation was when Lindberg crossed the Atlantic. There are thousands of new web sites cropping up every day, many that feature entirely new business models and new approaches to marketing. There are thousands and thousands of products and markets yet to be exploited just waiting for the right person with the right idea to come along. But figuring out where you want to go and what you want to do all starts with looking at the virtual landscape and understanding it.

How to Research Your Competition

The easiest way to research your competition is to use the popular search engines and product comparison sites that are related to your market. If you are going to open an Internet business, one of the first things you should do is survey your competition.

What should you be looking for:

- How much competition is there for your product?

- How many web sites are selling it? What are the competitive price points for the product you want to sell?

- How are others selling the products your wish to sell –are they bundling them with other products and selling them in kits or sets (Camera, tripod, flash, case, etc.).

- Are your competitors offering free shipping or service plans?

- Are they customizing or personalizing the product in some way?

This last method is how Michael Dell made his fortune and built one of the largest companies in the world. He was the first to offer computer buyers the Burger King model –have it your way.

If you are researching a consumer product I would first try the general search engines. Next go to the popular shopping sites such as shopping.com, nexttag.com, shop.com, ebay.express.com, and shopzilla.com. If you product is so specialized or an industrial product you can also try eBay's powerful search engine. Millions of specialty products and used products sell on eBay. Once you find an auction with a product you are looking for, click on the link in the auction that say "About Me" after the seller's username. This will take you to the seller's About Me page where sellers can often put links to their web sites.

One very useful tool for shopping the competition is the Market Research Wizard from www.worldwidebrands.com. This is a tool that searches both the Internet and eBay in one search. It is a little pricy at $97, but it gives you a tremendous amount of information including:

- How much demand there is on the Net for that product?

- How much competition you will be up against?

- What kind of advertising others are using to sell that product?

- Who your competitors are.

- How much they pay for advertising.

- eBay auction listings and bids for your product.

- The keywords your competitors are using.

To summarize, before you buy a lot of product with hopes of reselling it on the Internet and taking the time and expense to open a store, follow these three steps:

1. Determine if there is any demand for the product you want to sell.

2. Research the supply and demand situation to make sure you are not entering an impossibly crowded market.

3. Research your competition to determine the best way to sell your product.

Chapter 4

Niche Marketing for Success

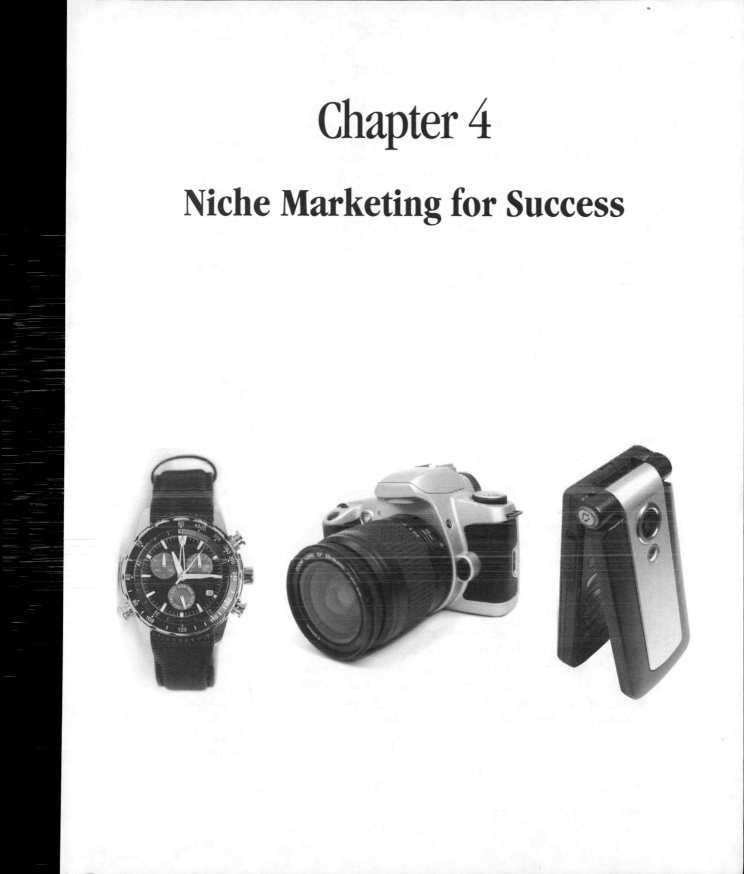

Selling to niche markets essentially means offering a highly specialized product. For instance, I have a friend who lives in Maine who started a business called Lobster Pot Direct (**www.lobsterpotdirect.com**) where he sells complete live lobster dinners delivered to your door. Other companies were already doing this, but he noticed that none of them were selling on eBay. He created a niche on eBay to capture the customers. Once captured, he directed them to his website (a Yahoo Store), where he marketed directly to them for repeat business.

Printer ink cartridges are a large seller on the web because almost everyone who owns a computer has a printer. Ink cartridges have become very competitive, but another friend of mine started one of the first websites selling the kits to refill your own cartridges. These are both examples of highly specialized product categories that qualify as a niche.

A niche can also be a way of selling. Millions of children's books are sold on the web each year on Amazon, Abebooks, eBay, and other large shopping sites. But several people have carved out a niche selling personalized children's books that you can order with your child's name woven into the story. The newest thing is books for which you send the seller a digital photo of your child and they even incorporate the image into the story.

Some sellers have found a way to sell highly competitive products by bundling them with other products and services. Others sell popular and highly competitive products, but they aim their products at a niche market where they have some special expertise. I do this myself. I have a website at **www.ezauctiontools.com** where I sell digital photography tools and information, but I target sellers who need to take product photographs for their websites and online auctions. Although I am selling products they could get from dozens of other websites, many of them run by large companies, I offer tons of free how-to information, product reviews, recommendations and advice. The site is quite successful because I target people with a specific interest.

One of my consulting customers explained that she has a fantastic overseas wholesale source for beads and bead-making supplies. But, even though her prices were very competitive, she wasn't getting much business.

When I looked at her website I saw that she was already getting pretty good traffic, but the site was nothing more than a big shopping cart full of thousands of products. I asked if she personally knew much about using beads to make jewelry and other products, and she said she did. I advised her to create a lot of free content, advice, instructions, links to other interesting websites, and photos of great things people had made from her beads. I even suggested she put up a photo album where her customers could display the things they had made.

It took her about two weeks to research and write the content and upload it. Within just a few days of adding the content her sales tripled. Within a few weeks, the search engines were indexing her content, and many new customers started finding her website. By the end of six months, her sales had grown from less than $1,000 a month to over $20,000 a month. And remember the photo album? Well, she expanded on that idea and let her customers list the products on her website for sale—she takes a 20 percent commission. Besides selling thousands of dollars worth of her own product, she now sells completed pieces of jewelry on consignment, which is highly profitable because there is no inventory cost.

You could say that selling beads is a niche and you would be right, but there are thousands of websites selling beads and beading supplies. What made her business a niche was providing the how-to information.

I have been selling a line of midpriced fire pit barbeque grills on eBay for the past year. This has been a very nice niche for me because I can up-sell the fitted covers, wood chips, recipes, and other related garden products. When we get to the next part and set up our Yahoo Shop, I am going to use these products to create my store.

Selling in an area where you have expertise is a vast differentiator on the web. People prefer to buy from other people who are knowledgeable, and they appreciate it when you share that knowledge with them. This brings us to another subject: developing a niche that just sells information.

People are hungry for information and have proven over and over that they will pay for it. When you mention selling information on the web, most people automatically think of all the books and CDs that sell get-rich-quick information. That is certainly a stable of information sales, but many people today are discovering that people will pay for all kinds of information. One entrepreneur assembled the top 100 most popular quotes from the Bible, put them into an e-book, and sold thousands of copies at $10 a copy. Other people create information-rich websites on topics such as buying a home or car or getting a mortgage. They provide tons of valuable free information and make their money from affiliate commission programs or companies advertising on their site.

Chapter 5

Researching and Finding Your Niche

The first step is look to yourself. Do you have any expert knowledge in a field from your career work experience or professional training that you can use to create a niche? Ask yourself these questions:

- What is your passion?

- What are your hobbies?

- What do you do for a living?

- Do you have any specialized training?

- What have you always wanted to do but never had the time?

Whatever your answers to these questions are, there is probably a niche market in them. Jermaine Griggs loved to play the piano. He was one of these fellows who could play any song once he heard it. He started a website called Hear and Play (**www.hearandplay.com**). He now sells CDs, workbooks, and videos that teach you how to hear any song and play it on the piano instantly. Germaine's website grossed over $2 million last year.

If you are a dental assistant, there are probably opportunities available selling supplies to dentists and hygienists or products and information to parents about tooth health and care. Perhaps you sell insurance for a living. A lot of insurance sales people have developed sites on which they now sell insurance online instead of in people's living rooms. The trick here is to find a narrow specialty such as boat or aircraft insurance or—here's an idea—contact an insurance company and develop a specialty insurance product for people like yourself who run businesses out of the home.

If you have any kind of technical or engineering training, there are many product and service niches that can be developed based on your training and experience.

A school principal was frustrated that his students had trouble finding all the supplies they needed and parents were always complaining about the prices. He used his knowledge to set up a website that packages school supplies in kits. What started out as a small web business selling supplies to parents in his district is now a large nationwide business (see Figure 5-1). He now sells supplies to over 3700 school districts.

Next look to your hobbies and interests. What do you really enjoy and like to do? Quilting? Fly fishing? Collecting old glassware, pottery, or almost anything? Painting, photography, printmaking, or ceramics? Crossword or jigsaw puzzles?

FIGURE 5-1   Educational Products, Inc. website

Fixing old cars? Almost anything a person does for a hobby or enjoyment can be developed into a niche opportunity.

> TIP
>
> *A man I know buys old British sports cars that are either wrecked or beyond saving. He usually pays between $100 and $500 for each car. He takes them apart and sells the parts on the Internet to others who are rebuilding old cars. He can turn a $300 wreck into over $3,000 in sales by selling the individual parts.*

Researching Your Niche

Now profile your customers. Who is your typical customer and where do they shop or congregate on the Internet? Are there blogs that they read? Are there websites with message boards or Yahoo Groups where they post messages and look for help or products?

Next, look at your competition and the supply and demand situation. Don't panic if you find a lot of competition. Remember, you can always find a subniche or do something better than someone else is doing it now. Just make sure the niche you want to work in isn't saturated or dominated by more than three or four major players.

Don't focus on only one niche. Using the steps just discussed, list several possible niche markets that interest you. Write them down or, even better, create a spreadsheet. List all the product categories and create columns for the competitive information so you can come back later and analyze them. Perform all of these steps for each niche you find until you land on the right one.

"How do I know when I have found the right one?" you ask. Here is a little test you can use. It's not foolproof, but it will help you eliminate the unprofitable niches and focus on the ones that can make you money. Just ask yourself these questions about each of the niche products or services that make it past your initial screening:

- Is this something that really interests me—something I want to do and would enjoy?

- Do I have, or can I easily acquire, expertise and knowledge in this area that I can share with potential customers?

- Is the competitive environment reasonable? Are there competitors that I think I can improve on?

- Is there a new way of selling these products that no one else is doing?

- Can I find a reliable supply of the products or materials at a reasonable price?

- Is this a lasting business or a one-shot deal—does it "have legs," as the marketing gurus say?

- Are there keywords available to promote the item in pay-per-click search engines that can be purchased at a reasonable price?

> **TIP** *I will show you how to do find keywords in Chapter 22. In the meantime you can perform three free keyword searches at **www.wordtracker.com**. The site is pretty much self-explanatory.*

- Does this niche have expansion possibilities including products that I can up-sell or cross sell?

Can You Supply Your Niche?

Once you have found your niche, you have to determine how you will source your products. If you are going to assemble or manufacture a product, then you will need a source of raw materials or supplies. If you are going to buy purchased products, you will need to contact wholesale manufacturers or distributors and obtain wholesale pricing, ordering, and shipping information. Once you have the pricing, you want to go back to your competitive evaluation or research tools such as the Market Research Wizard I showed you in chapter 3 and determine the price points you can get on the web in the current competitive environment. Now evaluate your cost versus the selling price. The question here is *can I make money selling this product?*

In terms of selling a product at a profit, the fact that you are selling on the web is your biggest advantage. If you own a retail store, you have to make a large enough margin to cover your overhead that includes rent, employees, benefits, insurance, advertising, and holding large amounts of inventory. Selling on the web minimizes these expenses. If you become large enough to need commercial space and employees, you will not need expensive retail space, you can operate out of inexpensive warehouse or industrial park space. You will also most likely not need high-priced employees or as many employees as you would need for a retail store. Additionally, as you will see in Chapter 24, promoting your site costs far less than expensive radio, TV, and newspaper advertising.

Understanding Your Cost Structure

Although the costs of running and promoting a website business are far less than a traditional brick and mortar store, there are costs, and you will need to know what they are. I suggest you set up a spreadsheet and list all your costs. The one main variable is promotion. I like to use 10 percent of sales as a rule of thumb. Table 5-1 shows a very simple example of a cost versus sales spreadsheet. You will need to modify it for your specific situation. Going through this exercise will help you determine if the product you want to sell is viable.

As you can see in this example, you would make approximately $3,500 a month with this level of sales and expenses. I didn't factor in shipping costs here, as I assumed you would calculate shipping and charge the customer your actual costs. But in actuality there is an opportunity to recover your shipping materials

ITEM	Revenue or Expense
Income	
Projected monthly sales	$12,000
Expenses	
Cost of goods sold	$6,000
ISP/DSL or cable Fees	$45
Yahoo Store fee	$40
Credit card fees (3 percent of sales)	$360
Website promotion (10 percent of sales)	$1,200
Shipping and packing materials	$600
Miscellaneous	$200
Subtotal of expenses	$8,445
Net Profit Before Taxes (Sales less expenses)	**$3,555**

TABLE 5-1   Sample Spreadsheet Showing Sales and Expenses

cost and even make a little money on shipping and insurance. I will cover these strategies in Chapter 10.

Once you have performed these exercises, you should be able to define and decide what your niche will be and if it can be profitable.

Chapter 6

Website Designs That Sell

Once your website (Yahoo Store) is up and running, it will be your sales person. If you owned a retail store you would want to make sure your sales personnel were knowledgeable, trustworthy, well dressed, and well spoken—and the same is true for your website. We will get into specific website design techniques when we get to actually building your shop in Section II. This chapter deals with the more general issues you need to consider before you get to that point.

Content Considerations

Let's look at those sales points again.

Knowledgeable

It always bugs me when I go into a store and ask a salesperson a product question and they don't have a clue. The same is true on a website. If I am considering buying a product, I usually have questions about the product. So I look for thorough and complete product descriptions that will usually preempt most of my questions.

If I still have a question, I first look for a *Frequently Asked Question* (FAQ) page where I hope I can get an instant answer. If I can't find my answer there, the next thing I look for is a prominent, easy to use *Contact Us* page. The contact page should be easy to find *and* easy to use. I really dislike Contact Us pages that require you to fill in a lot of information. Just provide a space where I can type in the subject line and a box to ask my question. Don't force me to fill out the model number, which version of a browser I use, what operating system I use and how I found the site.

Trustworthy

Trust is a large factor with Internet shoppers. Unless they are a repeat visitor, the customer is buying from a complete stranger. Almost everyone worries a little about fraud, but the larger worry is customer service. "Will I get exactly what I ordered and paid for?" and "Will you stand behind the product if anything goes wrong?" are the two most often specified worries people have.

The first thing you must do to inspire trust is to have a clean-looking professional store design. Forget flashing icons, pop-up boxes, long animated entry pages, spinning dollar signs, and other goofy techniques that have nothing to do with making a sale. They just annoy people and get in the way of building trust between you and the prospect. Spend the time to take good product photographs and write complete descriptions. Show that you have nothing to hide by providing your address and phone number prominently on the site. You can even personalize the site by creating an About Me or About Us page with photos of yourself and a description of your business.

The other factor is your policies. Place a link to a page that explains your shipping, payment, and return policy. Make sure they are fully explained, but write about them in plain, friendly language. All of these steps will help inspire trust by the customer in your website.

Well Dressed

Just as your salespeople in a store should be clean and well dressed, so should your web store. When you are setting up your store, Yahoo will present you with several templates. Take the time to select one with clean simple lines and uncomplicated color schemes, and try to create a clean look. Avoid busy designs, too many colors, reverse type (light colored type on dark backgrounds) and unusual or hard-to-read fonts (see Figure 6-1).

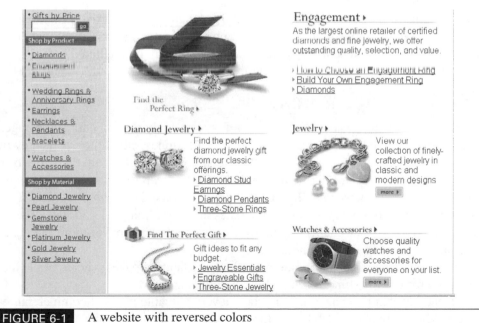

FIGURE 6-1   A website with reversed colors

Well Spoken

Words matter. What you say and how you say it can often make the difference in converting a prospect or winning or losing a sale. Pay attention to grammar, spelling, and style. Write in the active voice whenever possible and always use complete sentences. Avoid slang and jargon unless they are specific and well-understood in your particular niche. If writing in the English language is not your strength, get some help. If you live near a college or university, you can usually hire an English major for about $10 an hour to edit the copy on your website. One hundred dollars spent on editing will easily pay for itself in increased sales.

Avoid long, run-on sentences. Short sentences are best. If you write a long sentence, follow it with a short one. Write short paragraphs with white space between them. There have been plenty of studies that show that on the Internet people like to quickly scan pages for information that interests them. I like to boldface the topic or the first line of my paragraph to make it easy for readers to scan for topics, but don't overdo it.

Your sales copy should be loaded with features and facts, but should always stress the benefits of the product you are trying to sell. Features inform and benefits sell.

If you have to list specifications, use a numbered or bulleted list. I like to list the major specifications in the first paragraph so the person knows what they are buying, then list the rest of the specs after my sales copy in a bulleted list.

Design Considerations

When you see a newspaper on a newsstand, you see only the top half of the page. Newspaper people call this *above the fold*. The headlines and photographs they put above the fold are carefully considered to hook you into picking up the paper from the newsstand. The same is true on the Web. When a web page loads, everything the prospect sees without having to scroll down is considered *above the fold*. This is the first thing the prospect sees and creates their first image of your site. The old saw "you only get one chance to make a first impression" is never more relevant than at this point in your business venture.

You want to design your home pages and any landing pages where people hit your site for the first time very carefully with this in mind.

Treat your landing pages as you would a very valuable piece of commercial real estate. Maximize every inch for performance. Most web pages have an image at the top of the page with the name of the website. If this image is too large (vertically) it takes up room that you could use to communicate with your prospects to entice them to stay a little longer and look around.

One of the most common mistakes new website owners make is putting unimportant text such as "Welcome to my XYZ website" or slogans right at the top of their web page. The very first text a viewer sees when they hit your web page should be a description of what you are offering in a benefit-oriented statement. There are two reasons for this:

1. Web shoppers get to pages in a variety of ways. They might come from a banner or a search engine or an e-mail link. They often are not sure what they will find when they get there. A clear statement of what you offer or sell right up front is the best way to keep the real prospects reading

2. When large search engines such as Yahoo, AOL, and Google index your site, they reprint the first couple of lines of text on your page. If you have wasteful text such as "Welcome to my website where we aim to delight every customer," that is what the viewer will see in the search results instead of "The online store for unique handmade Swarovski Crystal jewelry."

If you want to put a welcome message or a business slogan at the top of your website, incorporate it into the image bar—the text in the image bar is not seen by the search engines.

The top fold of your website should include a clear statement of what the website offers and easy to read and find navigation links to the products and/or services you are selling. All text and pictures should be designed to instantly communicate your unique selling proposition or how you are positioned compared to your competitors.

For example, if you have hard-to-find products or the most complete product line in your niche, this is where you want to say it. If you are the bargain, the deep discounter, or the high quality provider, the top fold of your website is where you want people to learn this.

If you have a broad product line with several categories, place a photo of your best-selling item in each category in a row with a clickable link to the product category on the top fold of your site as opposed to just listing product links. Figure 6-2 shows a good example of this technique.

FIGURE 6-2   Website showing product category image links

If you have only a few products, be sure to show one of two of your best images on the top fold of your page. When you place images on your page, be sure to make the image itself a clickable link either to the specific product or the product category. I will show you how to do this as we set up your store.

Good web design will keep the customer long enough to explore your site. In the next chapter we will discuss how to convert the *lookers* into *buyers*.

Chapter 7

Making the Sale

In the previous chapter, we focused on design elements of your Home page to keep a person on your website long enough to start shopping. Once you start designing your store, the next important design elements are making the sale and getting the customer all the way through the checkout and payment process.

There are four steps to making an Internet sale:

■ Getting visitors to your site, known in the trade as "Getting the Eyeballs."

■ Providing confidence, trust, and enough information on the landing page to entice the prospect to start shopping.

■ Providing compelling product images and descriptions that make the customer want to make a purchase.

■ Guiding the prospect through the shopping cart or checkout and payment process to completing the order.

The first step, getting the eyeballs, will be covered in detail in Part III.

Catalog Designs that Sell

If you have done a good job providing confidence and trust and convincing your customers that your website has products they are looking for, the next step is to make the sale on your product pages. Web-based shopping is a primarily visual experience. Your product image is the first thing the customer sees. If the image conveys the correct impression, the prospect will usually continue reading the description. Just as on your landing page, clear, easy-to-read descriptions are critical to making the sale.

Here is a checklist for descriptions:

1. Start your description with a headline that clearly specifies what the product is. Be sure to specify any extra accessories or components that come with the product. For example: "Nikon 5100, 5 Megapixel Digital Camera Kit complete with camera bag, cleaning kit and tripod."

2. Next, describe the item in benefit-oriented text and list the key features.

3. Be sure and include a list of the minor features and specifications as well. If you don't want to interrupt the flow of your description, you can place a link to a pop-up page that contains all the detailed information that could be important to a customer but isn't essential to the central description.

4. Give the customer a reason for buying *now*. This is known as the *close*. The close could be text such as "Limited time offer" or "Free shipping this week on all orders over $*XX*."

The Checkout and Payment Process

Studies by the Internet Marketing Center have concluded that online shopping cart abandonment presently accounts for up to 40 percent of lost sales.

Think of this for a moment. The customer finds your website, looks at your products and makes a buying decision, adds the item to the shopping cart, and then abandons the sale at the last minute. This is a major problem with thousands of websites. I have heard anecdotal information that even large, sophisticated shopping sites such as Amazon.com and Bestbuy.com have experienced abandonment rates as high as 25 percent.

When customers are asked why they abandon sales at this point, the top three reasons stated are:

1. The process was too complex.

2. The vendor asked for too much information.

3. The buyer was not 100 percent positive that the transaction was secure.

If you can solve these three problems, you can measurably increase your business. The first two are actually related. I have seen shopping carts where you first have to fill in your name and billing information and then fill in your shipping information again even if the information is the same. On other shopping carts, they ask for detailed demographic information or questions about how you found their site. This information is nice to have but goes well beyond what you need to process the order. Another problem is requiring the customer to fill in some information on one page, then click to another page to fill out more information, and finally a third page to place the order. Anything you can do to simplify the ordering process will pay benefits.

The other big issue is security. On all my websites I have a statement in large bold letters at the top of my order page that says:

This is a secure transaction. Your ordering information is subject to our privacy policy and will not be shared, sold, or rented to any third parties. We require your phone number and e-mail address in case there is a problem with your credit card or your order. We do not keep your credit card information on file once the transaction is completed.

A statement such as this gives the customers confidence that this is a trustworthy place to do business. After putting a statement such as this on my digital photo products website, I saw an immediate 8 percent increase in sales with no other changes to the website.

Another important trust builder is to restate your guarantee or return policy right on the order page. Keep it short—this is not the place for several paragraphs of legal-beagle language. A statement such as:

You can order with confidence. We stand behind every product we sell and offer a 100 percent customer-satisfaction guarantee. Please <u>click here</u> if you would like to read our returns, warranty, or guarantee policy.

Having cautioned you against creating too many pages in the ordering process, this is one exception. When a customer clicks Purchase or Check Out on the shopping cart, I take them to a page with the preceding information. After these statements, I include a statement above the purchase button that says Click Here to Make Your Secure Purchase.

As you get into designing and setting up your store, be sure and remember these critical design issues.

Chapter 8

Payment Systems

The ability to accommodate credit card payments on your site is essential for doing business on the Internet, but there is still a small percentage of buyers who prefer to pay by check or money order and another group of buyers who will use a credit card but refuse to type it into a web form. These buyers usually prefer to purchase by telephone or fax. If you want to maximize your sales, it is important that you accept all forms of payment. There are also several choices to make when deciding on a credit card system to use.

In order to accept credit cards, you will need either a merchant credit card account or an account with a company known as PayPal (**www.paypal.com**). If you open a merchant credit card account, you will also need the services of a payment processing company.

Merchant Credit Card Account

Merchant credit card accounts are offered by most banks. Although almost every bank, including small community banks, offers this service, not all systems are equal. This is one area where it helps to deal with a large bank as they tend to have a broader range of services. There are also several independent companies that appear to offer merchant accounts, but in reality are brokers, as all of the accounts have to eventually be processed by a bank. Most brokers offer several choices depending on your needs and the type of business, but you can almost always get better rates by dealing directly with a bank.

There are several fees associated with a merchant account. These include one-time setup fees, verification fees, a monthly service charge, and transaction fees. Merchant credit card accounts are a huge profit center for banks. Because of this they can be very competitive, and it pays to shop around. Oftentimes the best deal can be found at your own bank because they will often waive or reduce some of the fees for their own commercial customers. Setup fees can vary from free to as high as $299. Monthly service fees tend to run anywhere from $9 to $25 per month. Transaction fees are a percentage of the transaction and can vary from as low as 1.3 percent to over 6 percent per transaction. Differences such as these make it worth your while to shop around.

Yahoo actually offers its own merchant credit card account service through a company called Paymentech. You can apply for Paymentech by logging into your store account and filling out an information form. It will take approximately 24 hours to find out if you are approved. Paymentech uses a gateway payment processor called First Data Merchant Services. If you have your own merchant card account, you will need to make sure it is compatible with First Data Merchant Services.

Just call your merchant card provider and they will tell you if they are. If they are not, then you will need a different card company to work with Yahoo Shops.

We will step through the process of setting up with Paymentech and First Data Merchant Services in Part II, when we set up your store.

Credit Card Processing Through PayPal

PayPal is a company now owned by eBay. PayPal (**www.paypal.com**) started out as a way for online auction buyers to pay for merchandise they bought on eBay and other online auction sites. In 2002, PayPal added the ability for their members to accept credit cards. Since then they have become the Internet payment transaction leader.

PayPal has over 85 million registered members worldwide and processes millions of online transactions daily. PayPal members can fund their accounts with a credit card, by linking it to a bank, or with cash. When you use PayPal to accept web payments and a buyer clicks your Check Out button, if the person buying is already a PayPal member, PayPal will recognize them and they can just pay through their PayPal account with one click after entering their password. If someone is not a PayPal member, PayPal simply brings up a credit card order form where the buyer enters their name, shipping address, and credit card info to complete the transaction.

PayPal has several advantages over traditional merchant credit card accounts:

- PayPal is fully integrated with Yahoo Stores.

- With over 75 million members, you have instant credibility when one of them visits your store and sees that you accept PayPal.

- There are no credit requirements to open a PayPal account. All you need is a credit card and a bank account.

- PayPal offers its members buyers' protection that protects them against fraudulent sellers.

- There are no membership fees, setup fees, or monthly fees.

- PayPal transaction fees are very competitive: 30 cents + 2.3 percent to 2.9 percent, depending on your monthly volume.

- If you process a refund, PayPal credits you 100 percent of the transaction fee.

- PayPal pays you interest compounded daily on any outstanding balances in your account.

■ PayPal sends you an instant e-mail with all the information you need for ordering and shipping within minutes of a buyer placing an order.

■ You can encrypt all of your payment information so it cannot be viewed in the web page source code.

■ PayPal has one of the most aggressive antifraud programs on the Internet.

To open a PayPal account, simply go to **www.paypal.com**. You will need a credit card to prove your identity. PayPal will not charge your card unless you authorize them to do so to make an online payment for something you have purchased. You will also need to register a bank account to become a verified seller. You do not have to become a verified seller, although I strongly recommend you do. If you are a verified seller, then any PayPal member who buys from you will be eligible for PayPal's Buyer Protection Plan. PayPal members put a lot of trust in this plan, so being a verified seller will give your buyers confidence in you.

PayPal provides an easy-to-set-up shopping cart with their membership. They charge $20 a month for the shopping cart which also includes a virtual terminal. Setting up the cart is very easy. It should take you about ten minutes to set up your first item and then less than one or two minutes per item to add more products. There is no limit to how many products you can add.

Because the shopping cart resides on the PayPal site rather than on your website, you do not need any software or web script to begin setting up your shopping cart. Setting up your shopping cart with PayPal is incredibly easy. Once you set up your PayPal account, log into your account and click the Merchant Tools tab at the top of any PayPal page. This will bring up the Merchant Tools page.

On this page, in the little box in labeled Key Features, click the link that says PayPal Shopping Cart. This will bring up a window like the one in Figure 8.1.

Now, just enter your product information, pricing, and item number. If you use stock keeping units (SKU numbers), you should also use them in your payment code, as this will make it easy to track products in your inventory system. Once you have entered this data, scroll down the page to select a payment button.

You can use the button provided or click the link that says Choose a Different Button, which will display a selection of additional buttons you can choose from.

You are almost done. Next, click the button that says Add More Options. This will take you to a page that looks like Figure 8.2. If you want to use fixed price shipping, simply enter it in the box provided. If you want to use calculated shipping (see Figure 8.3), click the Edit button and set up your shipping charges by weight. If you use this option, you only have to do this once and it will automatically populate to all of your items in the future.

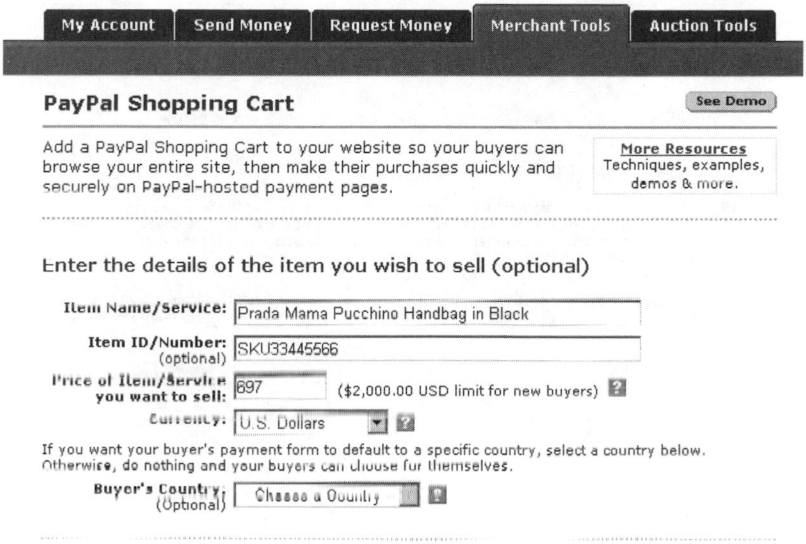

| My Account | Send Money | Request Money | Merchant Tools | Auction Tools |

PayPal Shopping Cart   (See Demo)

Add a PayPal Shopping Cart to your website so your buyers can browse your entire site, then make their purchases quickly and securely on PayPal-hosted payment pages.

More Resources
Techniques, examples, demos & more.

Enter the details of the item you wish to sell (optional)

Item Name/Service: Prada Mama Pucchino Handbag in Black

Item ID/Number: SKU33445566
(optional)

Price of Item/Service you want to sell: 697   ($2,000.00 USD limit for new buyers) [?]

Currency: U.S. Dollars [?]

If you want your buyer's payment form to default to a specific country, select a country below. Otherwise, do nothing and your buyers can choose for themselves.

Buyer's Country: Choose a Country [?]
(Optional)

FIGURE 8-1   PayPal Shopping Cart selection

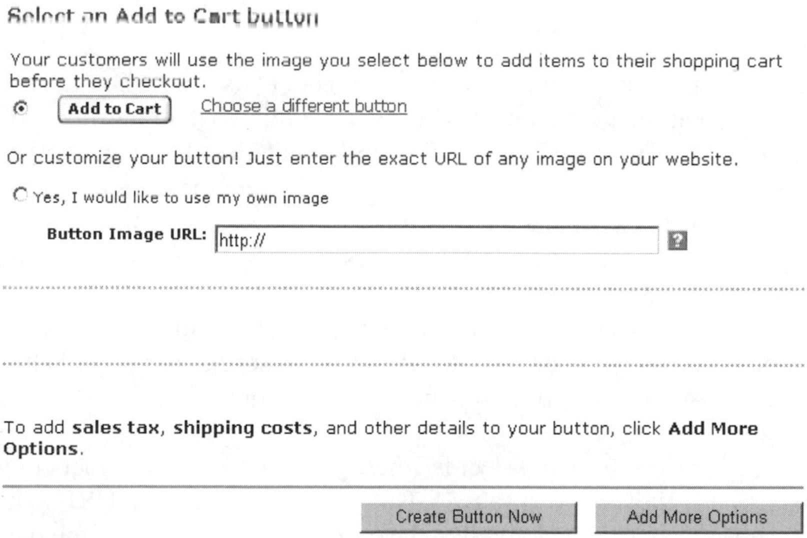

Select an Add to Cart button

Your customers will use the image you select below to add items to their shopping cart before they checkout.

(Add to Cart)   Choose a different button

Or customize your button! Just enter the exact URL of any image on your website.

Yes, I would like to use my own image

Button Image URL: http:// [?]

To add **sales tax**, **shipping costs**, and other details to your button, click **Add More Options**.

(Create Button Now)   (Add More Options)

FIGURE 8-2   PayPal Shopping Cart item creation detail

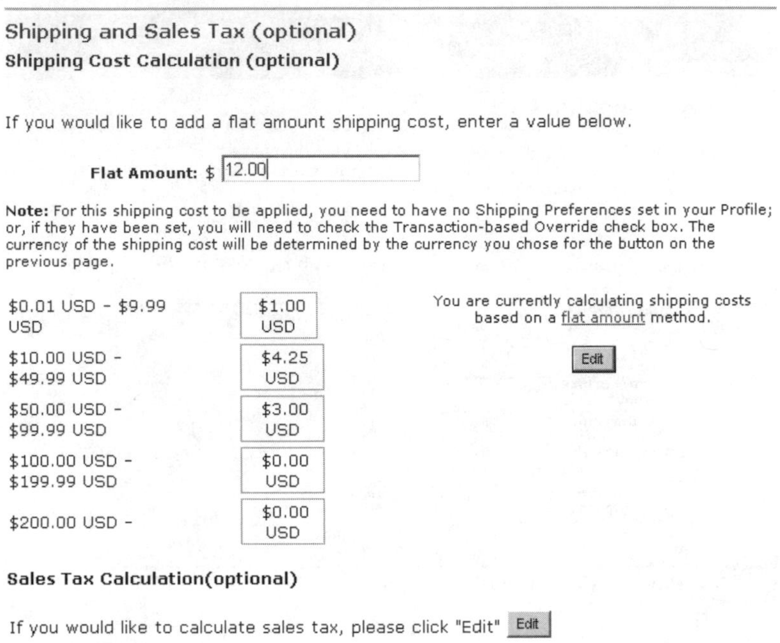

Shipping and Sales Tax (optional)
Shipping Cost Calculation (optional)

If you would like to add a flat amount shipping cost, enter a value below.

Flat Amount: $ | 12.00 |

Note: For this shipping cost to be applied, you need to have no Shipping Preferences set in your Profile; or, if they have been set, you will need to check the Transaction-based Override check box. The currency of the shipping cost will be determined by the currency you chose for the button on the previous page.

$0.01 USD - $9.99 USD	$1.00 USD	You are currently calculating shipping costs based on a flat amount method.
$10.00 USD - $49.99 USD	$4.25 USD	Edit
$50.00 USD - $99.99 USD	$3.00 USD	
$100.00 USD - $199.99 USD	$0.00 USD	
$200.00 USD -	$0.00 USD	

Sales Tax Calculation(optional)

If you would like to calculate sales tax, please click "Edit" Edit

FIGURE 8-3 Enter shipping information

The next item to set up is your sales tax. Figure 8.4 shows a box to enter your country, state, and sales tax amount. Once you set this up it will always populate to your buttons in the future. Whenever a purchaser enters a shipping address in the same state as you specify, PayPal will automatically add the sales tax to your item.

If your product is available in various colors or sizes, you can add option fields to your payment button. Just fill out the boxes as shown in Figure 8.5 to add any options to your product.

As you scroll down the page, you are next presented with a selection of buttons that will be displayed on your website when your customer is ready to check out (Figure 8.6). Just select one of these buttons and continue scrolling down the page to the next item.

The next item you have to select is where you want your customers to go once the transaction is finished (Figure 8.7). This is where you enter a URL to a page on your website where you would like the customer to end up once the payment process is completed. PayPal does give you the option of sending the customer to a page on PayPal, but I don't recommend this. You should instead create a "Thank

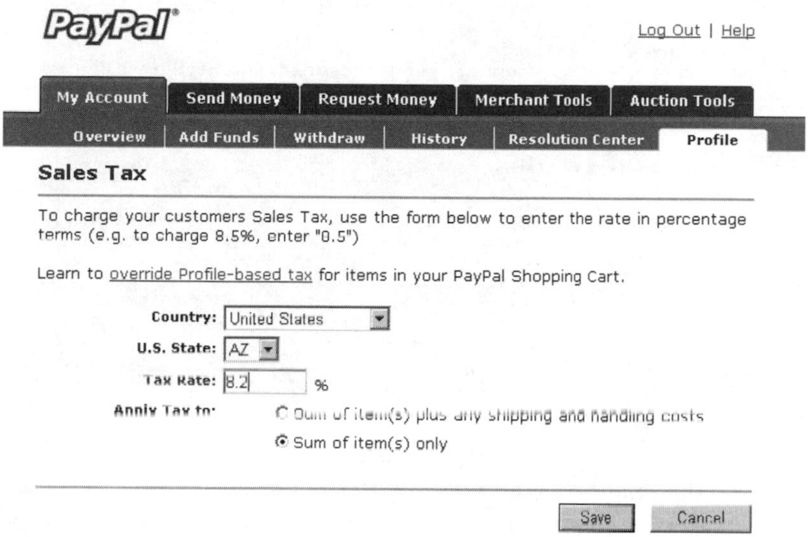

PayPal®

Log Out | Help

| My Account | Send Money | Request Money | Merchant Tools | Auction Tools |
| Overview | Add Funds | Withdraw | History | Resolution Center | Profile |

Sales Tax

To charge your customers Sales Tax, use the form below to enter the rate in percentage terms (e.g. to charge 8.5%, enter "0.5")

Learn to override Profile-based tax for items in your PayPal Shopping Cart.

Country: United States

U.S. State: AZ

Tax Rate: 8.2 %

Apply Tax to: ○ Sum of item(s) plus any shipping and handling costs

● Sum of item(s) only

[Save] [Cancel]

FIGURE 8-4   Sales tax calculation

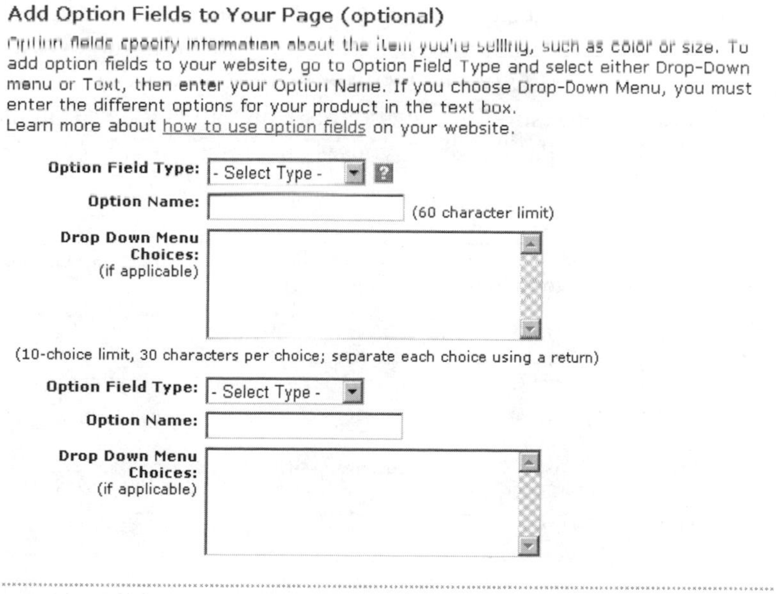

Add Option Fields to Your Page (optional)

Option fields specify information about the item you're selling, such as color or size. To add option fields to your website, go to Option Field Type and select either Drop-Down menu or Text, then enter your Option Name. If you choose Drop-Down Menu, you must enter the different options for your product in the text box.
Learn more about how to use option fields on your website.

Option Field Type: - Select Type - ?

Option Name: (60 character limit)

**Drop Down Menu
Choices:**
(if applicable)

(10-choice limit, 30 characters per choice; separate each choice using a return)

Option Field Type: - Select Type -

Option Name:

**Drop Down Menu
Choices:**
(if applicable)

FIGURE 8-5   Add product options

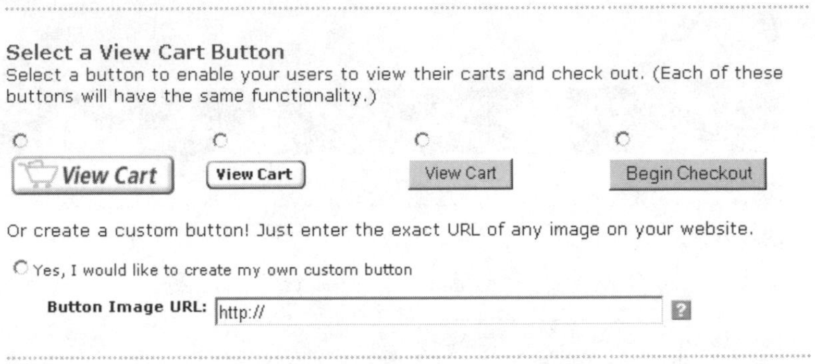

Select a View Cart Button
Select a button to enable your users to view their carts and check out. (Each of these buttons will have the same functionality.)

○   View Cart   ○   View Cart   ○   View Cart   ○   Begin Checkout

Or create a custom button! Just enter the exact URL of any image on your website.

○ Yes, I would like to create my own custom button

Button Image URL: http://   ?

FIGURE 8-6   Select View Cart button

you for your order" page on your website. Besides telling the customer that their order was processed successfully and thanking them for their business, you can also place other useful information on this page such as when you will ship, a number to call or an e-mail to send questions to, and other helpful information.

Figure 8.8 shows a couple more options you are presented with. The first item asks if you want to make shipping optional. Since you will need the shipping address, select the button that says Yes, Require Shipping. Below this is a section titled Collect Additional Information from Your Customers. If you choose Yes, when you customers make a payment, a box will come up where they can write a comment or ask you a question. If they do this, you will get their statement or question in the e-mail that PayPal sends you when a transaction is completed.

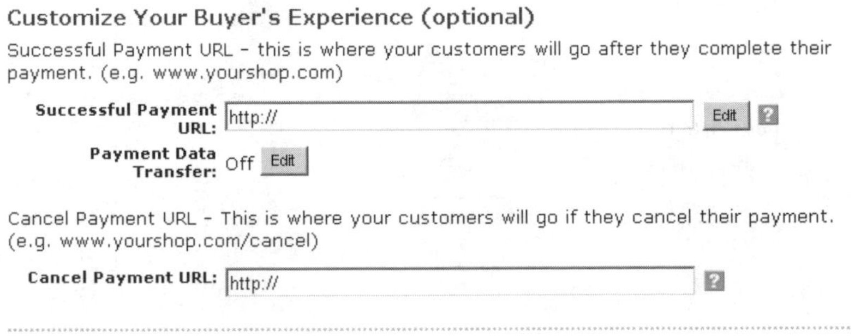

Customize Your Buyer's Experience (optional)
Successful Payment URL – this is where your customers will go after they complete their payment. (e.g. www.yourshop.com)

Successful Payment URL: http://   Edit   ?

Payment Data Transfer: Off   Edit

Cancel Payment URL – This is where your customers will go if they cancel their payment. (e.g. www.yourshop.com/cancel)

Cancel Payment URL: http://   ?

FIGURE 8-7   Return page URL

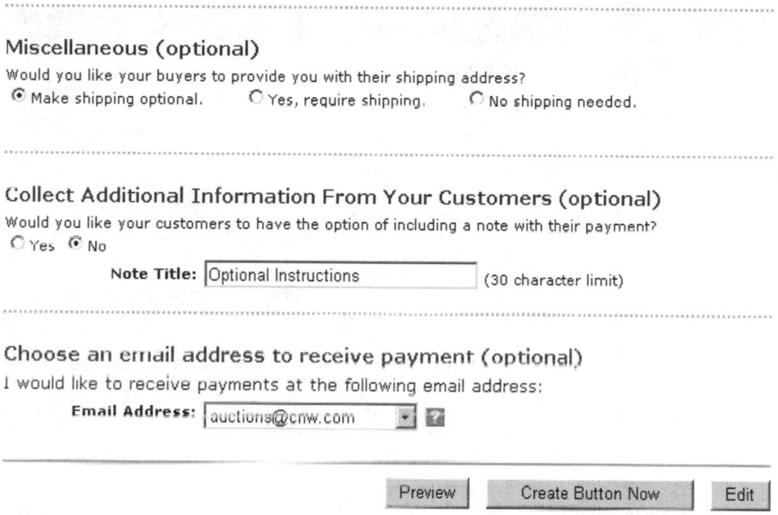

Miscellaneous (optional)

Would you like your buyers to provide you with their shipping address?

⦿ Make shipping optional.   ○ Yes, require shipping.   ○ No shipping needed.

Collect Additional Information From Your Customers (optional)

Would you like your customers to have the option of including a note with their payment?

○ Yes ⦿ No

Note Title: | Optional Instructions | (30 character limit)

Choose an email address to receive payment (optional)

I would like to receive payments at the following email address:

Email Address: | auctions@cnw.com | ▼ | ?

[Preview]   [Create Button Now]   [Edit]

FIGURE 8-8   Optional instructions

The final step is to enter an e-mail address where you will receive notices of payments. This does not have to be your main e-mail address you registered with PayPal, although it can be. If you have an e-mail program with an auto-responder, you may want to enter that e-mail address and compose a short e-mail that automatically goes out to your customers thanking them for their order.

Once you select your return payment URL, you are ready to create your payment button. Simply click the button that says Create Button Now, and you will be taken to a new page, shown in Figure 8.9. All you do is copy the text in from the first box (the Add to Cart Button code) onto your clipboard and paste it onto the page with your product. Then go back to the Add a Button to Your Website page, copy the text from the second box (the View Cart Button code), and paste the View Cart button onto your product and checkout page.

This probably looks like a lot of steps and work to create a shopping cart item, but all of the optional steps need only be performed the first time because PayPal will save this information until you come back to the site to create another button. In the future, all you will have to do is type in the product name, part number and price, select Add More Options, and click the Create Button Now to create your new item.

Add a button to your website

Copy your custom HTML code

The HTML code below contains your "Add to Cart" button. Copy the code and paste it into onto your webpage. When your customers press the buttons they will be taken to a webpage listing the items they have added to their cart.

Add to Cart Button code

```
<form target="paypal"
action="https://www.paypal.com/cgi-
bin/webscr" method="post">
<input type="image"
src="https://www.paypal.com/en_US/i/btn/
x-click-but22.gif" border="0"
```

View Cart Button

The HTML code below contains your "View Cart" button. Copy the code and paste it onto your webpage. When your customers press the button, they will be taken to a webpage listing the items they will purchase from you.

"View Cart Button" Code:
(Copy and paste this html code onto your website)

```
<form target="paypal"
action="https://www.paypal.com/cgi-
bin/webscr" method="post">
<input type="hidden" name="cmd"
value="_cart">
<input type="hidden" name="business"
```

FIGURE 8-9   Create button HTML code

Other Payment Methods

In addition to accepting credit cards over the web, you will also want to offer a phone number where people can call in and give their information over the phone. If you decide to use a merchant credit card account, you will have to rent or buy a machine to process your credit card transactions offline. If you use PayPal, you can set up a virtual terminal by logging into your PayPal account and then going to the web page **www.paypal.com/vt**. Just fill out the application on this page and, if approved, PayPal will set up a virtual terminal where you can type credit card information into their system from any computer to effect payments.

PayPal also allows buyers without credit cards to pay by electronic check. The buyer simply enters the name of their bank and the numbers from their checking account into a web form—or you can enter them from the virtual terminal.

Finally, unless you are selling very expensive items such as $10,000 Rolex watches, you will also want to accept money orders and personal checks. A lot of people do not like to accept personal checks because of the waiting period for the check to clear. This used to be a problem, but today most banks can clear a check in two or three business days as opposed to ten days or more from just a few years ago.

If you are selling very expensive items, you may not want to take personal checks due to the risk of fraud. If someone cannot pay with a credit card or e-check, just suggest they send a cashier's check. However, there is still potential for fraud with cashier's checks, as these are now sometimes counterfeited.

To protect yourself, whenever you get a cashier's check, have your banker call the issuing bank to verify the check is genuine and the funds are in place. If you simply deposit the check, the bank will immediately credit your account if it is a cashier's check, but if it turns out to be counterfeit (which they might not discover for a week or more) they will come back and debit your account. The same is true for money orders. Whenever I receive a money order, I always cash it first just in case it turns out to be counterfeit. If you cash it first, as opposed to depositing it with your bank, you are safe, and the risk lies with the institution who accepted it and gave you the cash.

By far, most of your customers will pay with a credit card online. As long as you make the process easy and reassure them that the transaction is safe, they will not hesitate to give you their credit card information if they want to buy from you. But, as I said at the beginning, there are many people who still like the personal touch. They will want to place orders by phone, and some will even want to pay by mail.

Chapter 9

Up-selling and Cross-Selling

Up-selling and *cross-selling* are the terms that refer to convincing a customer to increase the size of their order or add another product to their order at the time of the sale. Although the terms are often used interchangeably, in general, up-selling usually means getting the customer to increase the quantity or size of their order. Cross-selling, on the other hand, means to get the customer to buy a related product; for example, if you sell bird feeders, you get the customer to add bird seed to the order.

Not every product lends itself to up-selling and cross-selling, but for those that do, you should never miss an opportunity to try.

Up-selling

The most obvious form of up-selling is increasing the quantity of the order. If you are selling any type of commodity product, the sales page should offer quantity alternatives with incentives such as a discount or free shipping if they increase the size of their order. For example, if you are selling printer ink cartridges, you might offer three payment buttons:

Quantity 1 $14.90 + $1.00 S&H

Quantity 3 $42.00 + $3.00 S&H—save $2.70

Quantity 5 $70 + FREE shipping—save $9.50

That is a pretty strong incentive for the customer to order five units. Yes, you are making a little less money on each unit, but your average sale is larger. The theory is that is costs you X dollars to get a person to your website. By averaging up the size of the order, you make up in marketing costs what you lose in individual margin. Also, your variable cost to fulfill the order is lower. Your warehouse workers who pack the shipment and fill out the UPS shipping label can pack and ship five cartridges in the same time they can handle one.

Whether and how much to discount is really something you have to analyze yourself based on the realities of your particular product and business model. If you are selling books, which are fairly heavy and therefore costly to ship, or fragile glassware items that were expensive and difficult to pack, you may not be able to offer free shipping.

The idea is to look at your given situation and calculate your costs to best determine if and how to discount for increased quantity sales.

Cross-Selling

Cross-selling usually refers to adding an additional or related product to an order. An example of cross-selling is once a customer decides to purchase a cell phone, you offer them the opportunity to add a holster and car charger to the order at a special price if they buy now. You can do this very easily by creating a fake payment button. When the customer clicks the button to add an item to their cart, the fake payment button instead directs them to a page that makes the special offer alongside the original product standing alone. Below each item on this new page, you have a real payment button that will add either the original item to the cart or add the adjusted item with the additional accessories.

Once again, you want to give your customers an incentive to do this. If you just offer them additional items at the normal price, they may occasionally purchase the additional accessories but most often will not. However, if you offer them a discount not available elsewhere on the site, an incentive such as free or discounted shipping, or, even better, an electronic coupon to get 10 percent off their next purchase, your conversion rate will be much higher.

Now is the time—before you start building your site—to come up with these product offers and get the descriptions written and entered into your inventory list. It is much easier to create these systems in the beginning, rather than going back and changing a lot of pages later.

Chapter 10

Delivering the Product

Making the sale is only a part of the Internet sales process. Unlike a retail store where a customer usually takes their purchases with them, you have to deliver your product. This is another area you should give some thought to before starting to design your store.

There are four major shipping services used by Internet merchants to ship goods that weigh less than 70 pounds:

- United States Postal Service (USPS)

- United Parcel Service (UPS) Air and Ground Services

- DHL Courier Air & Ground Services

- FedEx and FedEx Ground (formerly RPS)

If you are selling to businesses and shipping goods to a commercial address, all four services are extremely competitive. USPS rates are fixed. Depending on your volume you can get competitive quotes from FedEx, DHL, and UPS. In my experience, the quotes from all three have been within 1 percent or 2 percent of each other. The larger issue lies with residential service. USPS Priority Mail is much cheaper, and usually ships faster to a residential address, than any of the commercial ground services for packages up to 7 pounds. Above 7 pounds, the other companies are much closer to USPS rates. Priority Mail has one additional advantage in that they supply you with free boxes, which can save you as much as $1 per shipment.

UPS Ground charges a premium for shipments to residential addresses. FedEx Ground Residential service is a little cheaper than UPS to these same addresses.

The choice of a shipper will largely depend on your volume and product weight. If you are selling smaller items (under 7 pounds shipped weight), USPS rates are much more competitive. This is important because a lot of customers shop competitively and are savvy enough to look at the shipping costs before buying. If your closest competitor is shipping via UPS and you can undersell him by shipping via USPS, this could be an important decision.

Speed is also an important component. Depending on where in the U.S. you are located, Priority Mail is usually much faster than UPS or FedEx Ground. People like to get their products quickly. If you use UPS, and you are in California and the customer is in Maine, it can take seven business days for them to get your package, whereas Priority Mail will usually arrive in three business days—and the USPS considers Saturday a business day, whereas UPS does not.

Automating the Shipping Process

If you are going to ship a high volume of products, then the ability to automate the shipping process may be a larger issue than the product price. Yahoo Stores offers the ability to integrate the shopping cart platform with UPS WorldShip, which is UPS's automated shipping platform. Once you open a UPS account (**www.ups.com**), you can download the WorldShip software for free and load it into your PC.

Available directly from your Yahoo Store Manager, UPS WorldShip enables merchants to ship and track packages, gather rate and service information, and validate addresses for UPS shipping services. By integrating these options into your store, you eliminate the need to manually enter or cut and paste data between your Yahoo Store and UPS shipping applications, which makes the shipping experience seamless and fast. The UPS tracking number is automatically e-mailed to purchasers so they can monitor the progress of their order. This is a big time saver, as you will not have to answer e-mails and phone calls from people wondering when their package will arrive.

With WorldShip, you can:

- Access the full portfolio of UPS shipping services, with the ability to ship to over 200 countries and territories around the world

- Generate UPS shipping labels with reference data, a custom barcode, or your company logo

- Display UPS published rates instantly or customized rates with the built-in rate calculator

- Import and export customer shipping data to and from other business systems for either manual or automatic processing of shipments

- Customize your default settings, such as package type and service level to match your shipping preferences

- Save frequently used addresses and assign profiles to your customers in an address book for future reference and faster shipment processing

- Receive and print proof-of-delivery information, including time of delivery and the name, address, and signature of recipient

- Generate required international export documents for easier and faster international shipment processing (if you are going to sell internationally this is a huge timesaver)

- Access immediate tracking status on packages

If you still want to use USPS, there is an excellent automation solution available from Endicia (see Figure 10-1) at **www.endicia.com**. Endicia provides most of the services for USPS customers that WorldShip does for UPS users; however, unlike UPS, as of this writing Endicia charges a monthly fee of $17.95 for their service and software. They also offer an integrated scale and postage label printer for about $250 that can be used with Endicia or WorldShip.

There are two Endicia features I really like. One is called Stealth Postage. This calculates the postage and prints it on the label with a bar code that the postal service can read but the customers cannot. This way if you are adding a handling fee, the customer cannot see what you really paid for postage when they receive their package. The other feature is a major cost saver. The USPS charges 45 cents for delivery confirmation. Endicia's system buys the postage and delivery confirmation online. When you purchase your postage this way, the USPS waives the 45-cent fee and you save this charge. This can really add up over thousands of packages.

FIGURE 10-1   Endicia Internet Postage solution

Streamlining Your Shipping

The other factor related to shipping is how you package and ship your goods. If you are starting your business in the home, you will need some room to set up a shipping station. This is a table with nearby storage for boxes and shipping materials, a scale and label printer, and everything you need to pack your merchandise all in one place. Packing and shipping is very time consuming, and the materials take up a lot of space. You will definitely want to organize this before you actually open your store.

Your shipping station should have everything you need to quickly and efficiently pack and ship your merchandise including tape guns, dispensers for Styrofoam, rolls of bubble wrap, and so on. Anything you can do that will save time will eventually save you money. If your volume increases, you may want to hire some help. The shipping process is usually one of the first processes that web store owners seek help to do.

Chapter 11

Bringing the Customer Back for More

Earlier we discussed the cost to capture a customer. Anytime you can sell to a repeat customer, it is always more profitable than selling to a brand new customer. The keys to doing this are first to provide a comfortable customer service experience throughout the sales process and then to capture your customers' names and market to them for future sales. If you don't create a positive and memorable customer service experience you won't have a chance to perform the second step. If you do, marketing to your existing customers, is easy.

Customer Service Experience

The customer service experience starts with the moment the prospect clicks a link that opens your site and ends when they receive your product. A positive experience is influenced by all of these factors:

- The look and feel of your site. Does this "feel" like a trustworthy place to do business?

- How easy was it to navigate and find products?

- Were your pricing and offers attractive?

- Ease of checkout. Was it straightforward and easy to understand the steps?

- Follow-up communications. Did your customer receive an e-mail confirming their order and letting them know when it will be shipped?

- When the product arrives, was it exactly what your customer expected, and was it professionally packaged?

If any of these steps were flawed, it amounts to breaking a chain. If one link in the chain fails, that is what the customer will remember even if everything else went smoothly. In the next part of the book, as you start to design your store, keep these steps in mind. Strive to create a store design and functionality that both entices and comforts the prospect. Then set up your processes—fulfillment, shipping, and communications—to insure an uninterrupted flow that reassures the customer from beginning to end. It is not enough to just design a great website, the entire shopping experience has to be flawless if you truly want to build a long-term profitable business.

Follow-up Marketing

Most follow-up marketing programs today are conducted by e-mail, although there are some large web operators that also use direct mail.

If you are going to market to your existing customers, the first thing you need to do is capture their contact information. At a minimum, you need to capture the customer's first name, last name, and e-mail address. Yahoo gives you several e-mail accounts with the standard store setup, but their tools for follow-up e-mail marketing are a bit limited. I use a program called Mail Loop from The Internet Marketing Center (**www.marketingtips.com**) that, once you download and install, resides on your computer. You can set Mail Loop up to capture the name and e-mail address from each customer. You can also capture e-mail addresses from people who use your store's contact form to ask you questions.

In addition, Mail Loop provides the ability to collect names for a newsletter or announcements of specials that you can send out periodically with electronic discount coupons. One downside to Mail Loop is the cost: about $400 as of this writing.

There are other online services that provide many of the same features. The largest is Topica (**www.topica.com**), which charges a monthly fee based on your number of subscribers. If you only have a few hundred names, this might be cheaper, but if you have to think you can develop a large list, owning your own system such as Mail Loop is a better choice. If you would like to research other alternatives, just do a Yahoo Search on the term "newsletter servers," and you will come up with links to dozens of companies that provide services and software solutions.

Offering Repeat-Business Incentives

Both PayPal and Paymentech, Yahoo's credit card service, give you the ability to create electronic coupons—a number or special word that a customer can enter in a box that you can enable in your shopping cart. The box is usually labeled Enter Promotional Code Here. You set the amount of the discount a customer gets when they enter the number or the term you specify. (I will cover this in more detail in the chapter on setting up your shopping cart.)

Once you build your customer lists, you should e-mail them on a regular basis with special offers if they buy something by a certain date. There are two ways to do this. You can set up a special page that is not published in the navigation links of your website where you direct only your return customers, or you can create a promotional code as I just described.

There are three ways to build a mailing list. First, you can create a check box on your shopping cart checkout that asks your customers for permission to send them special offers and news. Second, you can just send them an e-mail, but include an unsubscribe link they can click if they don't want to get your mailings. The third technique is to offer your customers, and anyone else who visits your website, a free newsletter on a topic related to what you are selling. This works best for specialty websites for hobbyists or special interests such as art, photography, sports, and so on. For example, if you sell fly-fishing gear you could write a monthly newsletter that talks about great fly-fishing spots, reviews new equipment, and features any new products you are selling. If your newsletter becomes large enough, you can also make money by selling advertising space to other companies that are in the same industry but not directly competitive, such as a travel company that sells guided fly-fishing trips.

No matter how you go about it, the key is to do it. Set up a plan to conduct follow-up marketing, execute it, and stick with it. If customers get used to regular mailings, you are developing a relationship and they will stick with you. But if you only market to them sporadically, they will see you as an opportunist and your unsubscribes will climb steadily.

Part II

Setting Up Your Yahoo Store

By Dennis L. Prince

Chapter 12

Introducing Yahoo Merchant Solutions

Certainly your mind has been busily whirring away with the discussion up to this point, and I hope you've been busy considering your approach to becoming a Yahoo Merchant. When you've determined what products you'd like to sell, how you'd like to market them, and how you'll manage the flood of good business you'll soon be enjoying, then you're ready to open your store.

Your Yahoo Opportunity Awaits

We've talked at great length about the opportunities a Yahoo Store can provide to you but now it's time to talk the nuts and bolts of why a Yahoo Merchant Solution is a good investment. First off, consider these interesting statistics as you consider actually throwing your hat into the online fray:

- 72 percent of American adults have considered starting their own business.

- 75 percent of those would-be entrepreneurs agree the Internet has made starting a business significantly easier than traditional brick-and-mortar means.

- And 47 percent of these merchants-in-training have indicated they'd never consider themselves "too old" to launch their own online venture.

    (Source: Yahoo / Harris Interactive Poll)

So if you've been a bit bashful about stepping forward with your best merchant's foot, why wait any longer? If you're still not convinced by those telling statistics that come straight from the hearts of your like-minded entrepreneurial peers, then consider specifically how choosing Yahoo can improve your experience, mitigate your risk, and help you realize your aspirations faster than you might imagine:

- Yahoo Inc. is the Number 1 Internet brand, globally.

- Yahoo.com is the most trafficked Internet destination worldwide.

    (Source: Harris Interactive Poll)

What this all means is that when you choose Yahoo Merchant Solutions, you're choosing to open shop in a highly trafficked, highly regarded realm on the Internet. Just as you wouldn't choose to open a brick-and-mortar store in a desolate area of your town or city, so too would you avoid making your leap into an online business in some dark corner of cyberspace. With the activity at Yahoo, it will be hard for you not to get noticed. So, let's learn about those Merchant Solutions.

A Look at the Foundation Under Yahoo Merchant Solutions

First off, let's see precisely why Yahoo Merchant Solutions will be a good choice for your online fortune mining:

- **Stability**   Yahoo has been on a continual growth path ever since its inception in 1994 and continues to be the Number 1 Internet destination in light of all other comers. Yahoo performs data backups of your store weekly, daily, and even hourly, mitigating the risk of lost information.

- **Security**   Of tantamount importance to today's online shopper is knowing that transactions will be secure and protected from mischievous meddling. The Order Form pages at Yahoo are managed via secure HTTPS connections, utilizing industry-standard information encryption. Moreover, your customers' credit card information is encrypted three times during their shopping experiences.

- **Dependability**   If there's one thing the folks at Yahoo have done well is to take a lesson from their online peers when it comes to the matter of customer/user support. That is, many other web "giants" have routinely snubbed their site users, visitors, and community members. Yahoo, with its suite of member solutions and tools (like Merchant Solutions), provides round-the-clock telephone support toll free, every day of the week, that you can count on. And, for new Merchants, Yahoo provides 30-day direct support by a designated consultant (yes, you'll have a direct line to a single individual as you start up your business).

- **Flexibility**   Perhaps the greatest allure of starting an online business is you can do so to suit your particular needs and income goals. Yahoo Merchant Solutions provides a suite of tools that can enable you to create and maintain your store in a variety of ways.

- **Expandability**   Although you may choose to start off small with your business (which is fine just as long as you *do* start), Yahoo makes it easy for you to grow your venture with tools and incremental solutions that are ready when you are.

- **Affordability**   Best of all, the Yahoo Merchant Solutions offer you a choice of store styles and features, allowing you to create your first store for less than $100 (setup fee plus the first of your monthly fees), so you can reach millions of online shoppers faster and easier than traditional land-based methods.

In addition, Yahoo is operating on state-of-the-industry server technology with nonstop monitoring and maintenance processes and procedures to ensure the site runs smoothly and interruption-free. Granted, Yahoo was target of the DOS (Denial Of Service) attacks in the late 1990s, but the company took the lessons learned from that unprecedented event to further bolster and safeguard its infrastructure to ensure that Yahoo Merchants and other users would be spared any impact of such unwelcome affronts. Yahoo

Let's move ahead into a look at the specific offerings with the Yahoo Merchant Solutions.

Comparing Yahoo Merchant Solution Packages

When it comes to comparing and contrasting the services of a particular provider, it's best if you can get an objective opinion on the matter. Well, here's your second opinion—from the authors firsthand experience, Yahoo Merchant Solutions *do* make for an excellent business platform.

As noted earlier in this chapter, Yahoo offers a tiered approach to its Merchant Solutions in an effort to provide entrepreneurs the amount of service that best suits their immediate needs (see Figure 12-1).

This approach is good but it's also something of a conundrum for first-time shop owners who may want a bit more clarity on how much service is enough, how much is too little, and how much is just money wasted on profit-siphoning bells and whistles. Each tier offers this common set of core tools and services:

- A free web domain name with your store (**www.YourStore.com**, perhaps)

- Free 24×7 phone and e-mail support (plus that 30-day consultant service)

- 20GB (gigabytes) of hosted disk space and 500GB of data transfer allowance per month

- Product catalog and inventory management tools

- A shopping cart solution that aids shoppers in selecting and "checking out" their purchases using credit card payments

- Website design tools

- Order management tools to provide sales transaction management

- Shipping solution integration using UPS (United Parcel Service) rates, package tracking, and label printing

FIGURE 12-1   Get ready to open your Yahoo Store by visiting the Merchant Solutions home page at http://sbs.smallbusiness.yahoo.com/merchant

■ Full statistics of store activity and traffic

■ Password protections

■ Fax and e-mail tools, allowing alternate customer order receipt and management

■ 1000 Yahoo BusinessMail e-mail accounts, each with 2GB of storage space (yes, you'll want to use several accounts to manage the different aspects of your business—maybe not 1000, but certainly more than one or two)

■ Spam and anti-virus protection for incoming e-mail

■ Access to marketing services that can boost the visibility of your online shop

	Starter	Standard	Professional
Fees			
Monthly hosting fee	$39.95	$99.95	$299.95
One-time setup fee	$50.00	$50.00	$50.00
Per-transaction fee	1.5%	1.0%	0.75%
Order Processing			
Fax/e-mail orders	E-mail only	Fax/e-mail	Fax/e-mail
Order data forwarding (real time)	No	Yes	Yes
Shipping Tools			
Export of orders to UPS WorldShip Tools	No	Yes	Yes
Merchandising			
Gift certificates	No	Yes	Yes
Cross-sell engine	No	Yes	Yes
Coupon manager	No	Yes	Yes
Affiliate/revenue sharing link tracking	No	Yes	Yes
Statistics			
Click trail tracking	No	Yes	Yes
Frequent searches (for your store)	No	Yes	Yes

TABLE 12-1   Comparison of Differences in Yahoo Merchant Solutions Service Levels

Wow! With that many standard features, it looks as if you're armed and ready to open a shop with just the common tools, right? All three variations of the Yahoo Merchant Solutions offer the foregoing features but Table 12-1 shows where they differ.

That's an impressive list of common services and some interesting "upgrade" features, but what does it all mean? It means you'll need to do some close scrutiny of these service plans (especially the associated monthly costs) as you're starting out. To help you out, the next sections break down the three tiers to help you determine which might be best for you.

Starter Level

The Yahoo team will tell you this is the best place to be if you anticipate you'll tally up to $11,999 in sales each month. That's not a bad haul, and it's certainly worthy of the comparatively paltry $39.95 monthly maintenance fee. In addition, consider all the tools that are common across the three tiers and you'll see that, as a new shop owner, you'll likely have more tools than you might immediately use. But that's the idea because the whole concept at work here, as noted before, is to provide you a tool suite and market opportunity that grows as your business grows.

For first-timers, it's best to go with the Starter level (hey, there's no shame in being a "starter" because it means you've committed to getting *started*). At this level, your monthly maintenance cost is lowest and you can take a bit more time learning how to own and operate your online venue without counting the dollars being spent with every hour. Rather, you can have the freedom to experiment with the tools, your store design, and engage the Yahoo support team without spending more than you need in the process.

Standard Level

This level, according to Yahoo, is best for sellers who expect revenues between $12,000 and $79,999 per month. There are several differentiators of note in this level as compared to Starter and, when you're ready to use them, they certainly justify the $99.99 monthly maintenance fee.

First, the ability to use gift certificates and coupons is rather significant since such promotions have become the industry standard of online shopping (think about the numerous websites and newsgroups devoted solely to legitimately disseminating money saving codes).

The Cross-sell engine is an industry-standard caliber tool that helps dynamically suggest additional items or potential "up-sell" (upgrade) items based upon what your customers might currently have in their shopping carts, often convincing them to purchase more than they may have originally intended.

The affiliate tracking tools allow you to monitor the volume of business (in visits and actual sales) from customers who were referred to your site by a partner site. When you establish an affiliate relationship with a site of similar content (perhaps a site that offers oil painting instruction if you're selling artist's supplies), you want to monitor how successful that relationship is proving to be and, more importantly, you want to reward the owner of the referring site by paying an agreed-upon percentage of revenues generated by way of the referral.

The fax order capability is, in my opinion, of lesser value, as more and more people (buyers and sellers) are gaining confidence in direct online purchase and payment transactions.

The click-trails feature is more significant, since it provides details of how customers navigated their way to your site and what sorts of search words or topics they entered while visiting your store, providing you a deeper look into your customers' wants, needs, and shopping predispositions. When you're ready to boost your revenues beyond your offerings alone, you'll use this sort of market data to help drive how you'll grow your business and how you may alter your product catalog.

Professional Level

If you're anticipating sales to add up to $80,000+ per month, then Yahoo would love to usher you up to their Professional level. If you look back at Table 12-1, you'll see there aren't any additional features to be gained (you got them all when you upgraded to the Standard level), but your per-transaction fee will be reduced to only 0.75 percent of each transaction (compared to 1.5 percent at the Starter level and 1.0 percent at the Standard level). When you can consistently maintain a level of sales near six figures each month, you have to consider the bite the per-transaction fee is taking out of your bottom line and, if the figures support it, make the transition to Professional level. The monthly fee is hefty at $299.95, but it's pocket change compared to $80K every 30 days.

As you can see, you have a choice to make. Recall the various discussion points raised in Part I of this book as you explored the different ways of creating and developing your business. Determine how the approach you began to devise then will fit into one of the Yahoo Merchant Solution tiers. When you've made your choice, it's time to start your adventure.

TIP

If you still have questions about the different Merchant Solutions tiers or you're uncertain which level might be right for you, give the Yahoo team a call, toll free, at 866-781-9246. Even if you haven't joined up yet, that support team is on the job and ready to help you.

Chapter 13

Getting Started

Okay. So you have an idea of the sort of Merchant Solution level you'll participate at (and, for the sake of the chapters going forward and in the spirit of starting from the start, we'll utilize the features of the Standard level), and you're now ready to get your business off the ground. Good. While there's much to do to get ready to open a store, this chapter gives you a checklist of things to do, things to consider, and things to avoid in step-by-step fashion. Follow this chapter faithfully and you'll soon be ready to stock your virtual shelves.

Let's get started!

First Things First

This to-do list approach begins with a precursory checklist of information you'll need before you begin the store creation process. Here's a list of those elements you'll need before you register for a Yahoo Merchant account.

Product Data

I'll show you how to create actual product listings in Chapter 16, but before you can do that, you'll need product information. And, in order to successfully create product listings for your Yahoo store, you'll need to have specific information identified to create a successful product in your online catalog. Therefore, here are the bits of information you'll need, named consistently with the Yahoo product catalog requirements:

- **ID**   This is a multipurpose identifier, unique to each product, yet used in numerous ways by Yahoo to establish the product's presence in your store. For example, an ID like "mug-01-02" may identify a coffee mug you're selling, design "01," and color or style of "02." Beyond this being meaningful to you, this same ID is also used as the identifier of the eventual product page where it will appear in your overall store design. And it's used to identify the corresponding product image that your customers will see. More details will be uncovered in Chapter 16 when you create a product listing.

- **Name**   This is a free text field where you can create a name for your product using letters, numbers, and some special characters.

- **Code**   This is a unique code that your customers will see when they view your products (unlike the ID field, which is used for cataloging purposes only). It's akin to a stock keeping unit (SKU) identifier—like a product number—but often includes use of an ISBN (if you're selling books) or UPC (if you're selling bar-coded products).

- **Price**   The selling price of your item. Use only numerals and decimal spaces here since the Yahoo catalog manager will not allow the use of commas or dollar signs.

- **Sale-price**   This price field overrides the aforementioned Price field in that its intended use is to display a markdown from a regular "list price," if you will. Only use this field if you intend to have a temporary sale or if you want to always promote the concept of "lower than retail" pricing.

- **Orderable**   This should default to Yes and is used to signify, within the Yahoo catalog manager, if the item is presently available for customers to order. This could be changed to No if the item is out of stock.

- **Ship-weight**   This important field is used to calculate shipping costs based on weight. You'll need to calculate this to know how much to charge your customers for shipping costs so they, too, can anticipate the additional charges.

- **Taxable**   If you're required to collect sales and use tax in your state of business, enable this field to Yes.

- **Image**   Specify the filename of the image for the product.

- **Options**   Here's where you'll be able to specify if a product is available in different sizes, colors, styles, or include some sort of customization (for example, monograms). We'll cover this in greater detail in Chapter 16.

Okay. That covers the core information you'll need when you actually create your Yahoo store product catalog items. Don't be too concerned if the terminology seems a bit foreign to you now; once you create a couple of items, you'll be well on your way in your understanding of Yahoo's naming conventions and the use and meaning of each term.

And, when you actually create a product listing (Chapter 16), I'll introduce some additional fields you'll potentially use. For now, this information ensures you have your products identified in a way that ensures you'll be able to list, load, and sell them to your prospective customers.

Product Images

Beyond detailed product information, you'll also need product images. It has become commonly understood and accepted that online shoppers are more inclined to make a purchase if they can first inspect an image of an item. And, while fewer and fewer online customers will even entertain the idea of purchasing an item sight unseen, even more are becoming inclined to make an otherwise *unplanned* purchase simply because an available image spurred a spontaneous buy. Images, then, help ensure positive customer activity on either end of the "shopping comfort" perspective and are absolutely mandatory if you intend to become truly successful in your online venture.

Thanks to simplified technology and cheaper costs, digital images are almost a no-brainer these days. If you resell a wholesaler's or manufacturer's goods, they'll usually provide a stock photo of the items you'll offer. If you're selling your own goods (whether hand-made or otherwise self-acquired), then you'll need to create your own images. While I anticipate you've had some experience in creating compelling product pictures, here are a few quick tips to ensure your pictures help prompt purchases:

- Choose either a neutral or a complementary contrasting background for your products (or consider cut-out images where you remove all background elements and enable the image of the product to "float" on your store page).

- Ensure good focus for good details.

- Light properly to avoid dark images and color skewing, yet don't flood an image so much that it will look washed out, have deep shadows, or show glare.

- Consider composite images that reveal multiple angles or highlight details, combined into a single image display.

Now, specific to your Yahoo store, you'll need to ensure the following regarding your product images:

- Images should be sized no larger than 800–1000 pixels in height or width.

- Images should be saved as either JPG ("jay-peg") or GIF ("giff") format files.

- Images should be named consistent with your product ID (that is, if your product ID will be "mug01" then your image filename should be "mug01 .jpg" or "mug01.gif."

- Image filenames should contain only letters ("a" through "z"), numbers (0 through 9), or a hyphen ("-"). Neither other characters nor blank spaces are permitted in the filename.

TIP   *It's a good idea to browse around at other merchants' stores and inspect their images to see which seem compelling and which don't. Remember, you can learn a great deal about marketing your own products when you study how your potential competitors are marketing theirs.*

Store Policy

Right behind your product information will be your policies of how you intend to do business as a Yahoo merchant. Decide up front what sort of policies you'll use in regard to payment methods, shipping methods, return and/or guarantee statements, and contact information. In addition, you'll be required to provide a statement regarding your Privacy Policy, which indicates what you'll do (and won't do) with customer data. I'll cover this in a greater detail in Chapter 15.

Merchant Account

While this seems to be the proverbial conundrum of the "chicken and the egg," in order to open a Yahoo Merchant account, you'll need to have a valid merchant account for managing orders received. Some folks come into the Yahoo space with a pre-established merchant account of some sort, while others don't. Not to worry, because if you don't already have a merchant account, you can elect to establish one with Paymentech (a Yahoo Merchant Solutions partner) or utilize a PayPal account. We'll discuss the pros and cons of each a bit later in this chapter.

Inventory Spreadsheet

While this is certainly an optional element, it's a good idea to have some sort of computer-based inventory listing (perhaps managed in a simple Microsoft Excel spreadsheet) to record and keep the details of your products. You'll need to have your product information captured in an organized manner and, using a spreadsheet, you can easily manage that information offline, later to upload the data into your Yahoo store product catalog. If you recall the information noted previously regarding the details of your products to be used for creating Yahoo catalog listings, you'll likely see the immediate value of a spreadsheet where you can maintain this information outside of the actual Yahoo Merchant Solutions toolset.

And Now...Registering for Your Yahoo Merchant Solutions Account

So, without further ado, here's the step-by-step approach to registering for your Yahoo Merchant Solutions account. Again, you'll register for the Standard account for the purposes of this book in order to discuss and explain some of the additional features of that tier. Remember, if you're just starting out, the Starter level account may be best for you, knowing you can easily upgrade to Standard level whenever you're ready.

FIGURE 13-1   Select your Merchant Solution store level to start your online adventure

To begin, visit the Yahoo Merchant Solutions area of Yahoo—either navigate from the Yahoo home page and click All Y! Services and then click the Merchant Solutions link, or simply type in this URL address in your web browser's address bar: **http://sbs.smallbusiness.yahoo.com/merchant/**. Either method will land you on the Merchant Solutions main page, shown in Figure 13-1.

You've decided which store tier will be best for you, so simply click the Sign Up button under the appropriate heading. Upon doing so, you'll see a screen where you will choose a domain name for your store. You may already have a domain name (if so, click the Already have a domain name? link shown in Figure 13-2). If you don't have a domain name already, here's where you can get creative as you establish your store's presence in the online world. Of course, there are a few

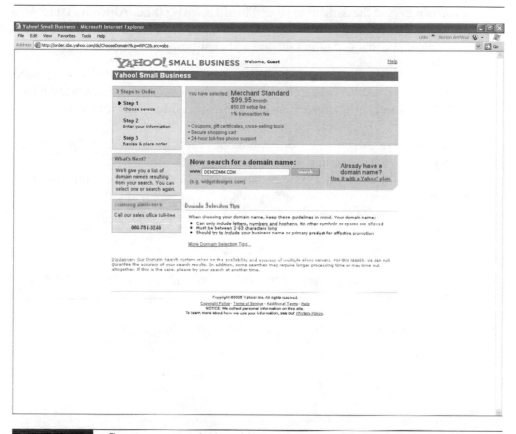

FIGURE 13-2   Create your store's domain name or use an existing domain

things to consider as you choose your domain name, elements that will make you more successful in your online adventure. Specifically:

- Choose a name that's readable, easy to spell, and easy to say (if you were to verbalize your domain name, would your listener understand how to type that correctly into a web browser and quickly find your store?).

- If you already have a business name, then choose a domain name that matches it. This can be problematic if the best domain name for your business has already been secured by someone else (first come, first served). If your business is Standard Products and you find that **www.standardproducts.com** has already been taken, you can elect to use a different extension (.net, .biz) or

you can extend the domain to something like **www.standardproductsonline
.com**. If you're just now choosing your business name, then work with a
domain name that will represent you and your business, online and off.

■ Try your best to secure a .com extension for your domain. While I've suggested
possible use of different extensions, research shows that customers are most
likely to anticipate a .com extension when accessing a URL online.

With that being said, choose a domain name, enter it in the Yahoo screen
(as shown in Figure 13-2), and continue.

Next, Yahoo will display a user login screen (see Figure 13-3). If you have an
existing Yahoo account (maybe e-mail), you can log in here and utilize that same
account to create your Merchant Solutions account. If you need to create a new
Yahoo identity, you can do that here, too.

FIGURE 13-3   Log in with your existing Yahoo account or create a new one

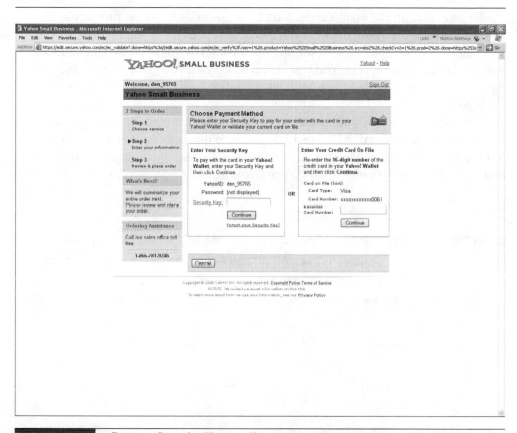

FIGURE 13-4   Create a Security Key to allow you secure management of your store

After that, you'll be asked to enter your Yahoo Security Key (see Figure 13-4). What's this? The Security Key allows you protected access to your Yahoo store account and, more importantly, allows you to establish your Yahoo Wallet, a virtual element where you can specify a credit card for payment of your Yahoo fees (including the initial setup costs of creating your Merchant Solutions account as well as the ensuing monthly fees to maintain your account).

TIP   *If you're nervous about having credit card information online, get over it. It's the way of the world today, but you can take steps to protect yourself by ensuring any site where you offer it uses encryption technology (Yahoo does), then checking with the card issuer to ensure they'll protect you against unauthorized charges if your information is ever compromised. A final self-defense step to take is to keep the card's limit low (maybe $3000) such that, if the information were compromised, a thief couldn't ring up too much activity before the limit was reached.*

Beyond creation of your Yahoo Wallet, the Security Key also protects access to your Yahoo store. With the key, you can access your store and manage it, yet you can also enable others with whom you'll work (business partners, contracted web designers, employees). You can create different levels of access to others by having them establish their own accounts and then adding them to your list of allowed users.

Finally, you'll verify your account selection and pertinent information on the review screen shown in Figure 13-5. Confirm this information and click the Submit Order button (at the bottom of the screen as displayed on your computer) and—just like that—you're ready to open your store.

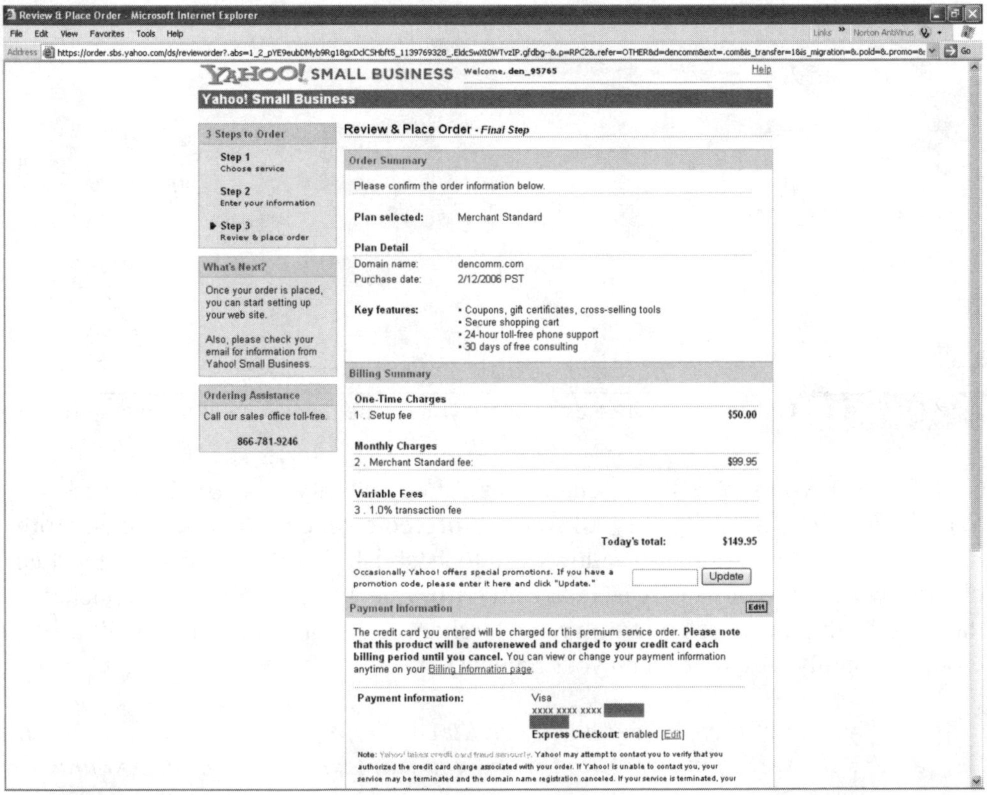

FIGURE 13-5 Verify your account selection and information to complete your Merchant Solutions account registration

Creating a Merchant Account

As noted earlier in this chapter, you'll need a merchant account in order to facilitate order payments and collections in association with your Yahoo store. In days gone by, "merchant account" implied setting up a credit card payment terminal to process credit orders. Today, the process has become infinitely easier to manage and afford. If you don't already have a merchant account established (some folks who create Yahoo stores are extending their existing brick-and-mortar establishments and, therefore, may already have established a merchant account), you have two new options to get yourself ready to accept credit card payments:

■ **Paymentech**   This preferred payment solution manager for Yahoo stores allows you to quickly establish a full-featured merchant solution for online credit card payment processing (see figure 13-6). The account setup process can take several days, so plan ahead.

FIGURE 13-6   Visit www.paymentech.com to establish a merchant account

FIGURE 13-7   Visit www.paypal.com for an easy alternative method for accepting credit card processing

■ **PayPal**   Yahoo has also enabled linkages to the PayPal solution to allow storeowners an alternative to a traditional merchant account. Visit **www .paypal.com** to create your account (see figure 13-7). Your account can be activated in as little as 24 hours, and usually less!

Chapter 14

Understanding the Elements of Your Store

Congratulations! You've successfully completed the first step to opening your own virtual business. Upon completing your registration for a Yahoo Merchant Services account, you have signed up for a thrilling and fulfilling undertaking, one that could certainly lead you down the path to personal fortune. Of course, every new adventure is typically filled with exciting yet unfamiliar elements, surroundings, and experiences. Embrace this element of your Yahoo store because it is certainly an achievable venture. No doubt you'll be wary of much of what you'll see as you prepare to build your online store, but don't fret: people do it all the time, and you can too!

In this chapter, we'll take you on a tour of the Yahoo store and the various areas and tools that will be at your disposal as you get ready for construction of your own sales haven. The tools might feel a bit awkward and even clumsy at first but persevere—you'll find you can get quite familiar with them in short order. While it's tempting to look ahead and discover how to start loading your store catalog, stay focused on learning how to use the tools first, *then* proceeding onward. This is a fun endeavor, so enjoy every step of the journey. First, though, let's get our bearings.

Manage My Services

With your account activated, all you need do to gain access to your store tool set is visit the Manage My Services page of Yahoo's Small Business area, either navigating from the Yahoo home page and clicking the Merchant Solutions link or entering the URL **http://sbs.smallbusiness.yahoo.com/services/**. When you do, you'll land on the main access page, as shown in Figure 14-1.

The Manage My Services page is your portal into your store and the veritable control center where you can access and manage all elements of your store, while you're building it and after you've published it and have begun receiving actual customer orders. To demonstrate the various store elements that you'll soon master in managing your own store, I'll walk you through the creation of the Summerdale House store, a destination for top-quality outdoor fire pits and grills, previously established under the domain of **www.firepitgrill.com**.

As a forewarning, prepare yourself that the Yahoo Merchant Solution tools haven't been designed for ultimate "user friendliness." That is, what you'll see may seem quite technical, often bordering on the edge of techno-babble, but it is the language of Yahoo Merchant Solutions, and you'll need to absorb and internalize it in order to be successful. Don't let the detailed nature of the store settings and parameters deter, dissuade, or otherwise discourage you. It's just terminology and once you understand what it means, you'll find you too can build a top-quality, professional-looking store of your own. Let's continue.

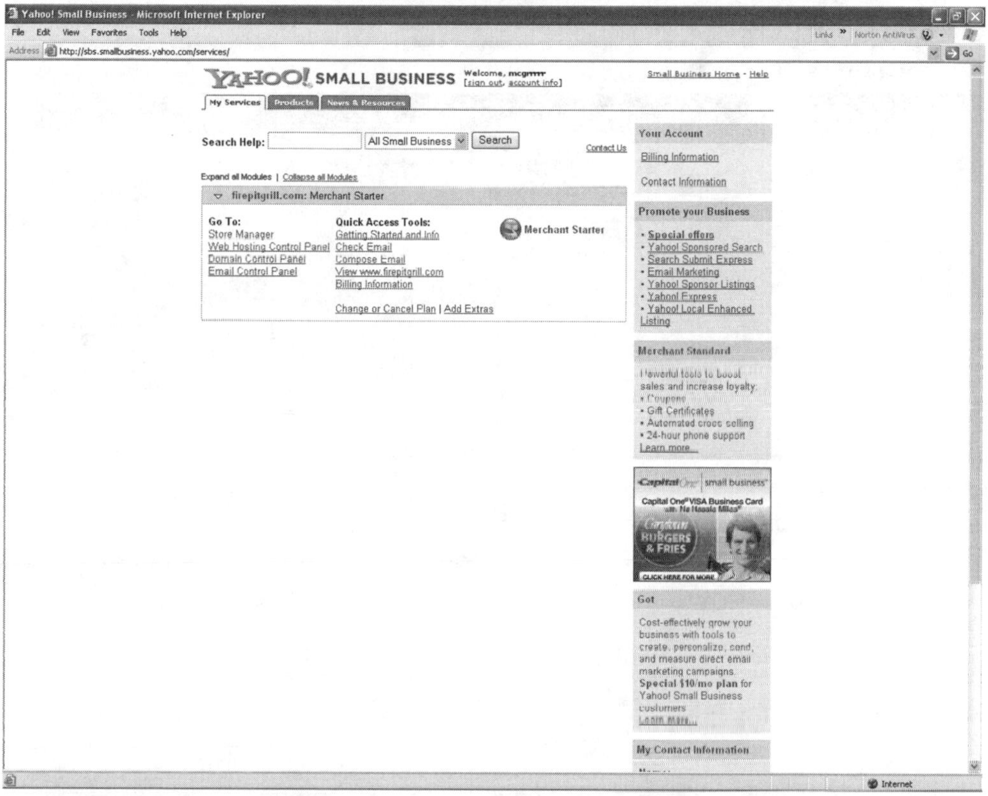

FIGURE 14-1   Begin your journey by getting familiar with Yahoo's Manage My Services launch pad

> TIP
>
> *Notice the text link on the Manage My Services page that reads, Change or Cancel Plan. If you've elected to start with the Starter level plan (and that's fine), this is the link you can use to upgrade to a Standard or Professional level plan as your business grows and your needs increase to include the additional features of the advanced store elements.*

Store Manager

Call this the heart of your Yahoo store, because it is the central location where you'll access and manage the various business functions associated with creating and running your store (see Figure 14-2).

Not only can you establish the design and overall content of your store, but you can also manage your catalog of products, your order processing, your

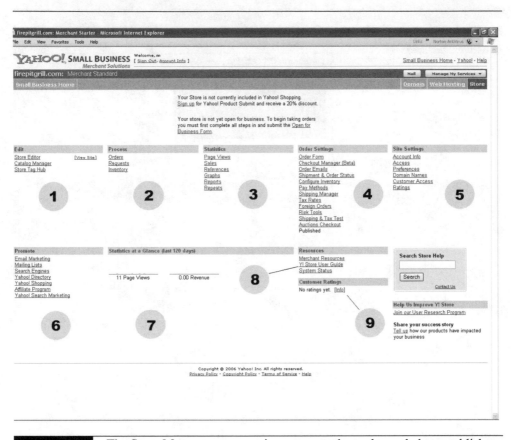

FIGURE 14-2 The Store Manager screen gains access to the tools needed to establish and manage your Yahoo store

special promotions, and your statistics of store activity. More specifically, here are the major business areas available to you, each with subelements, within the Store Manager. Each has been numbered in the following list to correspond with the numbered circles in Figure 14-2:

1. **Edit** Controls needed to create your store pages and manage your products.

2. **Process** Controls to view and manage your orders.

3. **Statistics** Controls to analyze your customer visits and purchases made.

4. **Order Settings** Tools to customize the manner in which orders are accepted, payment collected, and additional costs added.

5. **Site Settings**   Top-level settings that manage your account information, domain settings, and access controls.

6. **Promote**   Tool set to enable marketing and mailing communications.

7. **Statistics at a Glance**   Quick view of store activity, presented in graphic representation.

8. **Resources**   Access to additional tools and information to help in your store management.

9. **Customer Ratings**   Testimony from customers who have shopped your store.

> **TIP**   *Be aware that if you've begun with a Starter level store account, you'll have only limited access to the Promote features. Recall in Chapter 12 (Table 12-1) that many of the promotion tools were available only at the Standard and Professional levels.*

Catalog Manager

As you look again at Figure 14-3, you'll see that under the Edit area of the Store Manager is the link to access the Catalog Manager. Since that will be a key portion of your store creation and maintenance activity and an area where you'll need to gain mastery in relatively short order to maintain a flow of customers and orders, we'll discuss this one in more detail now. As mentioned, the Catalog Manager is your access point to product information—the product descriptions, details, images, pricing, and more. Look at Figure 14-3 and see how the Catalog Manager screen acts like another launching pad into further details of store management (much like the Store Manager screen itself).

Here are some further descriptions of the areas you'll encounter within the Catalog Manager main screen:

■ **Manage Your Items**   Here's where you'll access the product creation form, allowing you to create new product listings and manage them going forward.

■ **Manage Your Tables**   Tables are a method whereby you can group similar items for clean categorization within your store. You can create and manage these table groupings in this area.

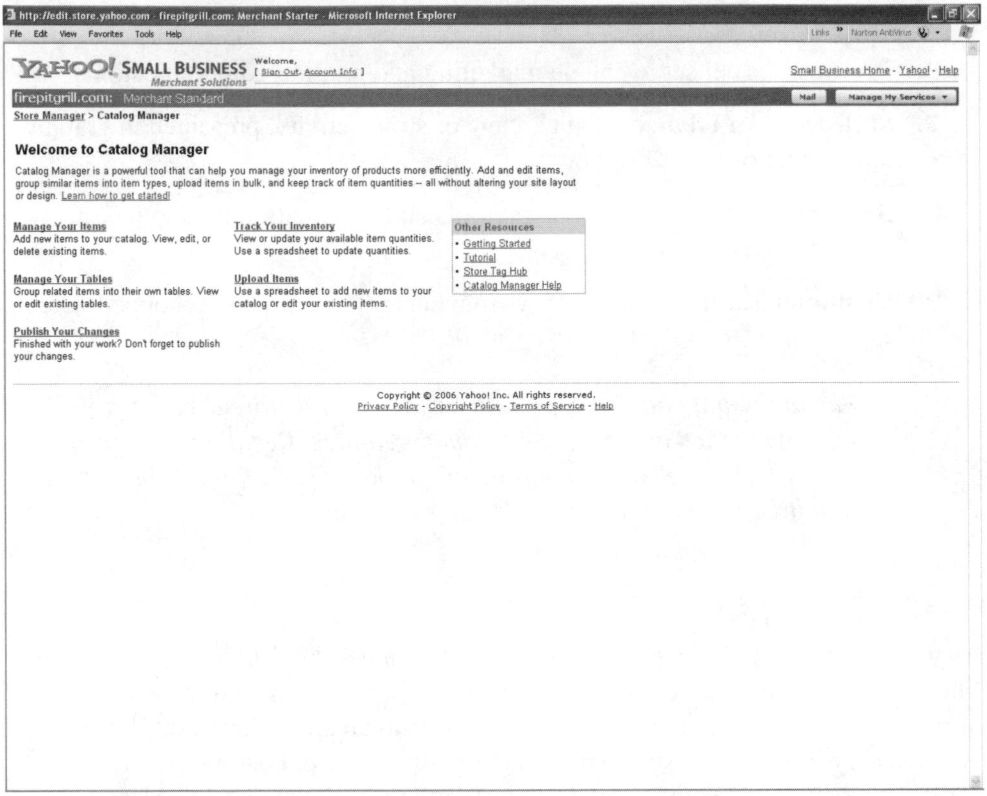

FIGURE 14-3   The Catalog Manager screen is where you'll manage and publish your product data and inventory levels

■ **Publish Your Changes**   After you've created or updated your catalog data, here's where you actually publish it to make it visible to your customers.

■ **Track Your Inventory**   Keep track of your inventory here and make updates to manage your inventory levels.

■ **Upload Items**   As noted in Chapter 13, here's where you can easily upload new product data or changes to existing product data from a spreadsheet you've maintained on your computer.

We'll get deeper into the details of each of the areas of the Catalog Manager screen as I demonstrate how to create and manage your product data in Chapter 16. For now, simply understand the navigation into this area.

Store Editor

If you return to the Store Manager screen, you'll see Store Editor text link, also located under the Edit heading along with the Catalog Manager link. Upon clicking the Store Editor link, you'll enter the area where you will assemble the elements that make up your store—the store title and header information; welcome messages and descriptions of the store in general; navigation buttons your customers will use to find, shop, and purchase products; and additional navigation points for customers to learn about your store policies and procedures. Think of the Store Editor as the place where you'll establish your "front door" and then how you'll set up your "store shelves" and "customer service center," just as in a brick and mortar store.

Look now at Figure 14-4 and you'll see that, upon first entry, your store is pretty much like an empty room with four bare walls and a collection of tools

Edit	will let you edit the proportion of index
Edit All	will let you edit all the items from this point down.
Section	will create a new section and list it here.
Item	will create a new item and list it here.
Link	will create a new link to an external page and list it here.
Image	will let you upload a logo
Look	will let you interactively change the look of your site.
Variables	will let you change the overall properties of the site.
Manager	takes you back to your store manager.
Publish	writes out a copy of your site to http://store.yahoo.com/yhst-91156304389766/.
Left Arrow	will let you switch to the regular interface.
Contents	takes you to a table of contents for the site.
Templates	leads to the templates page.
Types	leads to the types page.
Database Upload	will let you add to your site by uploading data files.
Config	will let you set properties of the Store Editor such as Editor toolbar location, default templates, and default items.
Controls	set Store Editor properties such as mode and editor entry page, or access advanced features such as search, multiple image upload, edit multiple items, and RTML documentation.
Alignment	determines how the elements on this page will be laid out.

FIGURE 14-4   In the Store Editor, you can establish the look and layout of your online venture

that will be used to fabricate the store elements. We've already hung up our sign, so to speak, to indicate this is the Summerdale House, but we haven't yet begun to use those tools—the rows of labeled box-buttons that will allow us to begin to define our store in more detail. We won't detail each of these box-buttons just yet, nor their function, as you'll see each in action as the store building process commences.

The most important thing to understand at this point is that the Store Editor is your interface for assembling your store, but it's not the only option for erecting your online sales place. That's right, the Store Editor is a Yahoo-provided tool yet you could, if you wanted, build your store using your favorite HTML editor. If you're more comfortable (and experienced) using a different tool to create store elements, you have that choice. We'll talk about this option in greater detail in Chapter 16. For now, recognize the use of Store Editor and where you can find it within the Store Manager main page. Onward.

Web Hosting Control Panel

Next up is the Web Hosting Control Panel. Look back at Figure 14-1 and you'll notice that, right below the text link we used to access the Store Manager is a text link labeled Web Hosting Control Panel. Click that link and you'll navigate to the aptly named screen as shown in Figure 14-5.

But what does Web Hosting do for you and why are you being presented this additional tool when it appears all you really need is Yahoo's Store Manager tool suite? Simple. Yahoo's Store Manager suite allows you to build one thing: a store (and a nice one at that). But, if you travel the web very much you've likely found several favorite sites where you can gain information about a product or service of some sort and also shop for goods, too. To that end, the Yahoo store has the "shop for goods" element covered, but it doesn't address the "gain information" element—that is, the website experience. Some of the best e-commerce sites out there provide additional compelling reasons to visit beyond shopping for goods. For example, since we're building the Summerdale House store that will offer high quality fire pit grills, we'd also be wise to provide our visitors with additional pages where they can learn more about fire pit grill safety, perhaps landscaping ideas to best showcase their fire pit grills, and perhaps even some great grilling recipes for their next outdoor feast. When you combine the website experience with the store tools, you create a complete "solution" for your customers and, if you keep the web content fresh and updated on a regular basis, you'll compel your customers to visit time and again to see what's new, and they'll be likely to buy more goods during their return visits.

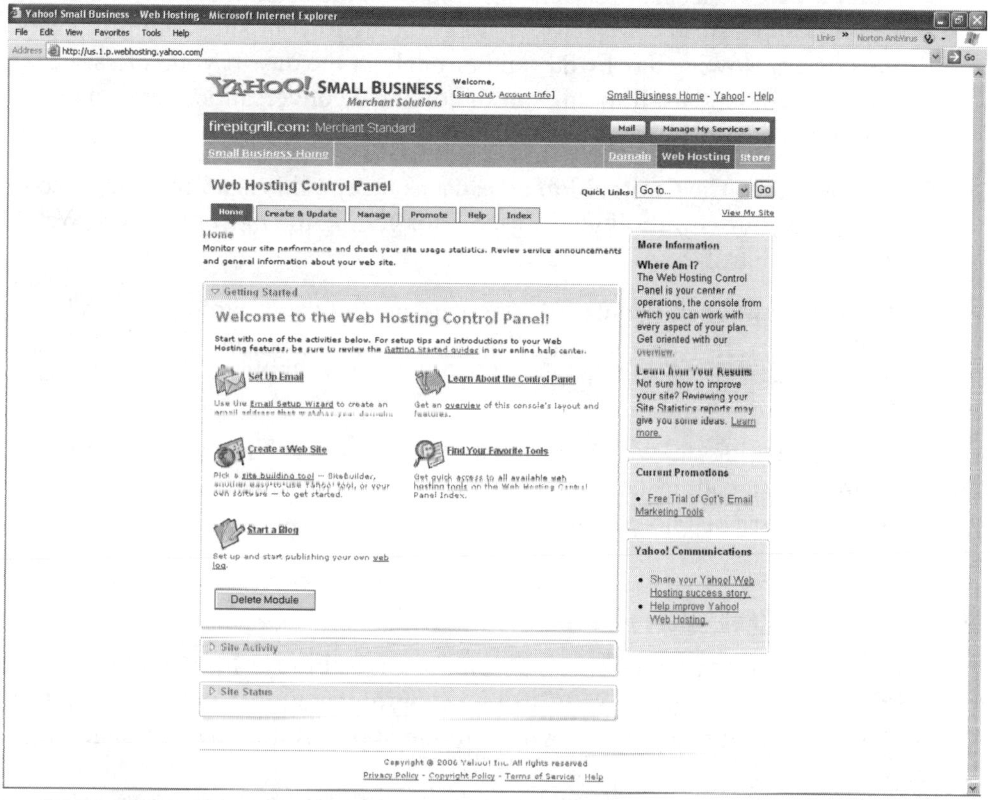

FIGURE 14-5 The Web Hosting Control Panel is your page to manage your Yahoo store from top to bottom

Turning back to the Web Hosting Control Panel now, a quick overview of its contents are as follows (refer to Figure 14-5):

- **Set Up E-mail** Here's where you'll create a usable e-mail address that matches your store or website name, giving your customers the ability to correspond with you directly.

- **Create a Website** Here's where you can access Yahoo's own SiteBuilder tool, a WYSIWYG (What You See Is What You Get) web page design tool that allows a fast and simple way to create a website to complement your Yahoo store.

- ■ **Start a Blog**   Seems everyone has "blog" on the brain these days. One way to keep a steady stream of visitors coming to your site/store is to keep the content flowing day by day and throughout the day. If your site/store concept will lend itself to this sort of continual conversation, here's a tool to create your very own blog.

- ■ **Learn About the Control Panel**   Just as it says, this is a link to help you self-tutor your way through the aspects of getting the most out of the Web Hosting Control Panel.

- ■ **Find Your Favorite Tools**   Acting very much like a "site map," this link will gain you fast access to al of the Web Hosting Control Panel tools in a nicely arranged text link index.

We'll be re-visiting the Web Hosting Control Panel in subsequent chapters. For now, recognize its location and intent and how it can help you create a total web experience to boost your store's bottom line.

Domain Control Panel

Revisit the Manage My Services page (refer again to Figure 14-1) and you'll see the next link in line, below Web Hosting Control Panel, is the Domain Control Panel. Click that link and you'll navigate to the appropriately named page (see Figure 14-6).

Recall when you registered for your Merchant Solutions account and were immediately asked to choose a domain name? At that point, you created (or specified an already existent) domain name where people will be able to find your store—as in **www.firepitgrill.com**. When you created that domain name, you automatically were registered in the WHOIS database, a central world-wide web directory that provides information of all the web domains that have been registered and the owners thereof. In the Domain Control Panel, you can make modifications to that information, if need be. Also, if you specified a pre-existing domain name when you created your Merchant Solutions account, you'll need to visit the Domain Control Panel to ensure that domain name, registered by a domain registrar provider outside of Yahoo (perhaps register.com or godaddy.com or countless others) will direct visitors to that domain to your new Yahoo store. Since this is a very important element of redirecting that you should manage sooner than later, here's how to redirect an existing domain name to your new Yahoo store:

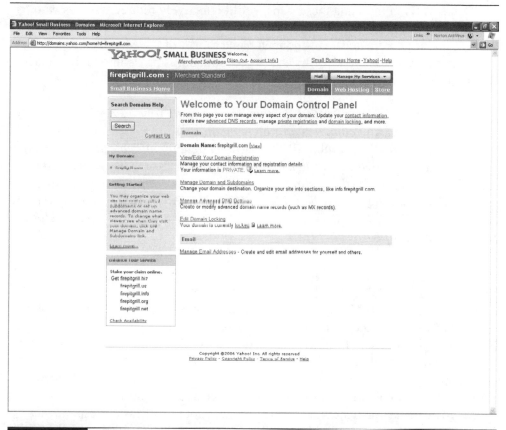

FIGURE 14-6   The Domain Control Panel is where you'll manage your store's WWW web address and details of it

1. From the Yahoo Domain Control Panel main page (refer to Figure 14-6), click the Manage Domain & Subdomains text link.

2. In the subsequent screen you'll see your established domain—that which you specified during the Merchant Solution account setup process—displayed. Click the text link next to it entitled Edit.

3. In the subsequent screen, select the Change the Destination to My Store Editor Home Page option button.

4. At the bottom of the screen, click the Submit button.

That's it. By completing these steps, you'll effectively redirect visitors who enter your pre-established domain name to your new Yahoo store. Remember, though, that if you created a new domain name as part of the Merchant Solutions account setup process, you won't need to go through this procedure; Yahoo made the connection to your store for you.

<table>
<tr><td>TIP</td><td>If you redirect an existing domain name to your Yahoo store as previously described, the change won't be immediate. Yahoo makes the actual redirections at midnight PST every night and, upon requesting the change, you'll deactivate your domain forwarding until Yahoo has completed the redirection. For this reason—it will disrupt any traffic to your existing web domain that you may be supporting—it's best to make this redirection at a day of lowest traffic activity on your existing domain name and as close to midnight PST as possible.</td></tr>
</table>

E-mail Control Panel

Lastly, this tour of the Manage My Services home page completes with at look at the E-mail Control Panel. As with the previous two pages, visit the Manage My Services page and click the aptly titled text link. When you do so, you'll navigate to the E-mail Control Panel page as shown in Figure 14-7.

Recall that when you signed up for a Merchant Solutions account you were afforded 1000 e-mail addresses with which to manage your business. Here's where you can establish those address to conduct your business correspondence in an efficient. What sort of addresses should you create? Consider the following examples:

- info@firepitgrill.com
- orders@firepitgrill.com
- feedback@firepitgrill.com
- customerservice@firepitgrill.com
- partners@firepitgrill.com

As you can see, using multiple e-mail addresses allows you to segregate your business correspondence, likely assigning responsibility to manage each account to employees of your company (or just to keep them all neatly separated if you're managing your store on your own).

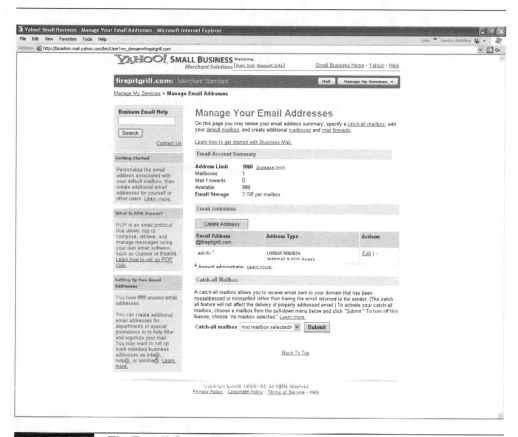

FIGURE 14-7 The E-mail Control Panel is where you'll establish all necessary e-mail nodes to manage your business correspondence

This completes the overview of the Yahoo Manage My Services home page. Next up, we'll take a closer look at the ways in which you might choose to build your store and accompanying website.

Chapter 15
Tools to Build Your Site

If you recall from the previous chapter, you learned a bit about the Yahoo Web Hosting Control Panel. Within that suite of tools you can access Yahoo's own SiteBuilder utility that enables you to rather easily create your own website, which can play companion to your Yahoo Store. But also recall that I mentioned that there are other options for building your website; there are other tools you can use to create a web page that may suit you better. For the purposes of this book, subsequent chapters will utilize the Yahoo SiteBuilder tool, but I'd be remiss if I didn't spend a little time explaining the other options available to you so you can decide for yourself.

Before We Begin: Comparing Web Hosting and Store Editor

Previously, I indicated all you really need to open a business was the Yahoo Store itself, which you could choose to build with the resident Store Editor tool (or other tools that you'll soon read about in this chapter). But beyond the discussion of whether Store Editor will be your design tool of choice comes the additional consideration of how Web Hosting features compare to those of the Yahoo Store Editor. Look at Table 15-1 to see the key comparison points between these two tool sets.

	Web Hosting	Store Editor
Page development	Pages are developed on your computer using a tool like Yahoo SiteBuilder or a third-party web development tool.	Pages are built directly in the Store Editor tool from an active web browser window, requiring you be actively connected to the Internet.
Page publishing	Completed pages need to be uploaded to your Web Hosting account using your development tool functions, an FTP client, or a File Manager upload utility.	Pages are published with a simple click of the Publish button from the Store Editor toolbar.
Page Location after publishing	Pages are published to your specified domain URL (for example, **www.firepitgrill.com**).	Pages are published to the Yahoo Store domain for your account (for example, store.firepitgrill.com).

TABLE 15-1   Comparison of Web Page Development Features between Yahoo Web Hosting and Store Editor

These comparative points are all fine and well, but what do they really mean? Succinctly, the table illustrates the effort involved in utilizing Web Hosting is more complex than that of Store Editor. Does that make Store Editor the easy choice, then? Actually, no. There are trade-offs to be made with whichever method you use to create and, more importantly, manage your store. While Store Editor is the easiest tool to use, especially to those new to building a store site, it does have limitations that can be overcome only by electing to use the Web Hosting tool (or other similar third-party web development tools). Let's look at these differences inherent to the maintenance of a store site, again comparing Store Editor and Web Hosting. Table 15-2 has the details.

	Web Hosting	Store Editor
Development Ease	If you're familiar with web hosting tools and methods, you can develop your own site template (look and feel) and will import your Catalog Manager data (products) as you choose. You'll establish links to your product pages directly. You'll test you store functionality as you choose.	When you update your Catalog Manager data, the Store Editor automatically creates new product pages for you. Page templates are ready made for you to utilize immediately. Testing matters have already been managed by means of the predeveloped catalog and template elements integration with Store Editor.
Customizability	You can exert full control over the content and functionality of your store. Also, if you're experienced in the use of advanced design tools like PHP/MySQL and Perl, you can utilize those features in this approach.	Detailed customizations are limited and sometimes a bit more cumbersome using Store Editor (especially if you're familiar with another web development tool). If, however, you're new to web design, Store Editor's limited customization options are offset by its relative ease of use and inherent integration.
Your experience with development tools	If you're already comfortable with web development tools, you can continue to use those as you design your store rather than learn a new Yahoo-provided tool.	If you don't have a prior web development experience, the Yahoo Store Editor is probably you best choice for starting out. You can elect to migrate to a different tool after you've gained more experience or find the need to incorporate more customized and advanced design elements.

TABLE 15-2   More Comparisons of Web Page Development Options and Considerations between Yahoo Web Development and Store Editor

Upon reviewing the points raised in Table 15-2, it should be easier for you to decide how you'll build your store. That is, you should consider focusing on the use of Store Editor exclusively if:

- You have no (or very limited) experience with web development tools and methods.

- You want to build and publish your store in the quickest manner possible.

- You don't want to be slowed by matters of site testing and debugging problems.

- You don't yet have an overriding need for total customization of your store, at least not yet.

TIP   *Before we get too far ahead here, understand there's one more limitation inherent to the Web Hosting SiteBuilder tool: you can only create a maximum of 100 product entries in SiteBuilder. For most folks just starting out, that's often of little concern. Even folks who manage products seasonally can be successful within this limit, swapping out catalog entries as the seasons change (keeping all product records safe and secure in a spreadsheet file on their computers to prevent the need from having to re-create them every year). If you feel this 100-product limit is too constraining to you, then you'll want to use both the Store Editor (to create and manage your product listings) and Web Hosting to better customize your web page content.*

When Worlds Combine

To this point, I've alluded to the creation of your store and possible accompanying page content in terms of both being integrated within the Yahoo realm. There is another option, though: you can have your Yahoo Store and your website peacefully co-exist as two distinct entities. That's right, you don't *have* to combine all of your content into one Yahoo basket.

If you have a website already, there's nothing that says you *must* combine it with your Yahoo Store in order to be successful; quite the contrary, in fact. Assume you've been hosting the website **www.firepitgrill.com** as a destination to learn ways to construct a garden setting that would be conducive for fire pits, providing how-to tips, planting suggestions, and fire safety information. Consider that your site has been very popular with folks who enjoy fire pits (and grills) and they've appreciated the information you've been able to pass along. You have a great base of visitors and perhaps you even started up a regular e-mail newsletter to continue to proliferate all the good things about fire pits in outdoor living spaces. Perhaps, though, your visitors began commenting that they just don't know where to buy their fire pits, or they want to know our recommendations of brands and styles that would be best in consideration to all that you've shared thus far. Well, you could redirect them to manufacturers or resellers of the sorts of fire pits and grills you endorse, or you could decide it would be more profitable to *sell them yourself.* Here's where two great ideas marry up, and suddenly your well established information portal has morphed into a retail destination. But you needn't board up **www.firepitgrill.com**, the sought out information site that's been hosted by a web hosting service elsewhere, in deference to starting over at Yahoo. Instead, you can simply create a Yahoo Store and link to it from our existing site, still hosted by our previous host provider.

Just thought I should mention this very important consideration to you.

Comparing Web Development Tools

As stated, we will be using Yahoo's SiteBuilder tool for the purposes of this book. I make this choice not because SiteBuilder is the *best* tool to use for building a website but, rather, because it's integrated within the overall Yahoo Merchant Solutions suite and is a very decent tool for those who are new to web design. The good news here is that even if you've never created a website before, you'll find that with a bit of patience, perseverance, and creative spark, you'll have a highly professional-looking site in a very short time.

Of course, I feel I should also introduce you to some of the other prevalent tools by which you could achieve the same (or even better) end result. While I certainly can't explain all the intrinsic workings of these other tools within the span of this book, I do want to acknowledge the options available to you so you may do further research of your own, if that's what you choose. Therefore, we'll consider the additional tools, beyond SiteBuilder, including Microsoft's FrontPage, Macromedia's Dreamweaver, or, collectively, the numerous other direct HTML editors. Take a look, now at Table 15-3 and its comparison of these different toolsets.

	Yahoo SiteBuilder	Microsoft FrontPage	Macromedia Dreamweaver	Other HTML Editing Tools
Cost	Free with your Merchant Solutions account activation.	Included with MS Office suite or $199 if purchased separately.	At this writing, Dreamweaver 8 is priced at $399.	Some free, some require purchase (prices vary).
Speed of development	Fastest because it's integrated into the Yahoo suite.	Relatively quick since it's a WYSIWYG tool but often requires direct HTML edits.	Much slower since it's so feature laden. You can increase your speed of use as your experience grows.	Depends upon the tool.
Flexibility	Least flexible in terms of comparative features, and you will not be able to directly edit the generated HTML code.	More flexible, yet still somewhat constrained to the Microsoft design.	Highly flexible and developed specifically for this purpose.	Depends upon the tool.
Know-how	Relatively easy to learn, and Yahoo support team can help you through any sticking points.	Also easy to learn yet requires some HTML skills to debug any direct HTML problems.	Quite complex with a steep learning curve.	Depends upon the tool.
Catalog support	Limited to 100 products.	No limit.	No limit.	Depends upon the tool but likely capable to support any number of products you want to create and manage.

TABLE 15-3   Comparison of Web Page Development Tools

Decisions, Decisions

So it's time to decide which approach you'll take in building your store and/or web pages and which tools you'll use to do so. Review this information a few times and spend some time at the Yahoo Merchant Solutions area to further investigate your options. Most importantly, consider your current experience level, your timeline for opening your store, and your potential product catalog both today as well as six months from now. And, remember, you can always make adjustments to the tools you use as your store development and maintenance experience grows over time. Yes, it's a lot to consider, and much of it could seem very foreign and potentially daunting to you. Don't throw in the towel, however. Subsequent chapters will walk you through the rest of the store creation and management phases, guiding you along the way to make your online fortune.

Chapter 16

Creating Your Product Listings

At last, it's time to begin building the product catalog for your new Yahoo Store. There's much to do here. We'll go into this exercise with the working assumption that you have adopted the idea of establishing and maintaining a spreadsheet of the items you'll offer. In this chapter, I'll show you the details of setting up a single product, explaining the various product data fields that you'll enter, why you'll enter them, and how to "publish" them so they'll be visible to your eventual customers. We'll also explain some of the inconsistencies—call them "idiosyncrasies"—of the Yahoo Merchant Solutions system. That is, you'll see a few things that'll make you go, "hmmm," as you create and publish your products. And, you'll learn that, while there are several ways to create and manage your products, some are definitely better than others. With that, let's start building your product catalog.

Two Paths to Product Creation

We've already taken you on a tour of the various tools of your Yahoo Store and, when it comes to creating your product listings, you'll find you have a couple of different ways—several really—to create and manage your catalog entries. Recall how I explained the method of building your site and your choice of using the Store Editor or using a web design approach using SiteBuilder or other third-party web development tools. The same holds true for creating your product listings—specifically, you can accomplish this task by using Yahoo's Catalog Manager, Store Editor, or a web development tool. And while it's true that having choices is a good thing, it can also incite be a bit overwhelming, as new store owners struggle to determine the best method to use.

Never fear—help is here.

To help you move along quickly and confidently at this stage of your store creation, I'll make this simple statement—I recommend you use the Catalog Manager when creating your product listings. Why? Well, rather than just tell you "because it's what I prefer," we'll offer these reasons:

- Viewing and sorting product data is easier. With Catalog Manager you can easily customize the views of your product data, choosing which data fields you want to see and in what order. If you want to sort your product data by a particular field (perhaps ID, name, or caption), alphabetically ascending or descending, you can do that.

■ Grouping of similar products is a breeze. Only Catalog Manager allows you to establish use of "tables"—grouping identifiers where you can gather all sorts of similar products to improve your customers' shopping experience.

■ Some key item management tools are only available through Catalog Manager. This includes functionality that allows you to easily regroup items into the previously mentioned tables. If you need to delete multiple items in a single action, you can do that with Catalog Manager, too.

Now, am I stating you cannot use Store Editor to create your product listings? Absolutely not. In fact, I suggest you experiment with both methods and use whichever suits your personal needs and tastes. As a general rule of thumb, if you have very few products, you might be satisfied creating products under the limitations of Store Editor. If, however, you'll be managing tens and even hundreds of products, the Catalog Manager is likely a better bet. With that said, let's proceed in showing you how to create your first product listing using the Catalog Manger.

Creating Your First Product

Recall that you'll access the Catalog Manager by navigating to the Manage My Services page, selecting the Store Manager text link, and then clicking the Catalog Manager link. When you do so, you'll arrive at the Catalog Manager home page, as shown in Figure 16-1.

Click the Manage Your Items link and you'll proceed forward to the Items screen of the Catalog Manager (shown in Figure 16-2).

Upon your first visit to the Items screen, you'll see a whole lot of nothing—you haven't yet begun building your product catalog. So, to begin, click the Add Item button. When you do, you'll see a new page, as illustrated in Figure 16-3.

As you begin to enter your item details, you'll notice the first block of data fields (that is, the specific pieces of product information I first explained in Chapter 13) is deemed Mandatory Fields. As straightforward as it sounds, these are the minimum data fields you need to provide input into in order to successfully create a product item record.

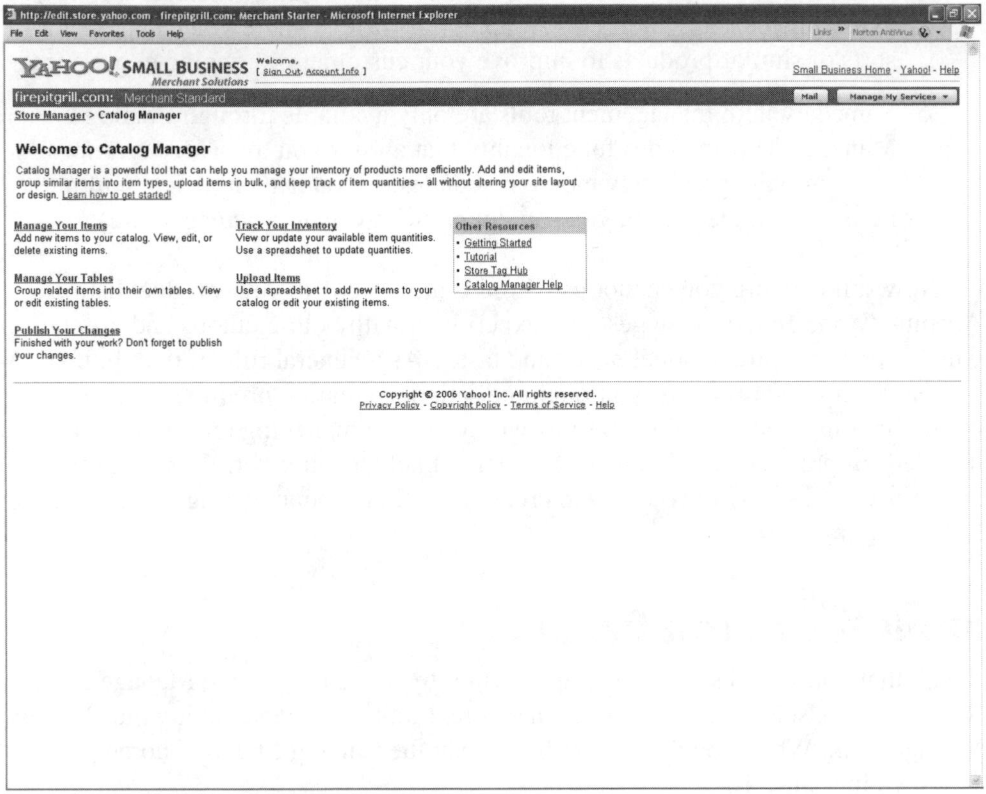

FIGURE 16-1   The Catalog Manager main screen is your launching pad for creating and managing your product listings

TIP

Already, here's one of those Yahoo inconsistencies we mentioned at the start of this chapter: while the block title is labeled Mandatory Fields, the only truly mandatory elements within this grouping are those denoted with an asterisk. Therefore, you must *provide input to the ID, Name, Orderable, and Taxable fields in order to successfully create a record. In order to actually* publish *the product item to your store, you'll need to complete the data entry in this block by also specifying the Code, Price, Sale-price, and Ship-weight fields.*

Following the mandatory block of fields is the block titled Store Fields. If you click the help button (the little question mark that follows the title), you see this is

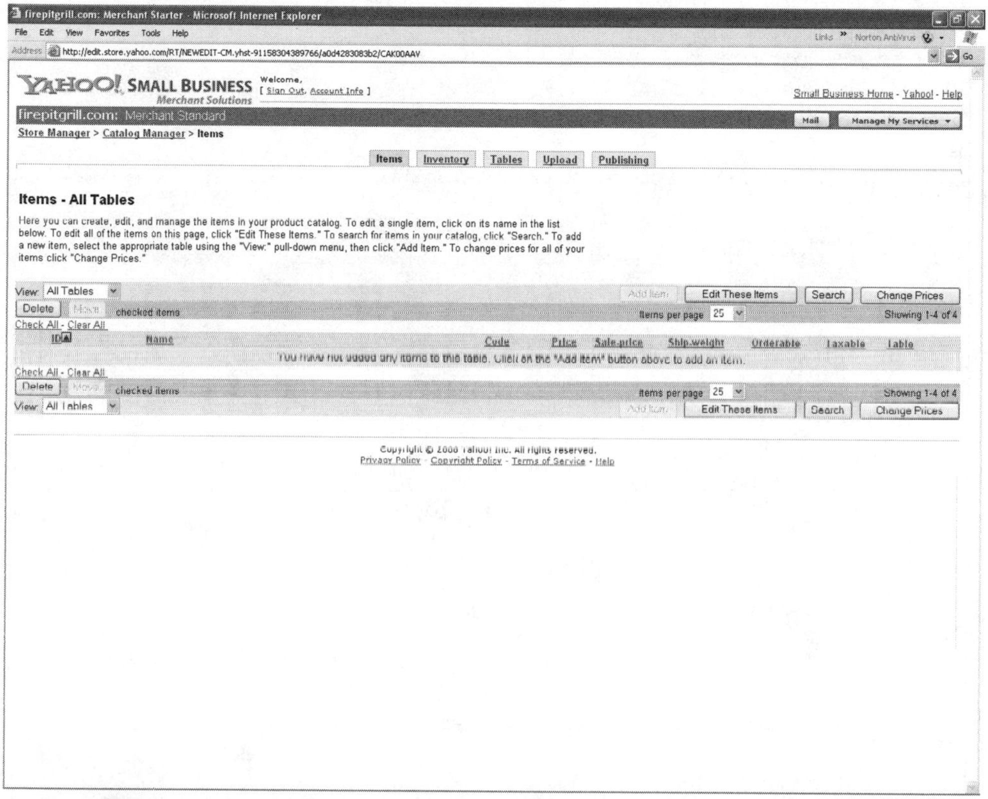

FIGURE 16-2   Here, you create and later manage the individual items within your catalog

alternately termed an "optional field." True to its name, these fields are optional (but *very* important) to your product listing. Here you'll provide an item image, option specifications, headlines, captions, and more. These are the fields you'll use to provide the informative data that helps your customers learn more about your products so they can determine if it's an item they'd like to purchase.

In total, there are 18 combined mandatory and optional product item fields, as described in Table 16-1.

As you look back to the screen capture in Figure 16-3, you'll see I've already filled in the data for our exciting product, the Western Design Cowboy Fire Pit & Grill. It's really as simple as this. To complete the process, simply click the Save button that you'll find at the bottom of the Add Item screen. The Yahoo logic will confirm you've entered the mandatory fields and then will create a product item

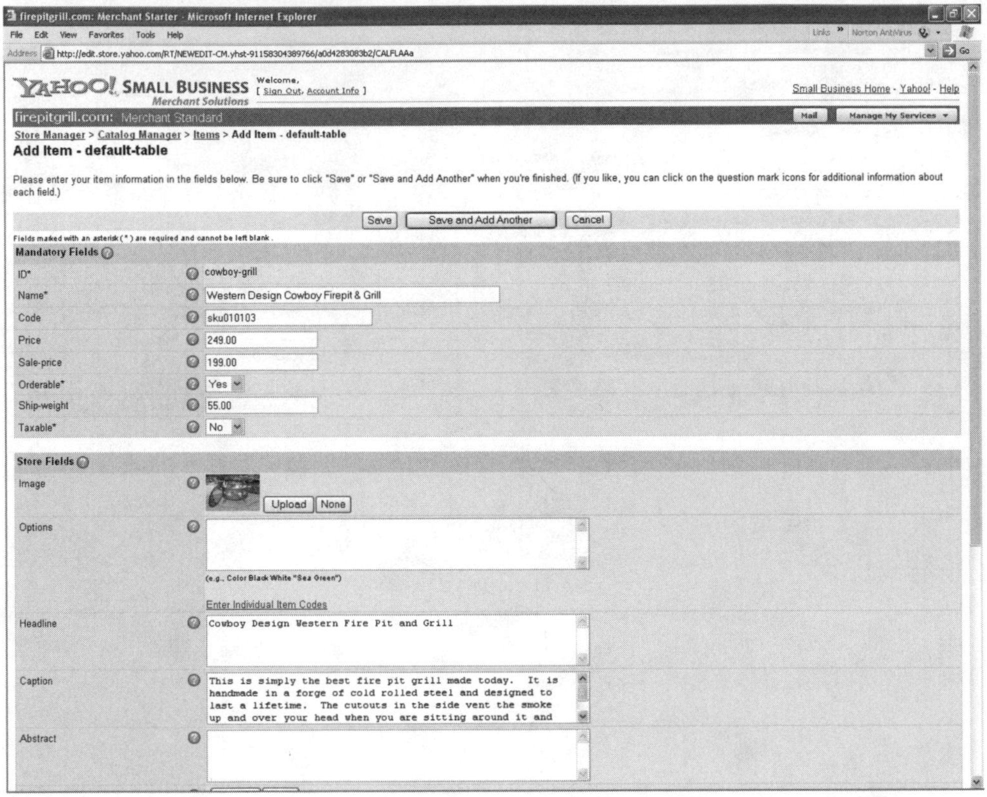

FIGURE 16-3   The Add Item page is where you can enter the details of your products

record within your product catalog. Once you understand the fields and the sorts of data you enter into them, the rest becomes just a matter of repeating the process for each successive product you'll offer. In fact, look at Figure 16-4 where you'll see I've now added several products to the Summerdale House catalog.

> **TIP**
>
> *While this method of creating product items is relatively efficient, you can imagine how time consuming it could become if you were planning on entering 50, 75, 100, or more products. If that will be your situation, you'd be better served by uploading a product data file, one that you will have previously created in spreadsheet format on your computer. Later in this chapter I'll show you how and where that upload can be done.*

Field Name	Field Use
Mandatory Fields	
ID	A unique identifier of a product item that is also used in the generation of a product page within the Yahoo Store.
Name	A free text field where you can create a name for your product using letters, numbers, and some special characters.
Code	A unique code that your customers will see when they view your products (unlike the ID field, which is used for cataloging purposes only). It's akin to a stock keeping unit (SKU) identifier—like a product number—but often includes use of an ISBN (if you're selling books) or UPC (if you're selling bar-coded products).
Price	The standard price of your product item.
Sale-price	A lower-than-Price value that will override your established standard price.
Orderable	Should default to Yes and is used to signify, within the Yahoo Catalog Manager, if the item is presently available for customers to order. This could be changed to No if the item is out of stock.
Ship-weight	Used to calculate shipping costs based on weight.
Taxable	If you're required to collect sales and use tax in your state of business, enable this field to Yes.
Optional Fields	
Image	The field where you'll specify a product item's accompanying image filename.
Options	Where you provide details for products that may be available in a variety of sizes, styles, or colors.
Headline	An optional title value that, when provided, appears above a product description (a.k.a. "caption"). When provided, this will replace the product item name.
Caption	Descriptive text that will appear on your product item page alongside an image (if you provide one). A misnomer of sorts, this is more than just a caption but, rather, allows extensive text entry, acting as a full product item "description."
Abstract	An alternate product item description that can be splashed on your store's home page to draw special attention to a product immediately upon entry into your store. The abstract information will not be displayed on the actual product item page, though.
Icon	An alternate image element that appears next to a product item name on a category (section) page. It can be an attention-getting graphic (for example, "Sale" or "New!"), or it can be a smaller-sized product image.

TABLE 16-1 Fields in the Yahoo Catalog Manager Item Screen

Field Name	Field Use
Inset	Acts as a thumbnail image of your product item and, when clicked, allows customers to view a larger-sized image of the product.
Label	An item that appears only on your store's home page and is useful as an attention-getting graphic.
Download	If you sell downloadable products (such as e-books or graphic files), this element will allow you to upload the content into your product item details.
Gift-certificate	If you elect to sell gift certificates as a product, here's where you'll make that specification.
Product-URL	If you intend to utilize Yahoo's Product Submit marketing service (an add-on service you pay for to help you increase product visibility), here's where you would submit the actual URL of participating product items.

TABLE 16-1   Fields in the Yahoo Catalog Manager Item Screen (*Continued*)

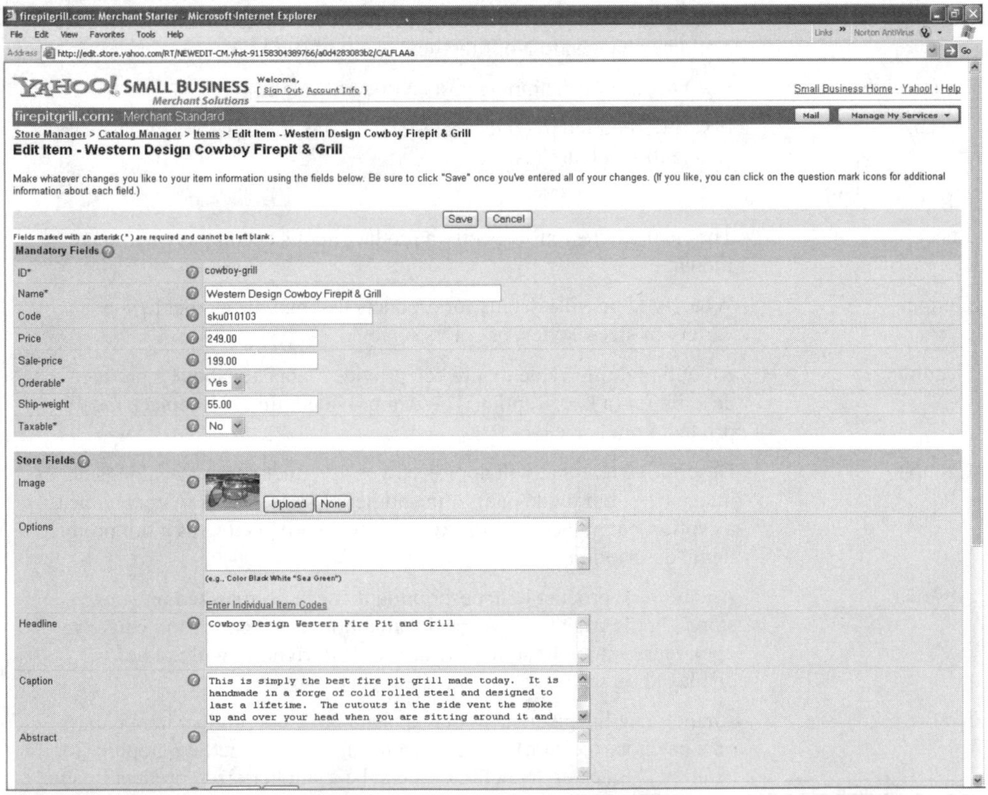

FIGURE 16-4   Once you have products created in your product catalog, the Catalog Manager provides an easy-to-review listing

Using Options to Effortlessly Increase Offerings

Okay. So there is a *bit* of effort required but it's not much and can allow you to provide your customers more choices that might translate into more sales. The good news is you can use the Options field in a variety of ways to achieve some very professional results. For starters, you can use the field to specify variations of a product you offer, perhaps color. Suppose you're selling T-shirts that you can supply in three different colors. Merely type the following in the Options field:

Color Red White "Royal Blue"

The first word you specify—here it's "Color"—will be used as the title of your pull-down selector, after which you'll enter your intended choices separated by a space (and notice that if a selection option consists of more than a single word, you simply enclose it in quotes). Upon doing this, you've easily created a pull-down option selector titled Color with selections of Red, White, and Royal Blue from which your customers can choose their color preference. But what about sizes? You'll want to make those offerings, too. You can do that in the same Options field and can create multiple pull-down boxes by simply ensuring a blank line appears between the different option selectors, like this:

Color Red White "Royal Blue"
Size Small Medium Large "Extra Large"

The blank line will be interpreted as the end of one option specification and the start of another. For the Summerdale House product, the Western Design Cowboy Fire Pit & Grill, we have size and color options from which our customers can choose. Figure 16-5 shows the entries in the Options field and the result our customers will see on the published product page.

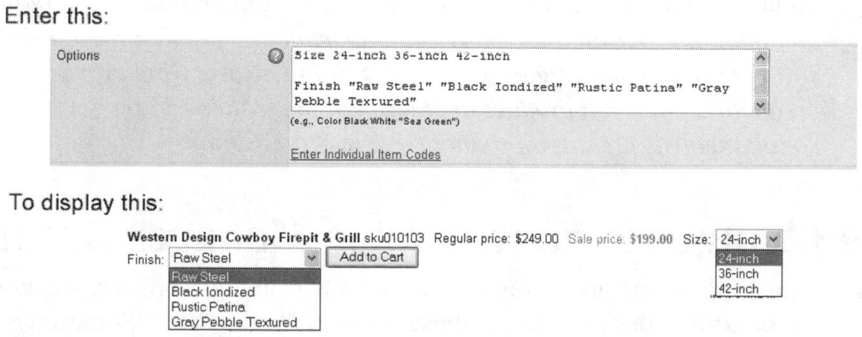

FIGURE 16-5 Using the Options field allows you to specify one or more pull-down selector fields

But the Options field can also be used in additional ways, as follows:

■ **Monograms**   If you offer embroidering or other such inscriptions on your product, simply type the word "Monogram" in the Options field and your item page will include a three-letter box where customers can specify a monogram specification of their choice.

■ **Inscriptions**   If you offer inscriptions of a certain character length, maybe 20 characters maximum, simply type the following in the Options field:

"Enter your personalized inscription here" Inscription 20

■ **Incremental Pricing**   If some of your selectable options will incur incremental pricing, you can make that specification in the Options field as follows:

Finish Natural "Black Ionized (+10.00)" "Gray Pebble Textured (+25.00)"

So you can see, adding customizable choices for your customers is a breeze in the Catalog Manager item page.

A couple of final notes here: if it helps you in managing your inventory, you can assign unique inventory codes to option combinations such as a T-shirt sized small of color blue. To do this, click the Enter Individual Item Codes text link that you see in the Catalog Manager Add Item page (seen in Figure 16-5). This provides you an area where you can specify available option combinations and assign a unique code to each. Then, consider if you'll only be able to provide certain combinations—perhaps your small T-shirt comes in all colors but the extra-large shirt is only available in white and navy blue. You can elect to create these as individual product items and bypass the options entirely. That is, you can offer a product called "T-Shirt: Small/White," another called "T-shirt: Small/Navy Blue" and so on.

TIP   *So while I mentioned I preferred to use the Catalog Manager to create and manage your product items, it's important to note that Store Editor still comes into play, regardless. That's right because whenever you create and publish a product item through the Catalog Manager, Yahoo simultaneously creates a product page in Store Editor.*

Making Changes to Your Catalog Manager Records

Upon creating and saving product items through the Catalog Manager, you will have begun building your product database for your Yahoo Store. Sometimes, you'll find it's necessary to make changes, either corrections or enhancements.

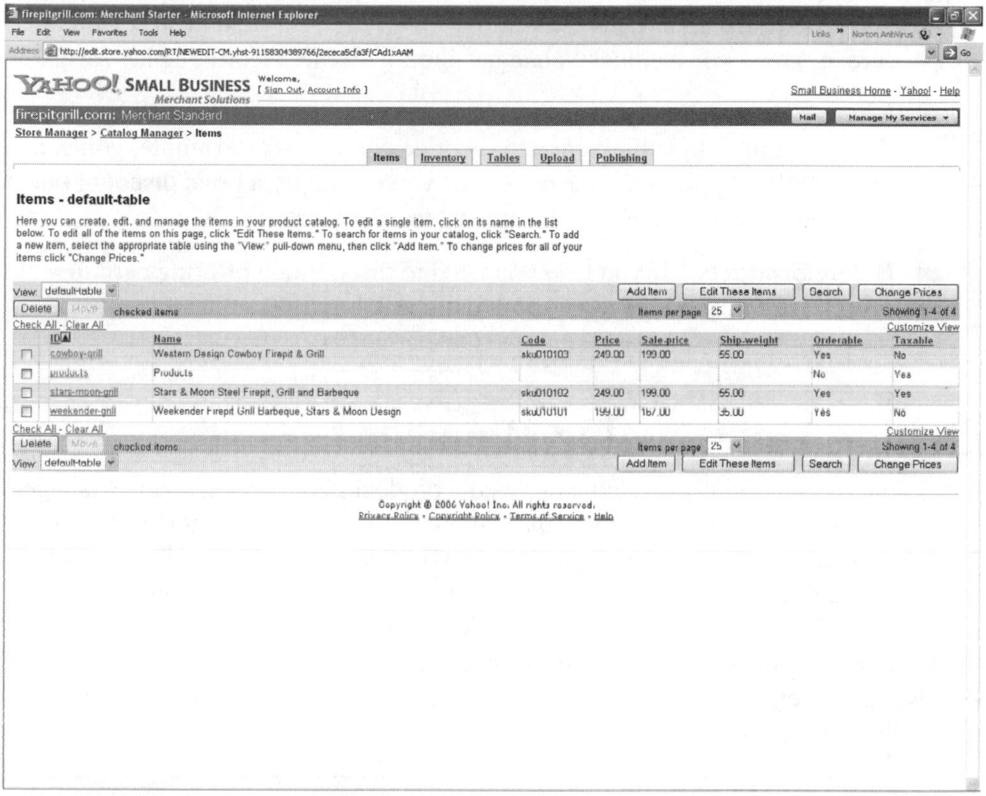

FIGURE 16-6 Using the Catalog Manager Manage Your Items screen, editing product item data is simple

As you recall from Figure 16-2, the initial Manage Your Items screen gives you an easy view to your product item records, but you might not have realized that it also allows updates within that same compressed view. Look now at Figure 16-6, and you'll see we have several products in the catalog and, from this Catalog Manager detail screen, it's easy to manage details about each.

Here's what you can edit:

■ **Single item editing** Just click the product ID (for example, "cowboy-grill") to display the same product item detail screen you used during the creation process. You'll be able to modify the information there just as you could while entering it the first time.

- ■ **Multiple item editing**   If you need to make changes to multiple items, click the Edit These Items button to open up the data fields you see on the screen where you can make changes directly in this record display format.

- ■ **Change item prices**   Click the Change Prices button and you'll be given the opportunity to implement a mass price change—for example, you can remove all sale prices in one action, or you can apply a price discount (such as 10 percent, 15 percent, or whatever) to all your items.

- ■ **Delete products**   If you find you need to discontinue offering certain product items, you can easily click the check box to the left of the item (refer to Figure 16-6) and click the Delete button.

Publishing Your Catalog Manager Records

Once you've successfully created and saved a product item in the Catalog Manager, you'll need to publish it to complete the setup process. If you look at the Manage Your Items page (refer again to Figure 16-6), you'll see a set of five tabs just below the page heading. You'll notice that, while managing your items, you've been utilizing the functions from the Items tab. Now, with that item data ready to publish, click the aptly named Publishing tab to complete the process. Figure 16-7 shows the Publishing screen where all you need do is click the Publish Catalog button to begin the publishing action.

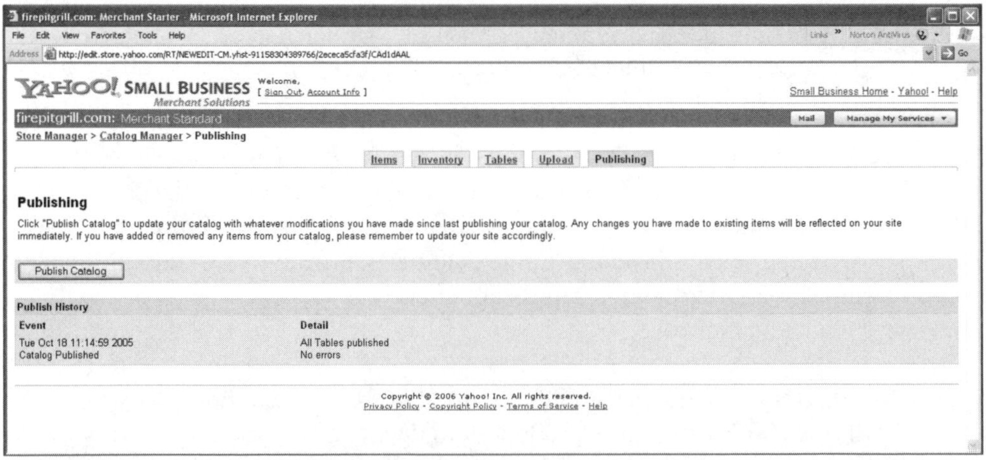

FIGURE 16-7   Visit the Catalog Manager Publishing screen to begin the process of finalizing your product item listings

Here's where another slight Yahoo idiosyncrasy comes into play. While it may seem logical to expect that publishing within Catalog Manager is all that's needed to release your new or recently edited product items to your store, there's actually one more step required: you also need to publish within the Store Editor. Recall the previous tip where I explained how a Catalog Manager product item record is automatically duplicated into the Store Editor as well. Well, because of that, your publishing work isn't complete until you exit the Catalog Manager upon publishing, navigate to the Store Editor, and publish there as well. It's a few extra mouse clicks on your part, but it's very necessary to fully release your product data to your Yahoo Store. So, in short order, here are the steps to take to publish your product item data:

1. From the Catalog Manager Manage Your Items screen, select the Publishing tab.

2. In the Publishing screen, click the Publish Catalog button.

3. Exit Catalog Manager and navigate to the Store Editor.

4. In the Store Editor screen, click the Publish button found on the rightmost location on the command bar (to see this, refer back to Chapter 14, Figure 14-4).

Upon initiating publishing within the Store Editor, the Yahoo system will chug away to validate and publish your complete store data, including your product items. After it has gone through several iterations of inspecting and preparing your store data, it will systematically complete the steps necessary to finalize your information. When it has completed its work, it will provide you an appropriate status box (see Figure 16-8) and—*voila!*—you've successfully created and published your product data. Congratulations!

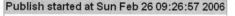

Publish started at Sun Feb 26 09:26:57 2006
✔ Preparing products for publish process
✔ Creating web pages
✔ Writing library files
✔ Creating product database
✔ Sending files to servers

FIGURE 16-8   The Yahoo Store Editor publishing process is complete when you see a status box like this

Managing Mass Product Data: Exporting and Importing

As mentioned earlier in this chapter, if you have many, many products that you'll be offering through your Yahoo Store, you'll likely be better served to upload them en masse rather that manage the Add Item function for one-by-one creation. If you're relatively familiar with spreadsheet programs like Microsoft's Excel, then you'll find managing larger numbers of different products is simplified when you do so *outside* of your Yahoo Store, uploading them later in one operation. Even if you're not well versed in the use of a spreadsheet application, you'll see it's very similar to what you saw in the Catalog Manager Overview screen.

At the outset, it's a good idea to create your first product within the Catalog Manager form to familiarize yourself with the different fields, the information that is to be input into them, and the result when you're finished. Beyond this, when you create at least one product item in this way, you simultaneously establish a template that will make creating additional products in an offline spreadsheet all the easier. Here's how it works. First, visit the Catalog Manager and navigate to the Upload tab (refer to Figure 16-6). Upon doing so, you'll see a very simplistic screen as shown in Figure 16-9.

Off to the far right of the Upload screen is a button labeled Download. As its name suggests, this is a utility whereby you can create a download file with your product item details. With as little as one item in your Catalog Manager, you can create a download file of CSV type (comma separated values) that will serve as the template to create and manage additional items in spreadsheet application. When you click the Download button, Yahoo will allow you to specify the product tables of data you wish to download (you're only using the single default table at this time), as shown in Figure 16-10.

Again, click the Download button and Yahoo will generate a CSV file and will display the result, in spreadsheet layout, on your computer screen (see Figure 16-11).

Notice the spreadsheet layout shown in Figure 16-11 is not running in a spreadsheet application but, rather, from a web page (note the title of the window, the long URL that finishes with "/data.csv." At this point, click File | Save As and save the data file to your computer. Next, power up a spreadsheet application (I'm using MS Excel), and you'll see the same layout. From here, you can see that the first row of the spreadsheet contains all the proper Yahoo product item field titles; it is critical to use these exact names as they're what Yahoo will use when you upload a larger file of data later. All you need to do now is enter the appropriate data for subsequent product item records within the spreadsheet cells below the proper field titles.

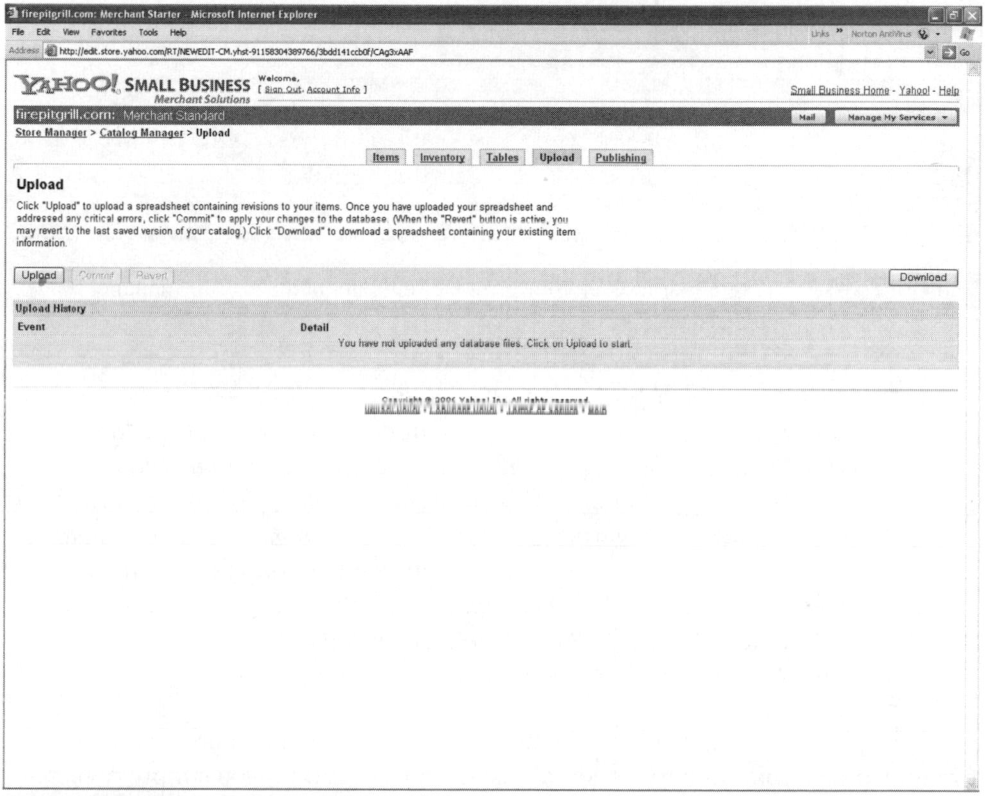

FIGURE 16-9   Begin developing your offline product item data file by visiting the Catalog Manager Upload tab

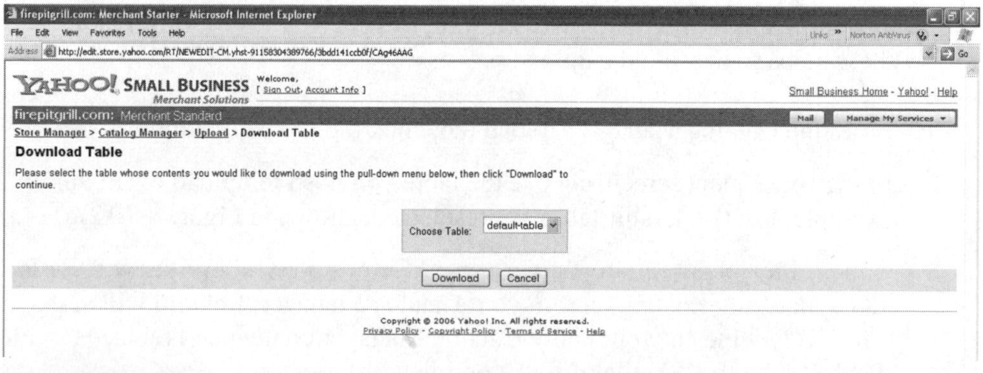

FIGURE 16-10   Select the product table of data you wish to download

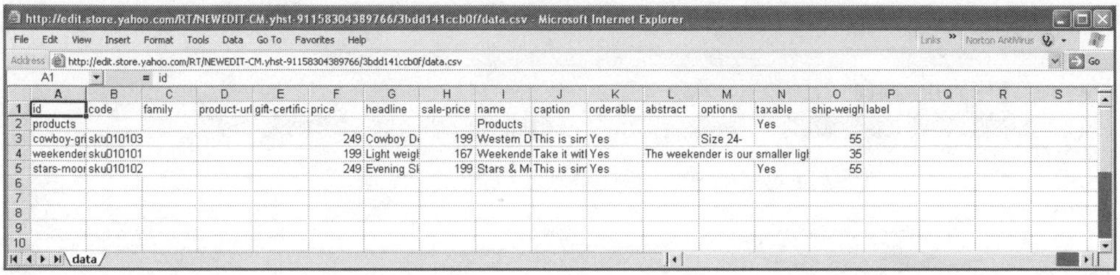

FIGURE 16-11   Take a first look at your product item data in an easy-to-manage spreadsheet format

TIP

At this point you may jump up to proclaim the fields aren't in the same order on the spreadsheet as they appeared within the Catalog Manager Add Item form. You're right! The good news here is that these fields (they're actually columns *in the spreadsheet) can appear in any order you choose—however they work best for you as you're adding new product item records—provided you always maintain the exact field (column) names as came in the Yahoo download file. When you later upload, the Yahoo logic will identify the column names and will insert the data in the appropriate product item record fields for you. Cool, huh?*

Once you've completed your spreadsheet, adding as many more new items for upload into your Yahoo Catalog Manager as you need to, you simply revisit the Catalog Manager Upload tab and reverse the process. Take note, though, that just as Yahoo provided you a CSV file when you downloaded, it likewise expects a CSV file when you upload. Upon completing your offline entry, save your spreadsheet file as a CSV and you'll do just fine (and ignore any warnings the application might pop up in front of you about using a nonstandard spreadsheet file extension; just confirm that, Yes, you want to save as a CSV). From here, follow these steps to execute the upload process:

1. From the Catalog Manager Upload tab, click the Upload button.

2. In the subsequent screen, choose the table you wish to upload to (in this example, use the default-table as preselected, shown in Figure 16-12).

3. Choose the upload action you wish to perform: Add will insert new records and update any existing ones in your Catalog Manager; Rebuild will effectively wipe out your entire Catalog Manager content and replace it with the data in your CSV file (use this option with care).

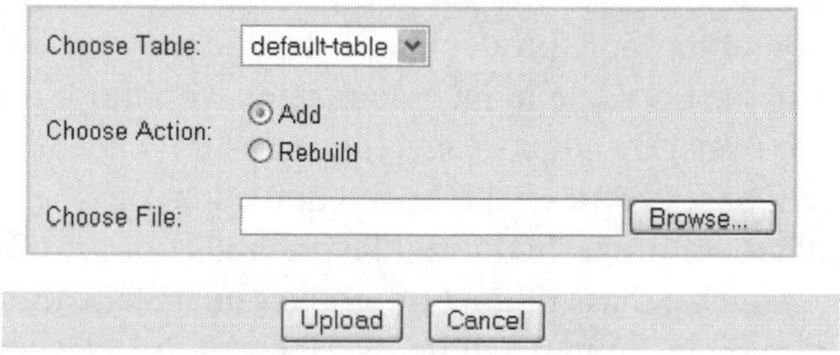

Choose Table:	default-table ▾
Choose Action:	◉ Add ○ Rebuild
Choose File:	[ ] [Browse...]

[Upload] [Cancel]

FIGURE 16-12 The Upload control window

4. Choose the CSV file to upload by clicking the Browse button and navigating through your computer's file structure until you've selected the appropriate file.

5. Click the Upload button.

6. Yahoo will examine your CSV file now and determine if there are any errors (improper field names, invalid field contents, mandatory fields not populated, and so on) and will provide you a look at the status of your upload. Any errors reported should be corrected in your CSV file, and you should restart this process.

7. When your file is error free, click the Commit button.

8. A confirmation screen will appear, again asking you to specify if this upload will be an Add or a Rebuild. Select the appropriate button.

9. Yahoo will complete your upload process, and you should immediately visit the Catalog Manager to ensure the upload performed to your expectations.

10. If you detect a problem in your product item data, return to the Catalog Manager Upload tab and click the Revert button to revert back to your product item data prior to the upload (this is useful largely in the case of performing product item updates that may have not gone quite right).

If your upload completed to your satisfaction, repeat the publishing process described earlier, publishing first from the Catalog Manager and then from the Store Editor.

Importing Multiple Images

During the discussion of multiple product uploads, you may have noticed there were no provisions in the CSV file to include images with those products. This is because the CSV file is merely a text-based file and is not capable of embedding graphics files (of GIF or JPG types); the Yahoo upload process would not recognize nor be able to handle those properly during the previous upload effort. Therefore, you'll need to now launch a mass upload of product images to accompany those product item records you just populated into your Catalog Manager. While this is an extra step, it's still more effective for multiple product records than using the one-at-a-time approach. Here's how you do it:

1. Establish product image files on your computer and name them *exactly the same* as your product ID name (for example, ID "cowboy-grill" must have an image file named "cowboy-grill.jpg").

> **TIP** *Best practice alert: while there are many different image types you can use these days, it's best to use only GIF or JPG with your Yahoo Store. Some folks' computers can't display some of the other types but* all *can manage these two common types.*

2. With all of your images available, collect these into a compressed (zipped) file.

3. Return to the Yahoo Store Editor page and click the red triangle/arrow at the rightmost of the Editor toolbar (see Figure 16-13).

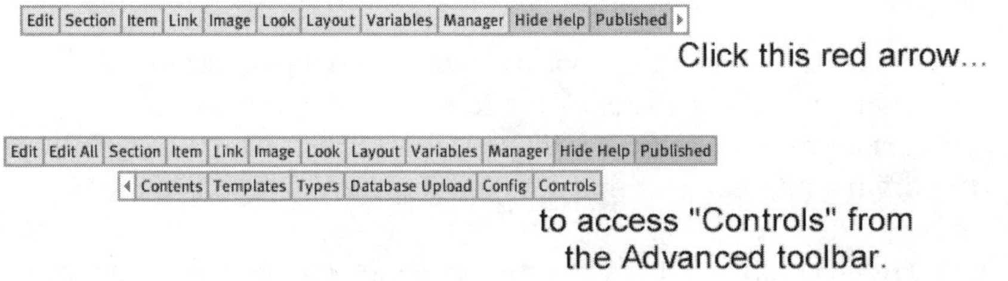

| Edit | Section | Item | Link | Image | Look | Layout | Variables | Manager | Hide Help | Published | ▶ |

Click this red arrow...

| Edit | Edit All | Section | Item | Link | Image | Look | Layout | Variables | Manager | Hide Help | Published |
◀ | Contents | Templates | Types | Database Upload | Config | Controls |

to access "Controls" from
the Advanced toolbar.

FIGURE 16-13 Navigate to the Advanced toolbar within Store Editor for uploading multiple product images

4. Click the Controls button and select Multiple Image Upload on the subsequent screen.

5. Click the Send button to effect the upload.

6. When the upload is complete, click the Update button at the top of the refreshed screen to return to Store Editor and review your listings, now with associated images.

7. Click the Browse button on the screen and locate your image ZIP file.

A Well Deserved Congratulations

And there you have it: you've created your product catalog! While this may seem like a lot to digest and many steps to take to gain the desired outcome, it does become easier on subsequent efforts. After a time or two, you'll be effortlessly navigating through the process and well on your way to readying your Yahoo Store to entertain customers.

Chapter 17

Creating and Editing Your Store Pages

With the know-how to create your product items in the Catalog Manager, it's now time to develop your overall store design to provide those great products a great place to be seen. Now, as sometimes convoluted and "tech-ese" the Yahoo Merchant Solution may seem to be, you'll quickly find it to be very adaptable to your individual needs. That is, you can create a simple yet effective store rather quickly (in a weekend, honestly), or you can completely immerse yourself into all of the bells, whistles, tags, and variables, which can result in a true work of art that would have Michelangelo wanting to drop by and stroll your virtual masterpiece. Or…you can start off simply and evolve your store *while you're open for business*. That's the approach we prefer, since having inventory sitting about without any means to actively sell it is just financial assets tied up. Rather than spend weeks or months (or more?) attempting to create a pièce-de-résistance storefront, you can invest a reasonable amount of time creating a decent looking shop and get the goods up for sale, allowing you to take in profits while you continue to tinker with your store's look, the inventory, and your overall approach to online business.

In this chapter, I'll show you how to utilize the basic store building features (and some nifty upgrades) in an effort to get your virtual doors open sooner than later. Along the way, we'll point out some paths for enhancement that you may likely want to explore further down the road. But, knowing you're here to start making your fortune on the fast track, we'll get you up and running at business speed.

Editing the Home Page

In the previous chapter you learned how to create and publish a product item in the Catalog Manager then, ultimately, publish it in the Store Editor to make it fully ready for inclusion in your store design. Consider that the backroom works—call it your managing your "employees-only warehouse" if you like—where customers are never intended to travel. Now you need to create virtual aisles where you'll stock the inventory of those products in ways that will be easy for your customers to browse and buy. To do this, you'll need to utilize the Store Editor again to create *section pages*—they're what make up those virtual aisles I just mentioned. You design a section page for the purpose of "hosting" products of your selection and then "assign" those products to the section page. Think of it as building a shelf specifically for a product or grouping of products, then filling the shelf with the goods. Again, the concept here likely isn't very mysterious to you; it's just a different terminology you need to get familiar with.

Log back into your Yahoo Merchant Solution account and navigate to the Store Editor (My Services | Store Manager | Store Editor). When you do, you'll arrive to the initial section page of your store, named by default the Index page (see Figure 17-1). To use a friendlier name, this is your store's Home page—it's the page your customers will be greeted by when they navigate to your domain URL. With this first exercise, then, you'll set up the entrance that will welcome your customers, provide them an initial overview of what they can expect to find within your store, and offer them buttons to navigate to your product pages and make their purchases.

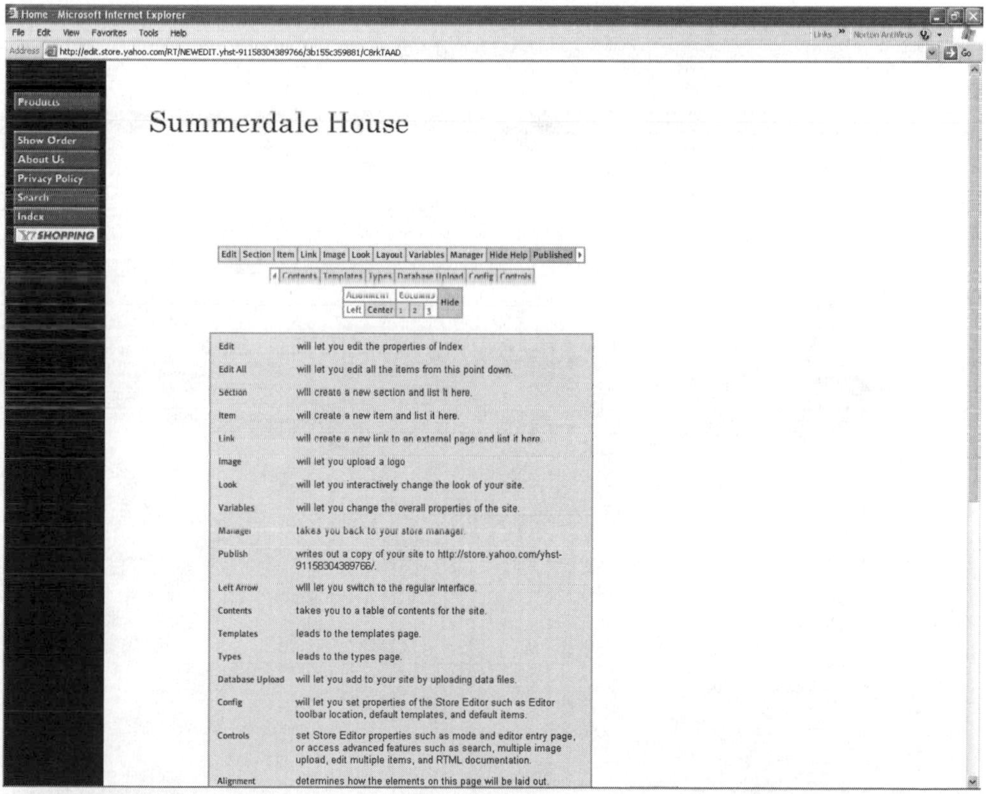

FIGURE 17-1   Return to the Store Editor to begin building the sections of your store

So, let's begin with your Home page. From the Store Editor toolbar, click the Edit button. When you do, you'll navigate to the Edit page where you can begin establishing your online presence, as seen in Figure 17-2.

TIP
Look closely at the main tool bar in Figure 17-1 and you'll see the end button formerly labeled Publish is now labeled Published. This indicates that you have published your store content (recall that activity from Chapter 16) and makes it easy to determine you have completed that task. Whenever you perform additional edits to your store—either product items or the section pages themselves—the button will revert to being labeled Publish. This feature allows you to, at a glance, determine if your store needs to be published. Nice touch, I think.

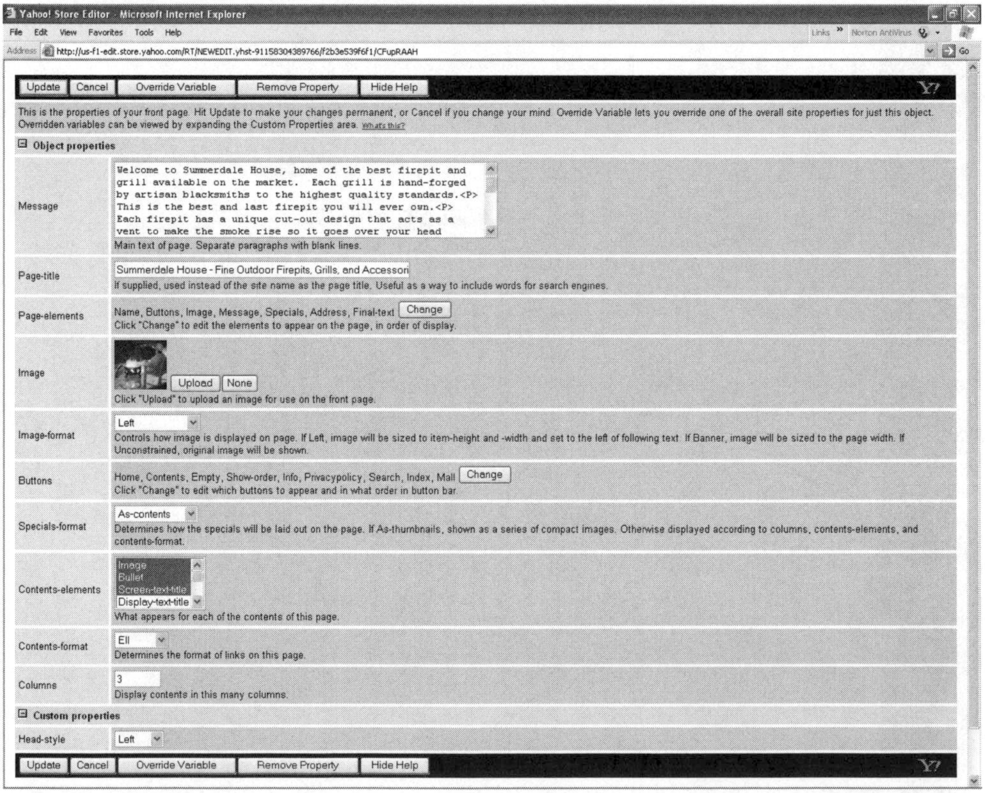

FIGURE 17-2   Create your store's Home page using this Edit form

For this exercise, we've entered some information that, while simple, nonetheless provides visitors with compelling description of the Summerdale House store and the products that await them inside. Remember that the goal in setting up your home and subsequent store section pages is to get to the point of what you're offering. Don't be concerned with creating the most technically and artistically adept store site; an overly enthusiastic effort can often detract from your customers' shopping experience. Simplicity is the key here, especially when you're just starting up.

At a high level, then, your task in editing the Home page is to provide a title for your store home, include descriptive text and images, and establish settings for the overall elements that will be included on the page. Think of any online store you've visited and you'll recall how you were greeted, how text and images were presented, and how you were able to navigate deeper into the store; that's what you'll be doing now with your own store home.

Okay. So let's see what elements on the Home page Edit form require your input:

- **Message** This is the welcome overture your customers will see when they arrive at your store. Consider this your two-minute elevator talk: you have a very short time to tell someone what your store is and why it is the destination to browse and buy the products you specialize in. When the elevator doors open, time's up! Did you convince that other person to shop your store?

- **Page-title** This seems pretty straightforward—establish a title for your Home page. It's important to note, however, that providing a compelling and descriptive title will increase visibility of your store and its products with online search engines. Therefore, take a few minutes to create something more evocative than just Home.

- **Page-elements** As previously noted, this is the function where you'll establish which Home page elements will be displayed on your store's entry page as well as in which order. Take a look at Figure 17-3 to see the new window you'll navigate to when you click the Change button to the right of this field in the home Edit form.

As you can see from Figure 17-3, you can specify which elements you want displayed on your Home page by entering a numeric value in the field that follows the element label. Notice that the numerals you enter will act as the determination

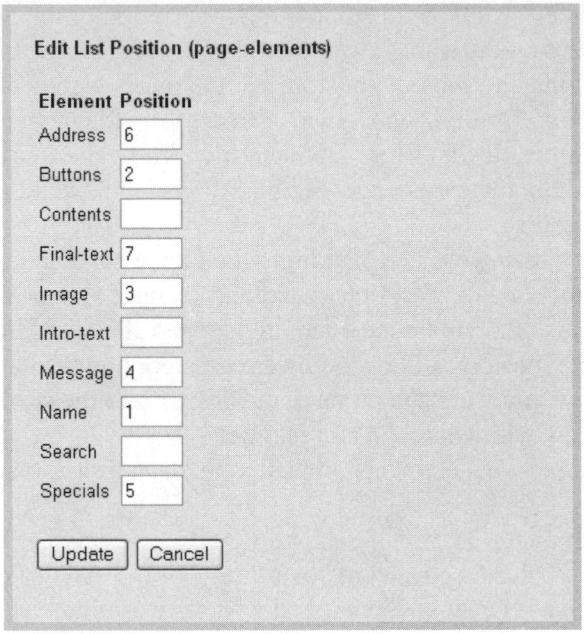

Edit List Position (page-elements)

Element Position

Address   [6]

Buttons   [2]

Contents   [ ]

Final-text [7]

Image   [3]

Intro-text [ ]

Message   [4]

Name   [1]

Search   [ ]

Specials   [5]

[Update] [Cancel]

FIGURE 17-3   Establish the elements to be included in your store Home page as well as control the order in which they'll be displayed

of how the elements will appear on your page (in this example, Name is first, designated by numeral 1, Buttons is second, and so on).

■ **Image**   Click the Upload button to access an upload dialog box (seen in Figure 17-4) where you'll locate and upload an image from your computer's files. Click the Send button in the upload box to attach the file to your store's Home page. Upon a successful upload, a small thumbnail representation of your Home page image will appear on the Edit form (as seen in Figure 17-2).

■ **Image-format**   Here you can control how the image is displayed relative to the other elements that will appear on your Home page. From the pull-down selector, Left will left-justify and size the image relative to nearby text. Banner will top-justify and size the image to page width. Unconstrained will display the image at its original dimensions.

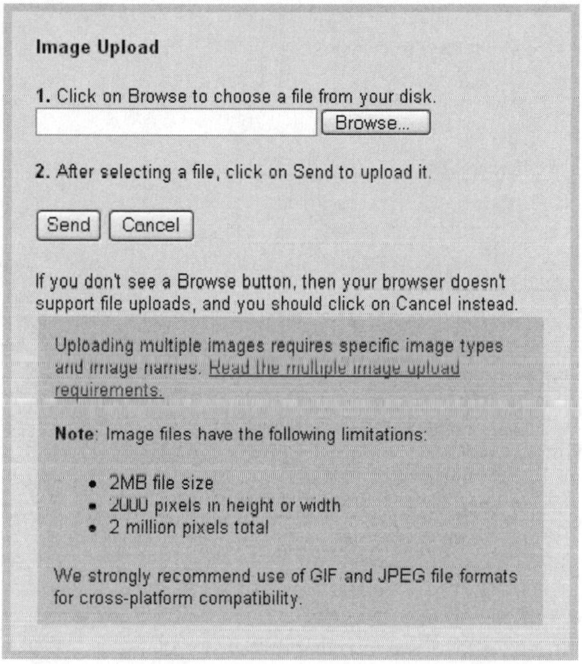

Image Upload

1. Click on Browse to choose a file from your disk.

[   ] [Browse...]

2. After selecting a file, click on Send to upload it.

[Send] [Cancel]

If you don't see a Browse button, then your browser doesn't support file uploads, and you should click on Cancel instead.

Uploading multiple images requires specific image types and image names. Read the multiple image upload requirements.

Note: Image files have the following limitations:

- 2MB file size
- 2000 pixels in height or width
- 2 million pixels total

We strongly recommend use of GIF and JPEG file formats for cross-platform compatibility.

FIGURE 17-4   Use this box to upload images from your computer for display on your Home page

- **Buttons**   Much like the Page-elements function, click the Change button here to display an editable form where you will determine which buttons will appear on your Home page and in which display order (see Figure 17-5).

- **Specials-format**   You saw Specials in the Page-elements control box. If you plan on specifying special offers, prices, or sales conditions, this field allows you to manage how those will be displayed on your Home page.

- **Contents-elements**   Here you can elect to pull and display data for each of the product elements you display prominently on your Home page.

- **Contents-format**   Following the preceding, here you'll define how Contents-elements are displayed on your Home page.

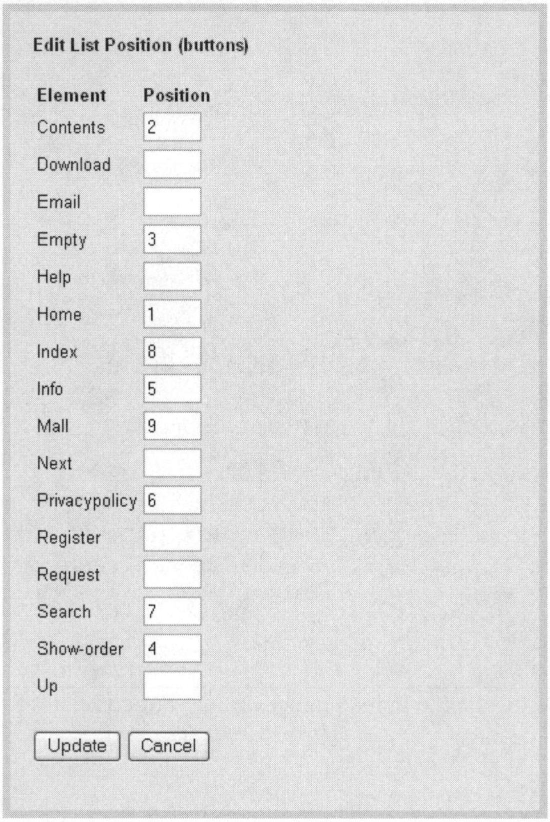

Edit List Position (buttons)

Element	Position
Contents	2
Download	
Email	
Empty	3
Help	
Home	1
Index	8
Info	5
Mall	9
Next	
Privacypolicy	6
Register	
Request	
Search	7
Show-order	4
Up	

[Update] [Cancel]

FIGURE 17-5   Determine the buttons to be displayed on your Home page and the order in which they'll appear

- **Columns**   Here's how you can display multiple elements in a nice columnar format (with invisible column lines) on your Home page. Just specify the number of columns you want to use in your design.

- **Head-style**   This determines the manner in which Head text will be displayed (that being text you've established in your product data).

It's quite a bit of information to manage but, as you can begin to infer, there's nothing truly mystifying about any of it. Once you're familiar with each element's name and its respective function, managing your store design will become successively simpler. And, to offer you a glimpse of what the simple elements

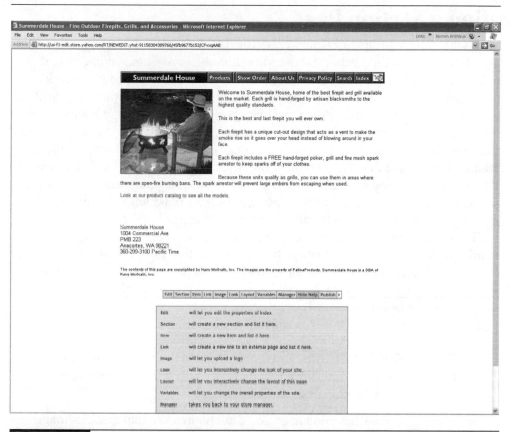

FIGURE 17-6   Simple but effective, this Home page design was created in as little as three minutes

specified in the example from Figure 17-2, look now at Figure 17-6 to see how quickly and easily I set up a simple Home page.

What's that you say—it's too bland a design? Well, it is rather simple but this exercise shows how fast you can enter your Home page information, proving it's not a daunting task. Later we'll discuss how to spice it up just a bit. Notice from Figure 17-6 how easy it is to edit your Home page design, view it and, if you like, go back and edit some more. It's a fast development with an easy review and re-edit capabilities at your fingertips.

TIP   *After you've gotten comfortable with using the various tools in the Store Editor toolbar, you can suppress the large block of tool descriptors by clicking the Hide Help button. The descriptor block will disappear.*

Creating a Section Page

With your store's virtual front entry established (or in a state of pending refinement, as you like it), it's time to build those virtual product aisles and supplemental information areas. In Yahoo Merchant Solution terms, these will be your section pages (and, truth be told, your Home page was also a type of section page). Section pages allow you to logically group and manage your store content, whether it's by type of product or type of information or service. In this way, you can design your store with usability in mind, providing a logical approach that will make sense to your customers and that will help them find what they're looking for faster than if there was no rhyme or reason to your layout (think of a garage sale where some sellers lay items out in an easy-to-shop manner versus those who lug out boxes of mixed goods and expect you to rummage through them).

To create a section page, return to the Store Editor page (refer to Figure 17-1 in this chapter) and click the Section button on the Store Editor toolbar. When you do, you'll navigate to a form similar to the Home page Edit form only this time you'll be creating a new page that will act as a section—some consider it a sort of *category*—page (see Figure 17-7).

Let's see what information you can enter to create an effective section page:

- **Name**   This is the only required-entry field in the section page form. This should be a short name since it will occupy a navigation button (such as Accessories, Lighting, or even Clearance.

- **Image**   For each section page you can import a section-specific image.

- **Headline**   Just like the Home page, this is a top-display text that should similarly be short enough to act as a sort of section signage.

- **Caption**   Provide a bit more information about what the section contains in this field.

- **Abstract**   Enter text here that will be displayed on other areas of your store where this section will be referenced and linked.

- **Icon**   This is useful if you'd like to use a catchy or otherwise recognizable image to serve as a link from elsewhere in your store to this section page.

- **Inset**   Use this to upload an image that will be displayed in thumbnail size on the section page.

■ **Label**   This is a special-use field whose contents are only applicable if you've established the section page from the Home page as a special. If that's the case, enter short text here that will appear from the page where this special has been designated.

In the example shown in Figure 17-7, I created a section page named Accessories and entered some text and an image. After doing that, I clicked the Update button at the top of the section form page and my section page is quickly created (see Figure 17-8).

Simultaneously, upon creating the section page, the Update function will also add a new button to your store's navigation bar with the section page name displayed (see Figure 17-9).

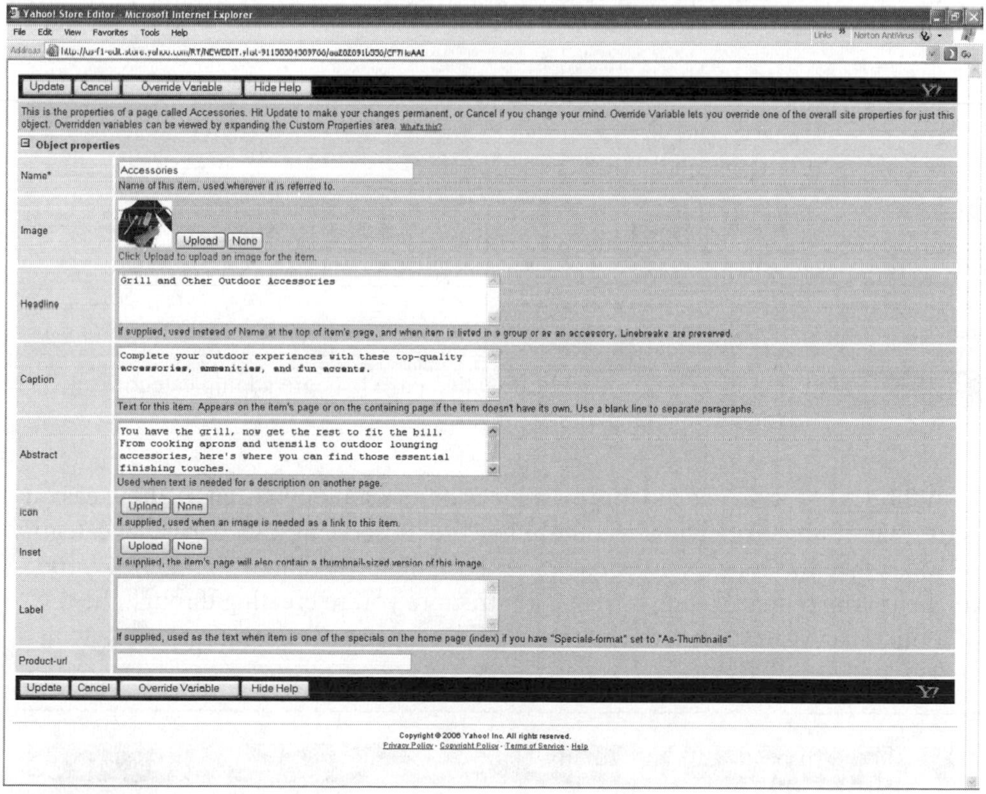

FIGURE 17-7   If you've got the hang of the Home page Edit form, creating new section pages with this form will be a breeze for you

FIGURE 17-8   In a snap, you can create a section page to begin adding categorical structure to your store

While the section page in this example is quite simple, you can see how easy it is to create, and you can now recognize how it will serve as a second-level category of goods that you'll offer in your store. At this point, take a look at Figure 17-10 for a pictorial representation of the store structure you're creating through the use of section pages and, soon, the linking of product pages (from your product items

FIGURE 17-9   As quickly as you create a section page, your store's navigation bar is updated to reflect the new addition

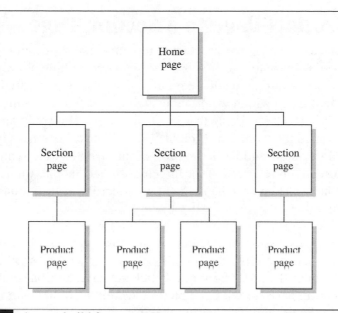

FIGURE 17-10   As you build from your Home page, your store will take on a structure
similar to this

created earlier in the Catalog Manager or uploaded from a spreadsheet) to the
appropriate section pages.

   Similar to the manner in which I encouraged you to draft up the details of your
product items before you actually began entering them into your store's Catalog
Manager, you may do well to draw up a store structure similar to that shown in
Figure 17-10, giving you the ability to envision how your store's major product
categories (section pages) will be named and which products (product pages) will
be associated with each category. Next time you're visiting your local market,
convenience store, or department store, take a look at the various signage and the
way the products are grouped; you'll be performing the same logical setup for
your Yahoo Store.

TIP   *Incidentally, it's okay to create an empty section page in a live store.
That is, if you want to begin heralding exciting new products that will be
coming soon, feel free to create a section page (thereby creating a visible
navigation bar button) and insert an image that indicates the goods will
be Coming Soon! This sort of tactic is always in use online as well as in
the brick-and-mortar world.*

Linking a Product Page to a Section Page

So now it's time to complete the structure to resemble that shown in Figure 17-10 by linking a product page to a section page. If you were looking closely, you may have seen that one of our navigation bar buttons was labeled simply Products—this is a section page to which we previously linked two of the Summerdale House fire pit grill products. Using that section/category name only temporarily, we've now renamed it to appear as Fire Pit Grills. When a customer visits the Summerdale House store and wishes to browse our inventory, they can quickly see that we currently have a section for fire pit grills and another for accessories. Figure 17-11 shows the updated naming of the former Products button on our navigation bar.

At this point, then, we previously created two fire pit grill items during the Catalog Manager discussion of Chapter 16 and now have a section page named Fire Pit Grills. It's time to link the fire pit grill products to the section page. To do this, simply enter the Store Editor and click the navigator bar button of the appropriate section page (in our example, it's section Fire Pit Grills). This will navigate you to the section page within the Store Editor. At this point, click the orange arrow located rightmost on the Editor toolbar to expand the toolbar and gain access to the remainder of the editor features. Now, click the Edit button (it's second to the left on the top bar) to access the expanded section edit form (see Figure 17-12).

Midway down the edit form you'll see a field named Contents—this is where you'll specify the product item IDs that you created previously when utilizing the Catalog Manager or within your imported product data file. In addition to the "cowboy-grill" created in chapter 16, another product, the "weekender-grill" was also added to the inventory.   Now, in order to link those two products to the Fire Pit Grills section page, you simply enter those IDs, each separated by a space, within the Contents field. Click the Update button and—quick as a flash—the products are now linked to the section page (see Figure 17-13).

| Summerdale House | Fire Pit Grills | Accessories | Show Order | About Us | Privacy Policy | Search | Index |

FIGURE 17-11   From the Products section page, simply click the Edit button in the toolbar to change the Name of the section page, here modified to read Fire Pit Grills

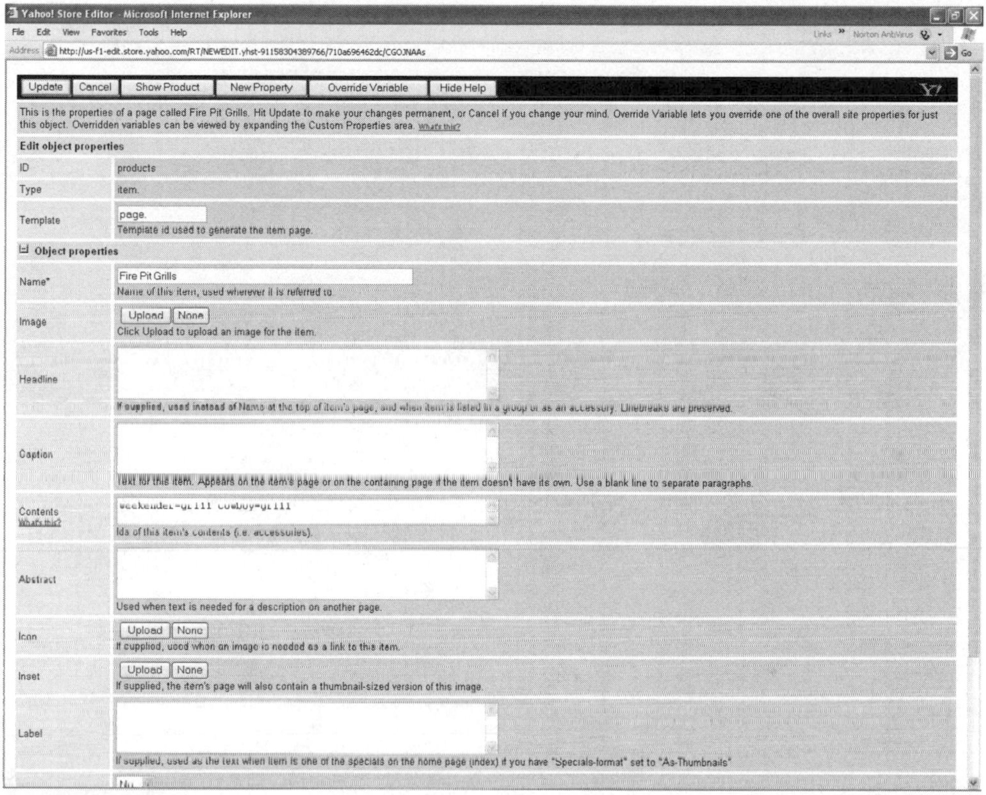

FIGURE 17-12 The expanded section edit form is where you'll link products pages to your section page

In its most basic function, that's how easy it is to create your store structure, from the Home page to section pages to linked product pages. Of course, you can achieve the same result in a couple of other ways, namely using a copy-and-paste function or a cut-and-paste function. Here's how.

First, if you hadn't recalled the name of our two grill product IDs, you could have elected to visit the product page of each. To navigate to a product page, simply click the Contents button from the expanded Store Editor toolbar. Upon doing so, you'll see a page that presents your store structure in a sort of outline format (see Figure 17-14).

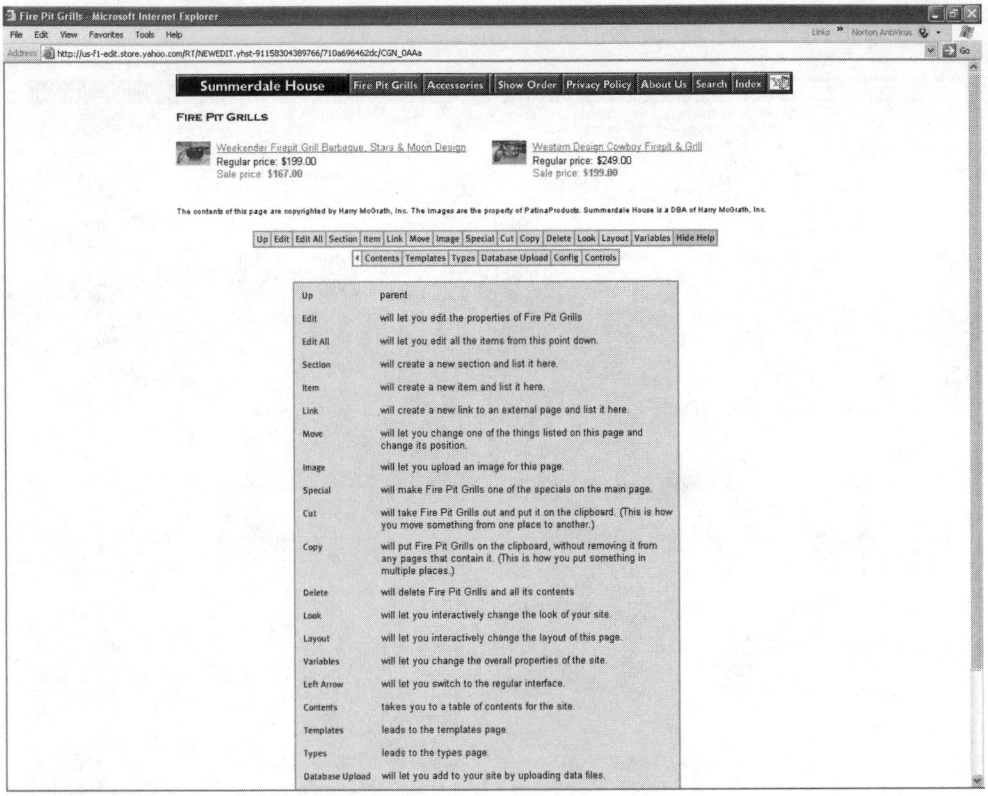

FIGURE 17-13   Products linked will appear on a section page

While Figure 17-14 shows that you have already linked the two grills under the section page, this demonstrates that you can access the product pages by clicking a displayed product ID.

TIP   *Wait a minute! That section page still reads products even though we changed the name to Fire Pit Grills. That's correct, but note that products in this view represents the section ID when we originally created it. It will retain that ID even though we can freely change the section Name field value. This is actually a good thing since the ID of products is a useful name when viewed from the Contents structure view, as shown in Figure 17-14. Here it exists as a useful maintenance view name for your purposes while still allowing you to rename the section in a way that will be more pleasing and useful to your customers.*

```
Contents | Variables | Templates | Types | Database Upload | Config | Controls | Weekender ...

New

⊟ index main. home.
     ⊟ products item. page.
          weekender-grill item. page.
          cowboy-grill item. page.
      accessories item. page.


     ind empty. index.
     nsearch search. page.
     stars-moon-grill item. page.
     info info. info.
     norder norder. order-page.
     privacypolicy privacypolicy. privacypolicy.
```

FIGURE 17-14   The Contents button provides you a view of your store structure and,
most importantly, gives you easy access to your product pages

When you click the weekender-grill product ID, you can easily navigate to
that product page. From there, while you're still in the Store Editor mode, you
can select the Copy toolbar button to effectively copy that product ID to a useful
temporary clipboard (Figure 17-15 shows the product page, the toolbar with
the Copy button, and the new Clipboard note that indicates the product we've
successfully copied, temporarily).

Next, navigate to the section page where you'd like to link the product
currently captured in the Clipboard and click the active product name link within
the Clipboard box and the product will be pasted into that section page. Yes, it's
that simple. You can also use this copy function to copy a product to multiple
sections within your store structure, if you like. And what if you decide you've
made a mistake and pasted the product item to the wrong section page (or you
later determine you want to discontinue a product offering displayed within a
section page)? Just as simply, click the Edit button in the toolbar and remove the
product ID from the Contents field. Click the Update button and the product will
be quickly removed from that section page.

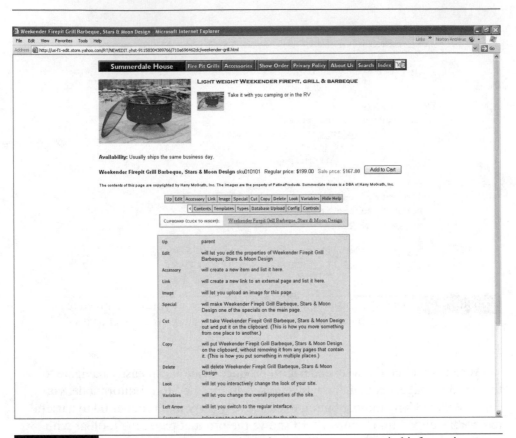

FIGURE 17-15   Use the Copy button on a product page to create copied information to soon paste—as links—into a section page

Lastly, if you want to ever move a product page from one section to another, access the product page of the item you want to move and click the Cut button on the toolbar. The item will appear in the same Clipboard box but will have been removed from its existing section page linkage. Navigate to the section page where you now want the product to appear and click the active product name link in the Clipboard box. Done! Oh, and if you had a product item appear in multiple section pages, the cut functionality just described will effectively remove it from all sections where it was linked, allowing you to move it to one or more different sections of your choice.

As you can see, the manual linkage and the copy/cut methods can be used interchangeably to link your products however you like.

> TIP
>
> *At this point, I have a small confession to make. During the discussion in Chapter 16 about creating a spreadsheet of multiple products to mass upload into your Catalog Manager, I purposely omitted mention that you can also establish section pages for those products within the same spreadsheet. If you'd prefer to create section designations within a spreadsheet and have the appropriate product items linked to those section pages at the time of upload, simply create an additional data column named path. For each product item you want to assign to a specific section page, just ensure the path column has an entry on that product item record line (such as specifying path value of Accessories for a product item record named Grill Brush. I deferred discussion of this feature since I didn't want to get you sidetracked from the product item creation steps. Now that you understand the use of section pages and linking of product items to them, feel free to experiment with modifying your next mass upload.*

Editing Page Layout and Navigation Properties

At this stage of your store construction, you might be thinking, "Well, that's fine, but what you've shown amounts to a store that has products yet only features a bare cement floor and unfinished sheet-rocked walls." No doubt about it, this store, while structurally sound, isn't much to look at, is it? Fair enough, because now we'll introduce you to the areas where you can modify your store appearance and then turn you loose to express yourself however you see fit. With carpet tacks and paint brushes at hand, let's get decorating.

Your decorating tools can be found in the Store Editor Variables section, accessed by the so-named button on the Editor toolbar. Upon clicking, you'll access a lengthy form that allows you to modify a page title, establish a background color or image, specify text colors, button colors and styles, image properties, and page layouts. The Variables page is laid out in logical areas, which we'll explore one by one.

Colors and Typefaces

First up, you can control the colors used in your store design as well as the typefaces (a.k.a. text fonts). Figure 17-16 shows the Colors and Typefaces fields in the Variables screen.

Each color selection element in the Variables screen displays a small color swatch as well as the designated RGB (Red, Green, Blue) numeric color value for

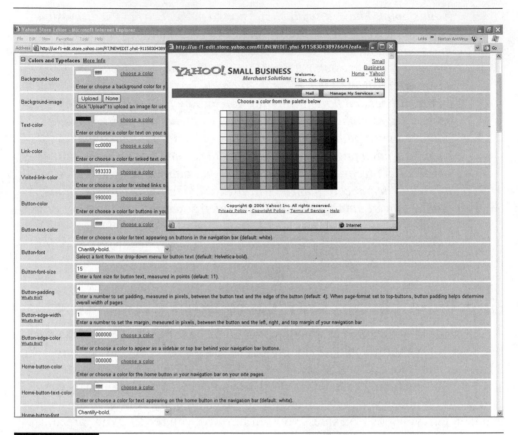

FIGURE 17-16   Begin adding visual style and flair by customizing the colors and typefaces used in your store design

the current color selected. If you'd like to change a color, you can either type in a new RGB value or click the Choose a color link to pick from a pop-up window color chart (as seen in Figure 17-16). There are no rules about how you should select your colors, so feel free to experiment away with the different field until you arrive at a color combination that will suit your store and be pleasing to your customers.

Likewise, you can change the font sizes and styles by either typing in a font name in the appropriate fields or clicking the down-arrow selector to choose from a list of available fonts. Again, experiment here until you find combinations that are suitable to your store design and easy for your customers to read.

Image Dimensions

As you may recall, there are several different image types you've seen up to this point: product item images, section page thumbnail images, and the secondary inset images that you may also elect to display on a section page where a product item is linked.

> **TIP**   *If you thought the inset images were sort of redundant to your already-selected product item image, recognize that the insets are excellent to use for alternate views of an item such as front-side, back-side, close-up, and so on.*

In this area of the Variables form, then, you can exert control over the sizes of the various images displayed in your store (see Figure 17-17).

The Image Dimensions section of the Variables form allows you to specify the height and width (in screen pixel representation) of each of the three image types. Experiment with sizing to ensure your pages provide useful and easy to see images without having them become too large (long time to display) or too small (indiscernible detail).

Page Layout

Figure 17-18 shows the fields pertinent to modifying your store's page layout. Here you can customize the appearance of the key page elements including the overall page size, navigation bar buttons, upload store logos, and more. Again, these elements can be easily modified and changed, allowing you to experiment with the layout and immediately review and revise your changes while in the Store Editor.

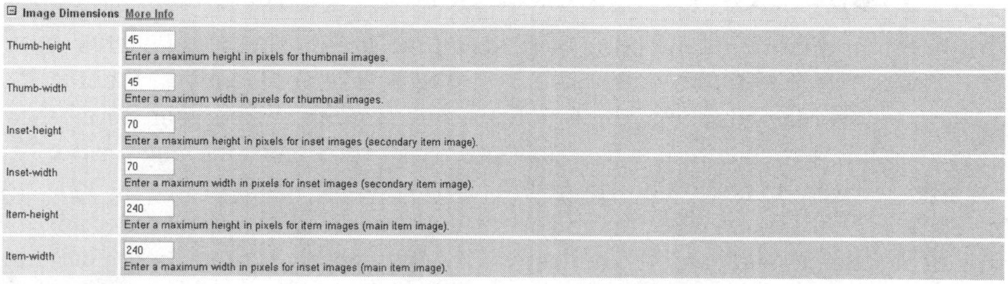

⊟ **Image Dimensions** More Info	
Thumb-height	45 Enter a maximum height in pixels for thumbnail images.
Thumb-width	45 Enter a maximum width in pixels for thumbnail images.
Inset-height	70 Enter a maximum height in pixels for inset images (secondary item image).
Inset-width	70 Enter a maximum width in pixels for inset images (secondary item image).
Item-height	240 Enter a maximum height in pixels for item images (main item image).
Item-width	240 Enter a maximum width in pixels for inset images (main item image).

FIGURE 17-17   Modify image sizes in this area of the Variables form

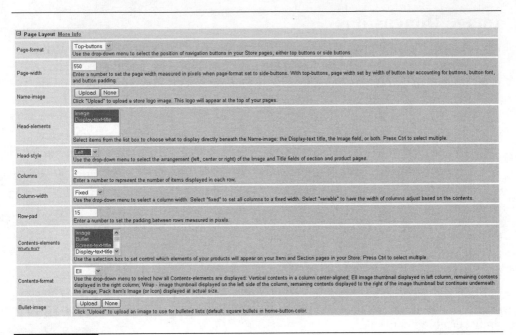

FIGURE 17-18   Modify key page elements in the Page Layout section of the Variables screen

Button Properties

Here's where you can adjust the design qualities of your store's buttons by adjusting the button style, color, text, and even embed images into a button display. As you study Figure 17-19, you'll see you can manage each button separately, providing you complete control and customization over every button element in your store.

Page Properties

This brief but important collection of fields allows you to specify elements that will appear on each of your store pages (see Figure 17-20). Here you'll enter valuable keywords, those that help Internet search engines to find your store based upon matching search criteria a user may specify (if someone's looking for fire pit grills, we want to be sure our store will be listed in the result of that query). In addition, here's where you'll note your business address as well as make any important statements regarding your store's content copyright protection (entered in the Final-text field).

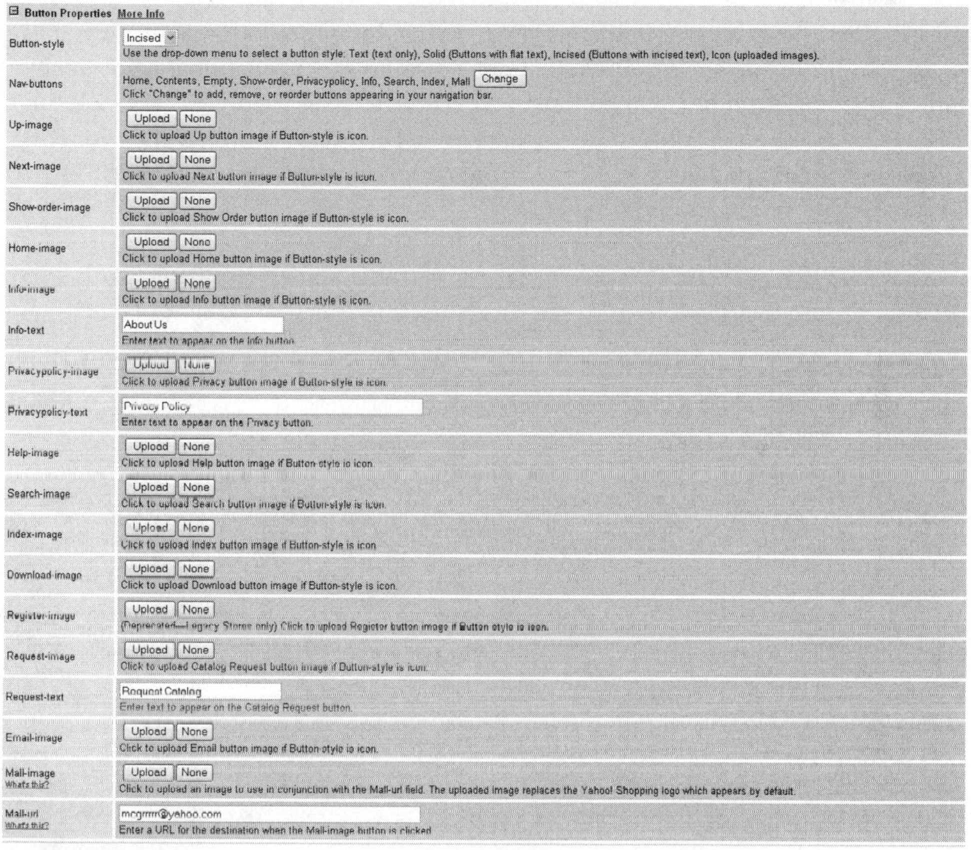

FIGURE 17-19 Modify button elements from within the Variables screen

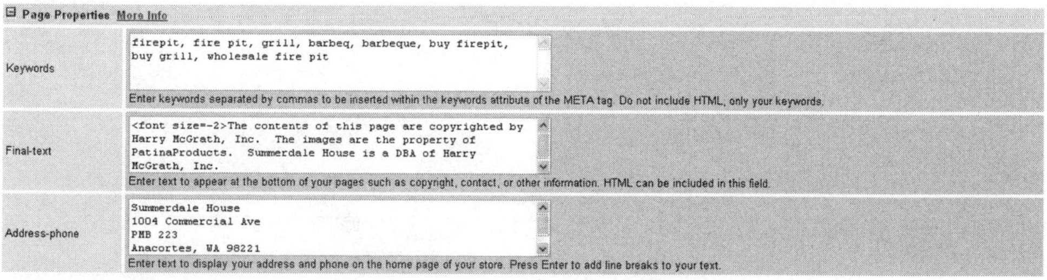

FIGURE 17-20 Enter keywords, address, and copyright-type statements in the Page Properties fields

Store Properties

Yes, there's still more to see in the Variables screen. Last up is the area where you can manage overall store settings including price display, order functionality, currency, minimum order quantities, and important cross-sell text (see Figure 17-21). Carefully review and experiment with these settings, then be sure to test their functionality before you finally publish your store (more on testing coming in Chapter 21).

⊟ **Store Properties** <u>More Info</u>	
Price-style	Normal ▾ Select a style to display prices: Normal-bold, Big-images in emphasis-color, Quiet-prices appear only on item, not section, pages.
Regular-price-text	Regular price: Enter text to appear before the regular price amount.
Sale-price-text	Sale price: Enter text to appear before the sale price amount.
Order-style	Normal ▾ Select a style from the drop-down menu for text appearing with the order button: normal, two-line, or multi line.
Secure-basket	Yes ▾ Select whether to use https secure mode for your checkout.
Compound-name	Yes ▾ Use the drop-down menu to select yes or no. When "Compound-name" is set to "Yes", then your accessory items will have their Names displayed in the shopping cart and on the Order Form.
Order-text	Add to Cart
Show-order-text	Show Order Enter text to appear on the Show Order button such as "My Cart", "My Items" or similar.
Families	Deprecated (Legacy Stores only) Enter names of families of related items for cross-selling.
Cross-sell-text	Enter text to appear above any cross-sell items such as "Other Items You May Like".
Currency	$ Enter the currency symbol to appear before prices. Note this is for display only and all orders will be calculated in dollars.
Minimum-order	20 Enter a number representing the minimum order amount. (default: none). For example, stores selling mostly low dollar items may wish to have a $25 minimum in order to process an order.
Minimum-quantity	1 Enter a number to set the minimum number of an item that can be ordered. Inform your visitors if greater than one.
Availability	Usually ships the same business day. ▾ Select an availability message to display for items. Choose "not set" to display no availability message or select an option to represent your standard order fulfillment time.
Need-ship	Yes ▾ Select whether to require a shipping address at checkout. If yes, item requires shipping address. (Set to no for downloads, subscriptions, or contributions.)
Need-bill	Yes ▾ Select whether to require a billing address at checkout. If yes, item requires billing address. (Set to no for items that are free.)
Need-payment	Yes ▾ Select whether to require payment information at checkout. If yes, item requires payment. (Set to no for items that are free, billed later, or shipped COD.)
Personalization-charge	Enter the charge (if any) for personalization. Personalizations include monograms and inscriptions, which can be defined in the Options field of an item. Override variable if charges vary by item.
Shopping-url	Deprecated: This field is no longer called by any standard templates.

FIGURE 17-21   Manage your overall store settings here

Wrapping It All Up

No doubt, this chapter has offered a lot of information and has exposed you to the many, many elements you can and will manage as you develop your store structure and style. If you're concerned that I didn't walk you through each and every element in excruciating detail, please don't be. The fact is that the Yahoo Store structure and layout tools become quite intuitive (yes, we said "intuitive") by this stage in your store creation. You should be familiar enough with the overall Store Editor navigation and manipulation such that you can focus on each element presented here and quickly determine its value to you. Along the way, you'll see Yahoo has provided plenty of help links directly within the various edit forms, giving you an additional information if and when you need it. But I've found the best teacher here is hands-on use and experience. Fiddle with the different forms and features described here and you'll quickly master their use. You're over the biggest hump in the learning curve here so enjoy the creation process. Remember, it's *your* store.

Chapter 18

Creating Additional Section Pages

The previous chapter was chock full of new terminology and plenty of new edit form screens that you may likely still be reeling from. Take the time to really work with the elements and techniques of establishing your store structure and managing the different variables that will make your virtual marketplace vibrant and enticing. The more you play, the sooner you'll achieve expert status.

When you feel ready to continue your store building efforts, it's time to continue with our study of your store structure and design. In this chapter, we'll leverage what you learned in Chapter 17 and discuss additional section pages you can create and additional ways to utilize them within your overall store layout. I'll also show you more ways to manage and manipulate the Variables page in Store Editor to gain you even more control over your store's blossoming "personality." Let's continue, shall we?

Creating More Section Pages

In the previous chapter I mentioned how section pages serve as the next level down from the home page in your overall store structure. I showed you how to create a section page from the home page using the Store Editor. Now, when you're ready to create another section page—that is, another useful major store category designation—simply navigate through the Store Editor to your store home page. Just as you did before, follow these four simple steps to create another section page:

1. Click the Section button in the Editor toolbar.

2. Enter the appropriate information in the Section form page (minimum requirement is you enter a section name).

3. If you want to upload an image to be associated with the section, click the Upload button in the section form, then click Browse from the pop-up window and click Send once you've specified an image file on your computer.

4. Click the Update button at the top or bottom of the Section form page to complete the creation.

Immediately you should notice that when you create a new section page, a new section navigation button appears on your store navigation bar. Recall that you can review the different buttons associated to your store navigation bar by clicking the Edit button when you're in your home page and reviewing the values contained within the Contents field. If your store structure requires, repeat the four steps to create as many section pages as you need (although the navigation bar can only actively display as many as 26 clickable buttons; more than 26 will be displayed as clickable text links within the body of your home page).

Back to managing section pages in your store, now consider the enhancement to the store structure diagram previously displayed in Chapter 17. The revised diagram is pictured here in Figure 18-1.

As you see in Figure 18-1, it's possible and often highly preferable to create section pages *within* section pages. Why? Well, let's consider the example of the Accessories section page created during the discussion in Chapter 17. From the home page, this will be useful to help your customers navigate to useful amenities

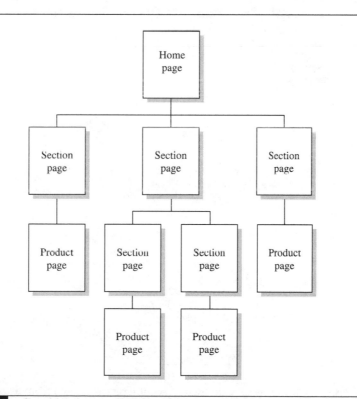

FIGURE 18-1   Consider the possibilities of your store design as you begin creating subsection pages as diagrammed here

that will enhance their use of the Summerdale House fire pit grills. It would be of even more use if that section page, however, was further subdivided into sections such as Utensils & Tools, Aprons & Mitts, and Grill Covers. Well, I've done just that by creating these section pages within the Accessories section page. The only difference in creating subsection pages versus the home page–linked section page is that you'll create the subpages from the section page of your choice. That is, I first navigated to the Accessories section page, clicked the Section button from that page, entered the section page name and uploaded an image. Upon clicking the Update button, I had section pages within our section page. Take a look at Figure 18-2 to see the results of my work.

FIGURE 18-2   Subsection pages are merely section pages created from a section page

From a newly created subsection page, you can link product pages just as I showed you in Chapter 17. It's simple and fast.

TIP *If you're wondering whether you can use the copy-and-paste and cut-and-paste functions we demonstrated in Chapter 18 as an alternative method to create subsection pages,* you can!

Editing Section Headline and Abstract Fields

Again, customization is at your fingertips as you tame the various functions in your Yahoo Store. When you create section pages and even your product pages, you'll find there are a couple more modifications you can establish that will provide a bit more marketing punch to your products.

We'll start by looking at the Headline field, found in both section page forms as well as product page forms. For this example, we'll modify the product page form for our Western Design Fire Pit & Grill. If you'll take a look at Figure 18-3, you'll see how this particular item is displayed from the Fire Pit Grills section page.

While we're quite satisfied with the product name as displayed on the section page, we might like to alter that a bit when our customers are actually reviewing the product within its own product page. From the product page, then, we'll edit the item and add some alternate text in the Headline field to read "Old West charm in a rustic design fire pit & grill." Upon clicking the Update button on the product item edit form, we've effectively replaced the appearance of the text in the Name field with the alternate text now populated in the Headline field. Figure 18-4 shows how we're able to improve the displayed text on the product page.

Where you may consider use of the headline text a minor alteration, it nonetheless gives you additional freedom and control to further customize your store page content and appearance while giving you latitude to punch up the pitch, so to speak.

FIGURE 18-3 From the Fire Pit Grill section page, the Western Design Fire Pit & Grill is displayed using the product name

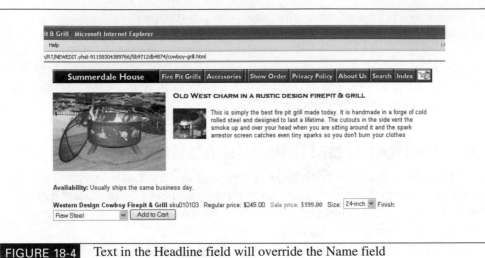

Text in the Headline field will override the Name field

Next up and worth mentioning is the Abstract field. Here again, as with the Headline field, you can easily and effectively embellish the content in your item or section pages beyond what initially greets customers from your store entry pages. For this example, we'll add some abstract text to a section page. From a section page, we'll edit the page and add some additional text in the Abstract field within the section Edit form. Upon clicking the Update button on the section page edit form, the abstract text is now included in the content of the section page. The text, however, may not show up from the home page view immediately. In order to effectively activate the appearance of this text, there are a couple of steps to be taken. First, you'll need to include the Abstract item within the "Contents-elements" list box from the home page. Here's how:

1. Navigate in Store Editor to the home page.

2. Click the Edit button on the toolbar.

3. Locate the Contents-elements list box, which likely already has selections like Image, Bullet, Screen-title-text, and other already selected (highlighted in dark blue). Scroll down the list until you find Abstract. Hold down your keyboard's Control (CTRL) button while clicking the Abstract selection to include it in the overall list of selected items.

4. Click the Update button.

Next, it's necessary to modify your store variables to also account for the use of abstract text (especially if you want this abstract to appear wherever a section page is linked throughout your store). Here's how:

1. Navigate in Store Editor to the home page.

2. Click the Variables button on the toolbar.

3. Locate the Contents-elements list box (it's found under the Page Layout section heading).

4. Using the CTRL key, activate the Abstract selection.

5. Click the Update button.

With that, your home page should now display the abstract text you entered. In this example, we added text to our Accessories section page. In Figure 18-5, you can see how our Fire Pit Grills section page appears without abstract text whereas the adjacent display of the Accessories section page link displays the abstract text.

The Abstract text allows you to add more compelling information from your home page

Overriding Variables

And speaking of variables, you have yet more control over your store design and display when you choose to override your store variables selections. As you've discovered, the settings from the Variables page allows you to make design and display choices that can be easily proliferated throughout your store. There may be times, however, when you wish to override those settings, perhaps for a particular product or section page. No problem.

I liked that I could display the subsection page titles from our Accessories section page, yet I wasn't satisfied with the tiny size of the accompanying images (the Thumb-height and Thumb-width settings under the Image Dimensions section heading on the Variables page). While those dimensions were suitable to other

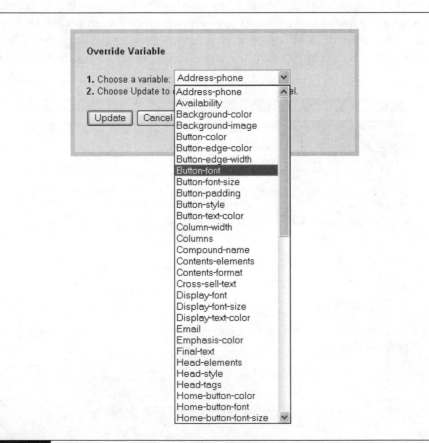

FIGURE 18-6 Find and select a variable to override

areas of the store where the thumbnail images appeared, I wanted them to be a bit larger within the actual Accessories page. You enable an override, then, as follows:

1. From any page where you wish to override a storewide variable, click the Edit button on the toolbar.

2. At the top of the edit form page, locate and click the button labeled Override Variable.

3. In the subsequent screen, click the pull-down arrow to the right of the Choose a variable field to find and select the variable you want to override (see Figure 18-6).

4. Click the Update button on the Override variable selection box (also shown in Figure 18-6).

5. Upon being returned to the edit form page from where you started, you'll see the variable field you selected is now available for modification, the effects of which will be specific to the page you're presently editing only.

Figure 18-7 shows the results of the overrides to the thumbnail image size overrides.

Understand that overriding variables is strictly an elective action and is certainly not required if you're satisfied with the effect variable settings already have within your store. If, however, you want to tweak and touch up specific areas, then again you have that control at your fingertips within your Yahoo Store.

FIGURE 18-7   A successful override of the storewide thumbnail image dimensions allowed resizing of the images on this section page only

Chapter 19

Creating Supplementary Pages

So far, so good: with what you've read up to this point, you're able to create the backbone of your Yahoo Store. You understand where, how, and why to manage a product catalog, product pages, a Home page, section pages, and the linking of products and images to the appropriate pages. Slowly but surely your virtual aisles will be filling with great products, and you'll certainly be experimenting with different variables to infuse your store with your own personal touch. Now, though, you need to consider some additional pages that should also exist before you open your store. In this chapter, I'll describe the supplementary pages you'll need, explain why you need them, and explain how easy they are to create, leveraging from what you already know about Yahoo Store construction.

A Quick Review

While you've seen and done quite a bit up to this point, let's take a moment to quickly review what it is that you've achieved so far:

- ■ You've registered and created your account with the Yahoo Merchant Solutions suite and have established (or associated) a web URL address for your store domain.

- ■ You've created a product spreadsheet outside of the Yahoo Merchant Solutions suite to determine what inventory you'll be offering in your new store and collecting all the necessary details that enable you to create an orderable item in your store.

- ■ You've created product listing pages within the Yahoo suite using the Catalog Manager, understanding the necessary elements that will result in a useful and enticing listing for your eventual customers.

- ■ You've learned how to manage mass uploads of multiple product items and even multiple product images, offering you an alternative to populating your store's product offerings.

- ■ You've learned how to create your store's Home page and how to utilize the different design elements within the Yahoo Store Editor.

- ■ You've learned how to create an overall store structure using a combination of the Home page, section pages, and, ultimately, product pages.

Yes, you've learned quite a bit and no doubt you're continuing to work with the various Editor forms and the Variables settings to further embellish your store with a unique feel and functionality. Frankly, you've successfully poured a solid foundation upon which to launch your store, yet there are just a couple more tasks you must complete before your online shop is ready for the masses.

Completing Yahoo's Required Pages

Before you begin to wonder whether you even want to create supplementary pages, understand that a couple of them are actually required before Yahoo will allow you to open your store for business. That's right—there are two pages that Yahoo deems mandatory and that must be completed before a store can be opened. Don't fret too much, since neither is terribly difficult to complete and, in fact, both can be quite helpful to your overall business success.

The Info Page

You may recall seeing a button labeled About Us on the navigation bar in the various Home and section page images shown throughout this part of the book. That button is commonly referred to as the Info Page button by Yahoo (and we actually modified the button test to read About Us rather than the standard Info label). Yahoo requires this page since it's where you'll list your contact information should a customer need to reach you in connection with a product offering, a sales policy, or an order placed. It's required of all Yahoo Store owners to provide such information in order to better ensure good business is being done within the Yahoo realm (and with all that's been said and done about online fraud on the Internet, we think it's pretty clear why Yahoo has set this stipulation).

You needn't do anything special to create a space in your store for the Info page—it already exists just by the mere existence of the corresponding navigation bar button. Click the Info button on the navigation bar to advance to the space where you'll establish appropriate details. You'll arrive at a blank page that looks very much like a new section page; simply click the Edit button in the Store Editor toolbar and you'll traverse to the Edit form you see in Figure 19-1.

Looking at the Info Page edit form, you'll find the following fields:

■ **Greeting** Believe it or not, this is a critical element to any online merchant site as it is the virtual equivalent to the employee who greets a customer in a brick and mortar store and who may also remain ever-ready to answer a customer question. Smile broadly, then, and reach out a welcoming hand, crafting a bit of text that tells the online shopper more about who you are, what your mission is, and what they can expect to encounter when shopping at your store.

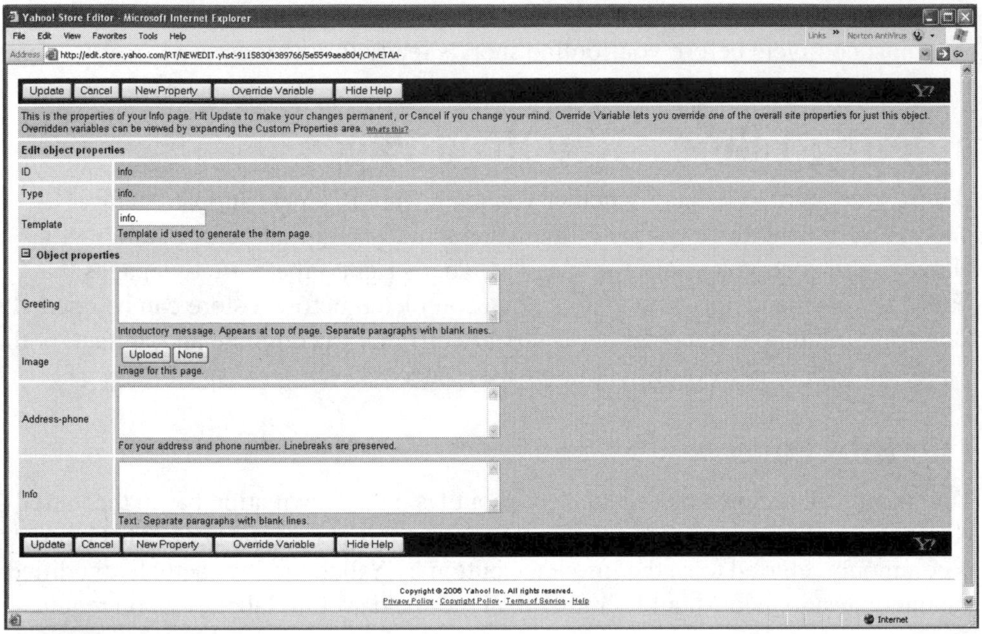

FIGURE 19-1   The Info Page edit form is brief yet important to complete before you can open your Yahoo Store

- **Image**   If you have a special image you want to share at this point, simply upload it (and this is a good place to upload a picture of a brick-and-mortar shop if your Yahoo Store will be an online extension of your existing business).

- **Address-phone**   This is the all-important contact information that will make it possible for your customers to reach you directly or generally gain a better understanding of where you physically reside and/or operate from.

- **Info**   Here's where it's a good idea to make statements about your overall operating policies and practices. Don't skimp here because this is where you can likely answer many of your customers' questions *before* they ask. Therefore, be sure your info includes an e-mail address (or several if you'll offer different addresses for different customer needs—orders@yourstore .com, product-inquiries@yourstore.com, returns@yourstore.com, and so on), your shipping policies (including methods, usual turnaround time, holiday schedules, and so on), and a Refund/Return Policy (very important to establish trust in your new customers).

> TIP
>
> *Incidentally, if you're familiar with HTML, you can use that in the Info field to create tables and other useful layout effects to better communicate details about your store and its operating procedures.*

The Privacy Policy Page

This page probably needs little explanation in regard to its purpose or importance in the realm of online shopping. You saw this page referenced by the appropriately labeled navigation bar button, Privacy Policy, from the Home or section pages we've managed thus far. Like the Info page, this is a pre-established page element in your store design and one you need to complete. Again, you can't open your store without it, as Yahoo indicates in the following official statement:

Yahoo! Merchant Solutions guidelines require that your Merchant Solutions account post, maintain, and adhere to a privacy policy that informs customers about the disposition of personal information collected by your company and how it may be used.

As with the Info page, again you needn't do anything special to create a space in your store for the Privacy Policy page—it already exists. Click the Privacy Policy button on the navigation bar to advance to the space where you'll establish appropriate details. You'll arrive at a blank page that looks very much like a new Section page; simply click the *Edit* button in the Store Editor toolbar and you'll traverse to the Edit form you see in Figure 19-2.

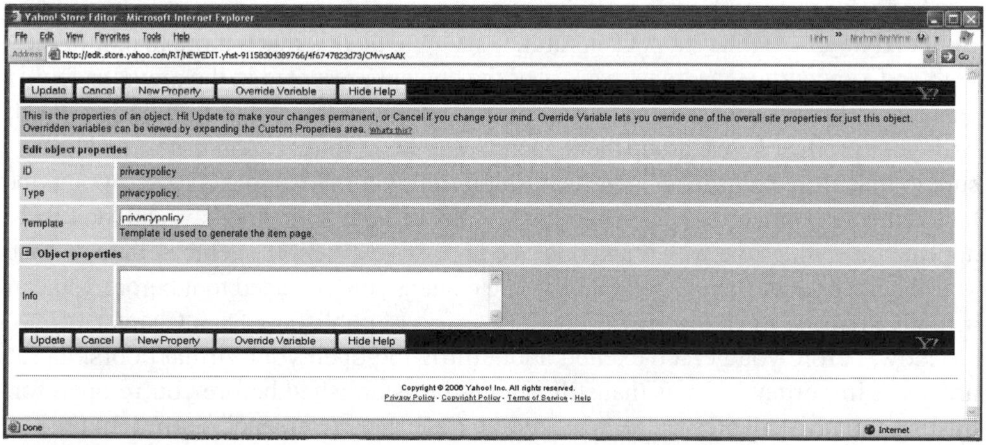

FIGURE 19-2   The Privacy Policy Page Edit form contains a single field that will contain your important customer protection details

Looking at the Privacy Policy Page edit form, you'll find the only field requiring input is that labeled Info. And, just like the Info page field of the same name, you can utilize HTML tagging to nicely format the policy statements you'll make here. What sort of information should you communicate regarding a privacy policy? How about these:

- Announce your commitment to your customers' privacy and that you won't share, sell, or otherwise use their personal details without their prior consent.

- Assure your customers' privacy by stipulating how their data is kept secure on your site and elsewhere in your processing of their information to complete store-relevant transactions and communications.

- Itemize exactly what information you collect from customers and how that information is used in managing their interactions with you and your store.

- Provide clear instructions on how customers can review the data you've collected from them and how they may make additions, changes, or deletions to it.

> **TIP** *If you'd like a bit of help getting started with crafting your privacy policy details, we recommend all new online shopkeepers visit the Better Business Bureau Online to examine their sample template. You can find it at* **http://bbbonline.com/privicay/sample_privacy.asp**.

And with that, you've successfully created a store structure and enabled a viable front end to your online shop. Congratulations! Yes, there's much more to still fiddle with and I encourage you to go back over the content presented in the previous few chapters to further enhance your store content, arrangement, and overall design. Work with your product items, group them accordingly in various section pages, and be sure to link all sections in an intuitive fashion from your Home page. At this point, the ball's in your court, so to speak, in regards to solidifying your store's visual look and appeal. Take your time with it and don't be afraid to explore. Remember, though, that you'll need to publish your store and all the content you've added to it before you can actually be ready to go live (review the discussion of publishing from Chapter 16).

Now, before you get too excited about throwing open your virtual doors, there are some important settings that still need to be established before you're open for business. In this chapter we've wrapped up the basic "front end" setting. In the next chapter, we'll introduce you to the "back end" content where you'll establish how you'll accept and process actual customer orders. There's still quite a bit to do, but with every step you take, you're that much closer to launching your online store. Read on!

Chapter 20

Order Form and Checkout Settings

U p to this point, I've toured you through the features and functionalities of the Yahoo Merchant Solutions product management toolset (the Catalog Manager) and the store site creation toolset (the Store Editor). Recall that I indicated you can manage both of these portions of your online store either directly within the Yahoo space or you can elect to manage them outside of the Yahoo tools; your product items can be itemized, detailed, and ultimately uploaded using an external spreadsheet application and, likewise, you can opt to create your web content of your store using a third-party development tool such as FrontPage or Dreamweaver. As you venture into the final area of creating your Yahoo Store, you'll now find you must stay within the confines of the Yahoo suite of tools. That is, in order to create and manage the "back end" of your store functionality, you'll need to work exclusively within the Yahoo Store Manager. Fear not—you'll see it's very much the same as the functionalities you've used in previous chapters. And, if you're ready to put the final touches on your end-to-end store operating content, then here's what you'll need to know about establishing your store order form and checkout settings.

Returning to the Store Manager

You'll likely recall that you first navigated to and traversed the Store Manager back in Chapter 14. There you learned about how this is the heart of your store and the core area where you'll manage the business aspects of your online shop. Now that it's time to address matters of product ordering, shopping cart function, and other financial and business details of your store, the Store Manager is where you'll be doing your work. Specifically, here's what you'll accomplish through use of the Store Manager in this stage of your store development and readiness:

- Customize your store's order form and checkout flow

- Set up your shipping rules

- Establish your tax rules

- Set up your payment methods

Of course, the Store Manager allows access to additional functions but, for the moment, we'll focus on the key items just noted as you get ready to open for business. For a quick refresher, recall you can access the Store Manager by navigating to the Yahoo My Services page (**http://smallbusiness.yahoo.com/services/**), then click

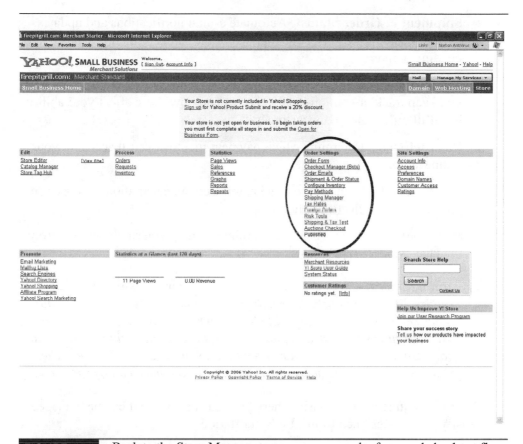

Back to the Store Manager to manage your order form and checkout flow

the Store Manager link on the page. When you do, you're ready to utilize the Store
Manager functions as shown in Figure 20-1.

You'll notice that Figure 20-1 features an oval drawn around the area labeled
Order Settings—that's where you'll be focusing your efforts in this chapter.
Specifically, you'll work with the following text links within the encircled area:

- **Order Form**   Create settings pertinent to the display and functionality of
  the on-screen order form your customers will see and use as they shop at
  and purchase items from your store.

- **Order E-mails**   Establish receiving e-mail addresses for new orders
  received as well as catalog requests.

■ **Shipment & Order Status**   Automate e-mail notifications and updates so your customers can be kept apprised of the status of their purchases and pending deliveries.

■ **Configure Inventory**   Establish inventory notifications and alerts to help you keep track of your on-hand balances and how those affect your ability to fulfill orders placed by customers.

■ **Pay Methods**   Determine which payment methods you'll accept at your online store.

■ **Tax Rates**   Make the appropriate automated tax calculation settings if you'll need to collect sales taxes.

■ **Risk Tools**   Establish rules and warnings to help you safely and securely manage credit card payments.

> TIP
>
> *You'll notice the final selection under the Order Settings column in Figure 20-1 is "Published." When you begin managing your order and other settings, the selection will change to read Publish Order Settings. Much as how you needed to publish your store settings in the Store Editor, you also need to publish your order settings in the Store Manager when you first establish the details and every time you make changes to them.*

Yes, there's quite a bit to consider here but you'll soon see it can be managed very easily in well-designed forms. Let's get started.

Customizing the Order Form

Start from the start by clicking the Order Form text link as shown in Figure 20-1, navigating you to the order form edit page (see Figure 20-2).

On this lengthy form, you'll set the following:

■ **New Checkout Flow**   Enables the improved Yahoo checkout flow logic, navigating customers from item selection to cart review through order details settings, and finally to the order confirmation page. I recommend you utilize the default setting in this section.

■ **General Order Form Options**   Establish whether you want customer names to be captured as a single field value or if you want to capture first and last names in separate fields. Also, specify which currency you'll manage.

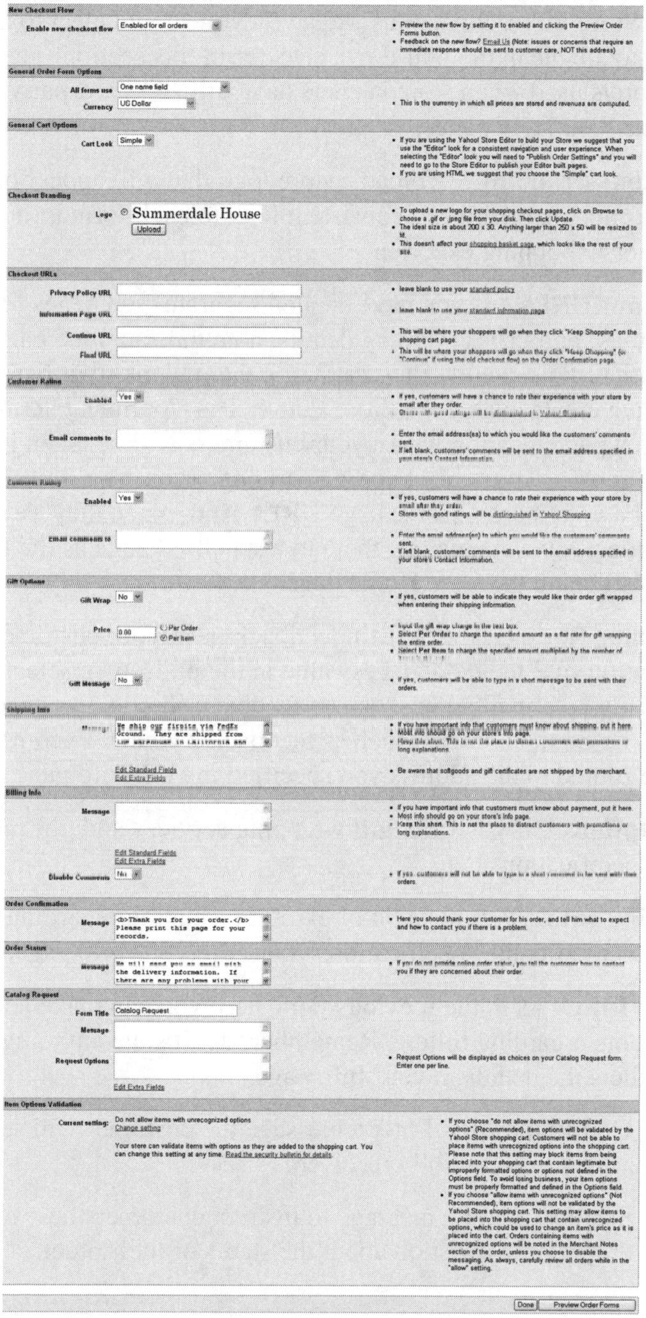

FIGURE 20-2 Managing the settings of your orders begins in this order form page

- **General Cart Options**   If you've created your store pages using the Yahoo Store Editor toolset (as we have), you should elect to use the Editor setting available in the pull-down selector in this section. The Simple selection is used when store keepers have utilized third-party HTML tools to create their store pages.

- **Checkout Branding**   Upload a store logo that will appear on your order forms, maintaining a consistent look to each form throughout the customers' shopping experience.

- **Checkout URLs**   If you have created separate web pages for your Info (About Us) and Privacy Policy details, note those unique page URLs in the appropriate fields here; otherwise leave them blank to utilize the pages you may have created using the Store Editor. The Continue URL field should contain a page location where your customers will be taken if they click Keep Shopping from the shopping cart page (you would likely want to set this to be your store's Home page URL). And, when they've completed their order, you can navigate them to a specified page as the Final URL, often also being the store Home page.

- **Customer Rating**   Easily gain feedback from your customers by enabling this section (use the default Yes value in the pull-down selector) and specifying an e-mail address where feedback should be routed. If you don't specify an e-mail address (such as feedback@yourstore.com), the e-mail will be routed to the address you specified in your Info page.

- **Gift Options**   If you offer gift wrapping services and gift messages, make those specifications here.

- **Shipping Info**   Provide a bit of extra information regarding shipping. Try not to contradict the specifications you set in your Info page, however.

- **Billing Info**   As in the previous field, here you can make additional statements regarding billing. Remember; don't state anything that contradicts the details in your Info page.

- **Order Confirmation**   Enter a message the customer will see when an order has been successfully received.

- **Order Status**   Enter a message to instruct customers how to contact you should they have a question about the status of their order.

- **Catalog Request**   Create a useful request form through which customers can inquire for a catalog of other products or make general inquiries. Enable this function completely by returning to the Store Editor Variables settings and adding the Request item to your buttons table.

- **Item Options Validation**   Make the setting to prevent any invalid options from being specified during the ordering process. In this way, customers will be stopped from completing their order if an option they've specified is not properly formatted in a way that you can successfully fulfill the customer purchase (such as inscriptions or monograms).

When your settings have been made, click the Done button found at the bottom of the order settings form. When you return to the Store Manager page, you'll see the bottommost link under the Order Settings column now reads Publish Order Settings. Click the link to complete the incorporation of the order settings you've just specified.

Setting Order E-mails

Next up, Yahoo enables you to create up-front settings for e-mail communications from your store to your customers. Rather than be strapped to your online In Box day in and day out, sorting through your various messages received to extricate important new order or customer request notifications, here you can specify distinct e-mail nodes where such communications should be routed for fast and efficient management.

To manage your order e-mails, click the Order E-mails text link under the Order Settings column on the Store Manager page. When you do, you'll advance to the appropriate settings form as shown in Figure 20-3.

Within the form page shown in Figure 20-3, you'll manage the following fields:

- Automatic Order Processing

  - **E-mail To**   Specify the e-mail address you want to receive order notifications from your store (such as neworders@yourstore.com).

  - **Encryption Settings**   Although this is rarely used anymore, encryption is available if you request customers provide their credit card information within the order form. If you're managing credit card payments via Paymentech or PayPal, this won't be necessary.

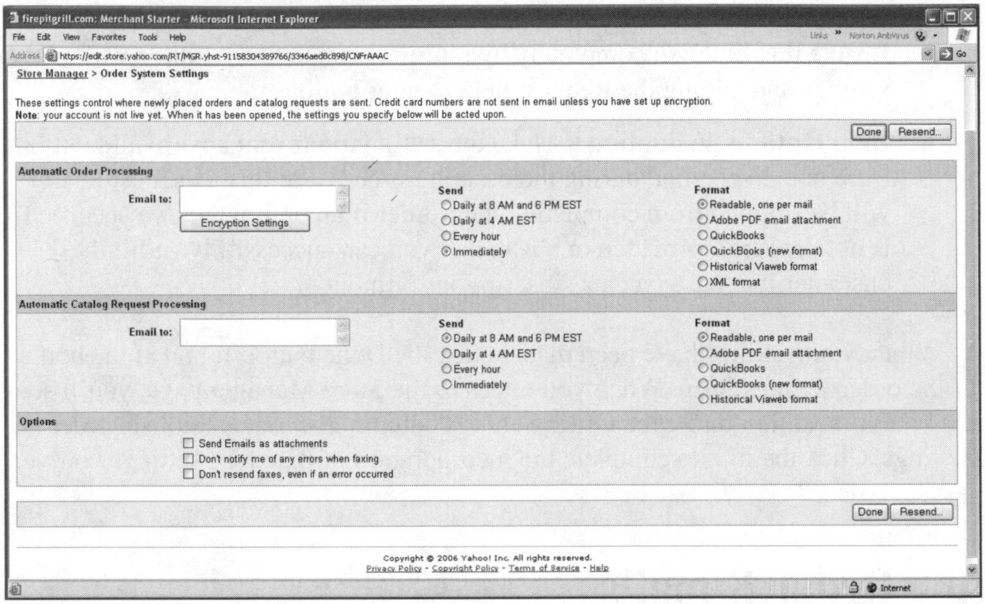

FIGURE 20-3   Use this form to set your order e-mail responses

- **Send**   Specify when you want this type of message sent to your receiving e-mail address. Usually you'll elect to send these immediately, although your process might also benefit from a batch sending specification.

- **Format**   If you select messages be sent immediately, you may simply choose to have them formatted as Readable, one per mail (which creates a simple text message). If you prefer to use a batch-send methodology, you may choose one of the other formats available to possibly group multiple orders in a single file for manipulation.

- Automatic Catalog Request Processing

  - **E-mail To**   Specify an e-mail address where you'd like requests to be routed (such as catalog-request@yourstore.com).

  - **Send**   Specify how and when you'd like such requests forwarded to your specified e-mail address.

  - **Format**   Specify the format of the request e-mails.

- Options

  - **Send E-mails as Attachments**   Check this box if you want the received messages to be captured as text files within the e-mail rather than as the textual body of the message.

  - **Don't Notify Me of any Errors When Faxing**   If you'll be accepting online fax orders, check this box if you don't want to be notified when a customer's attempted fax fails (the customer will be notified at the time of ordering, though). If you want to monitor this activity, however, leave this box unchecked.

  - **Don't Resend Faxes, Even if an Error Occurred**   If you don't want the Merchant Solutions programs to attempt a resend of a failed fax order, check this box.

Now, as simplistic as the preceding settings may seem, these are actually key elements that will help you organize and manage your incoming message flow. I highly recommend you establish discrete e-mail nodes for your incoming orders and requests (remember, you gained the potential for 1000 e-mail addresses when you signed up with Merchant Solutions) to keep your business running smoothly.

Configuring Shipment and Order Status Communications

Moving down the list of text links under the Order Settings column from within the Store Manager main page, now click the Shipment & Order Status link. When you do, you'll gain access to the page shown in Figure 20-4.

In this page, you'll make settings that can enable automated e-mail notifications to be sent to your customers every time you make a change to the status of their order (such as upon order receipt and upon order shipment). The settings here are quite intuitive:

- **Shipment Tracking**   Check this box to turn on automated e-mail messaging to your customers whenever you update the status of their order.

- **Order Confirmation E-mail**   Enter a valid e-mail address from your store to serve as the sender mail address (such as orders@yourstore.com) and to operate as a reply-to address if your customer has a question after receiving an automated confirmation message.

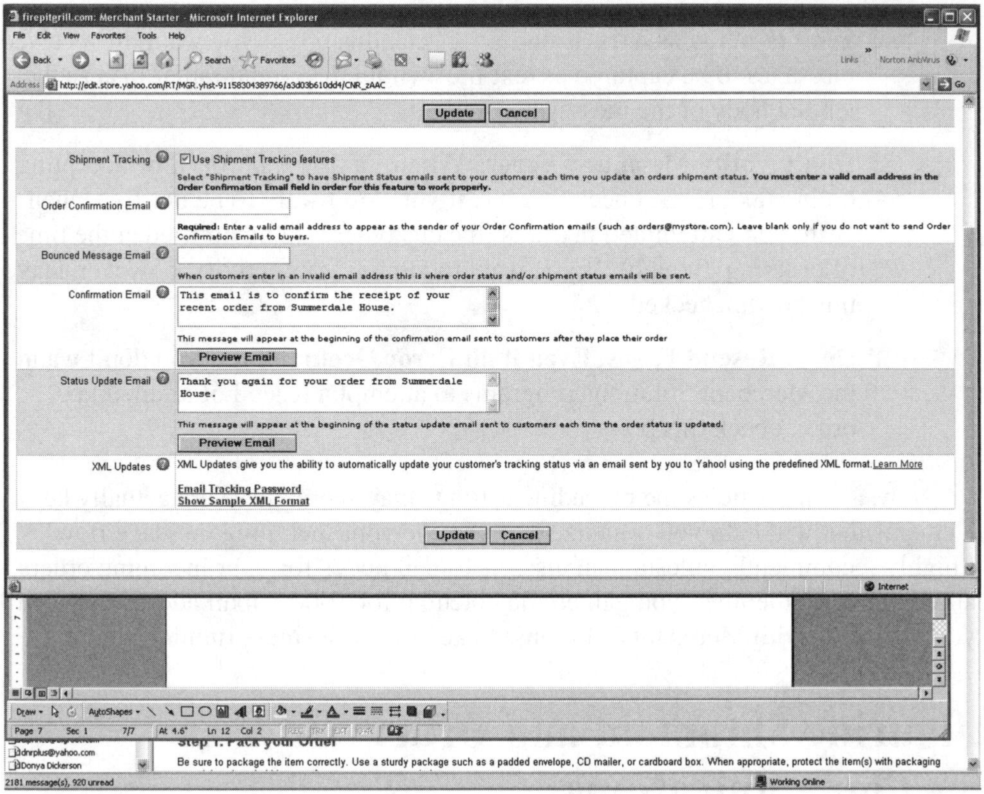

FIGURE 20-4 Use this form to enable automated shipment confirmations and order status updates for your customers

- **Bounced Message E-mail** If your customer specifies an invalid e-mail address when placing an order and the confirmation message cannot successfully be sent, the bounced (that is, undeliverable) message will be routed to your store e-mail address that you specify in this field.

- **Confirmation E-mail** The basic text that will appear at the opening of every confirmation e-mail message sent.

- **Status Update E-mail** The basic text that will appear at the opening of every order status update e-mail message sent.

- **XML Updates** If you'll be using the embedded UPS shipment management functionality in Yahoo's Merchant Solutions, you can enable complex status updates here. This technique won't be covered in this book.

Configuring Inventory Notifications

This very important feature allows you to establish settings that will indicate how the Yahoo Merchant Solutions toolset is to interpret the availability of your products. You'll determine your inventory method in this form, accessed by clicking the Configure Inventory text link from the Store Manager main page, so Merchant Solutions knows how to instruct your customers regarding whether the items they want are available or not. Moreover, you can also enable alerts to yourself to notify you when your on-hand balance reaches a certain level, prompting you to acquire more products to sell. Figure 20-5 shows the form you'll see when you click the Configure Inventory text link.

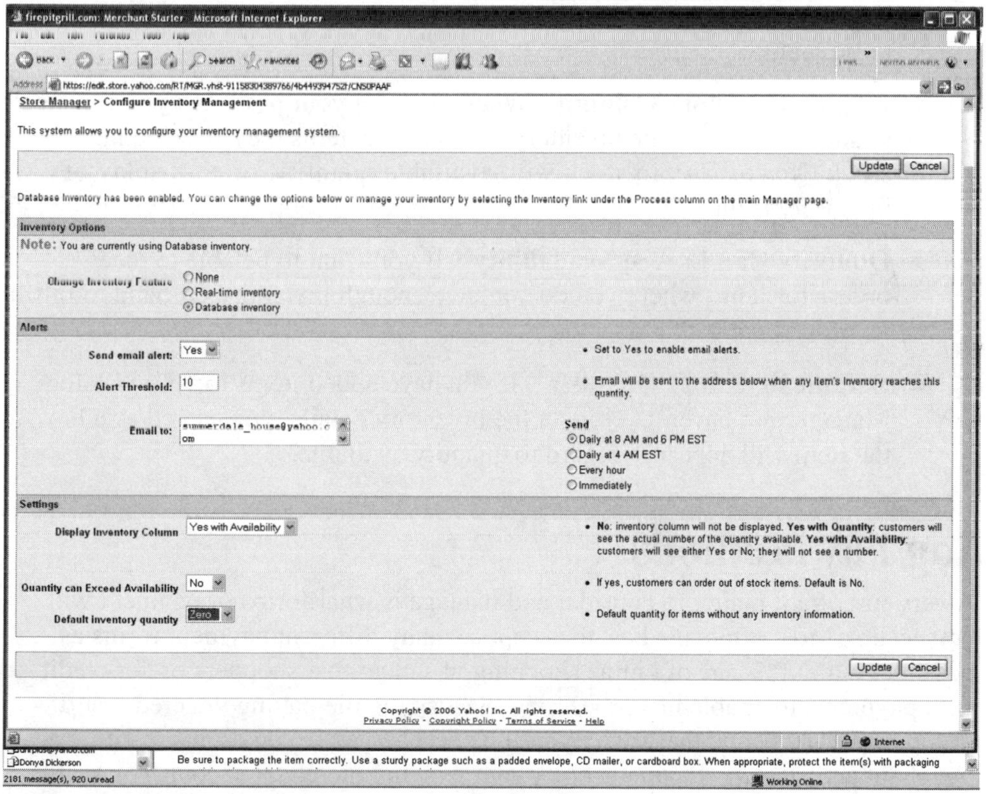

FIGURE 20-5 This useful form allows you to receive automated notifications related to your inventory status

■ **Change Inventory Feature**   If you're managing your inventory levels through Yahoo's Catalog Manager, you'll select the Database Inventory option (as I have). Selecting Real-time Inventory indicates you manage your inventory details offline using a web page of your own (and you'd specify that web page for Yahoo upon making this selection). If you choose not to enable inventory management, click the None option.

■ **Send E-mail Alert**   Here you specify if you want e-mail alerts sent regarding your inventory status.

■ **Alert Threshold**   This is where you can establish at what level the inventory will drop before an alert message is sent to you. This is often referred to as the *reorder point*—the on-hand balance level at which you need to order more inventory.

■ **E-mail to**   Here you specify the e-mail address where inventory alerts are to be sent.

■ **Display Inventory Column**   When ordering your products, you can elect to show customers the inventory status of the items they're selecting—in stock (Yes or No), in stock with available quantity, or no display of inventory status.

■ **Quantity Can Exceed Availability**   If you want to be able to receive orders for items where you do not have enough inventory on-hand to fulfill an order, enable this selector.

■ **Default Inventory Quantity**   If you have added items to your Catalog Manager but haven't yet input the inventory details, you can choose how the item will appear in regard to quantity available.

Setting Pay Methods

A very important matter to consider and manage is what forms of payment will you accept. Most often, it's best to accept as many different payment forms as possible, but in this age of online shopping, it's clear that shoppers prefer credit card payments to enable fast processing. Security while paying via credit card is of top importance, and that's why you'll be best served if you establish either a merchant account (via Paymentech or your existing merchant account) or enable PayPal secure payments. Click the Pay Methods text link from the Store Manager page to begin.

First, you'll need to establish the details of how you'll process credit card payments. Figure 20-6 shows you the page where you can link to Paymentech or PayPal to make your account specifications; just click the appropriate "setup" text link associated to either method of your choosing. If you already have a merchant account, you'll be able to specify that from the appropriated Paymentech link shown as well. Simply follow the subsequent on-screen instructions for whichever method you choose.

Next, click the bold text link Payment Options, to specify which options you wish to have appear on your order form. Figure 20-7 shows the different options Yahoo currently supports.

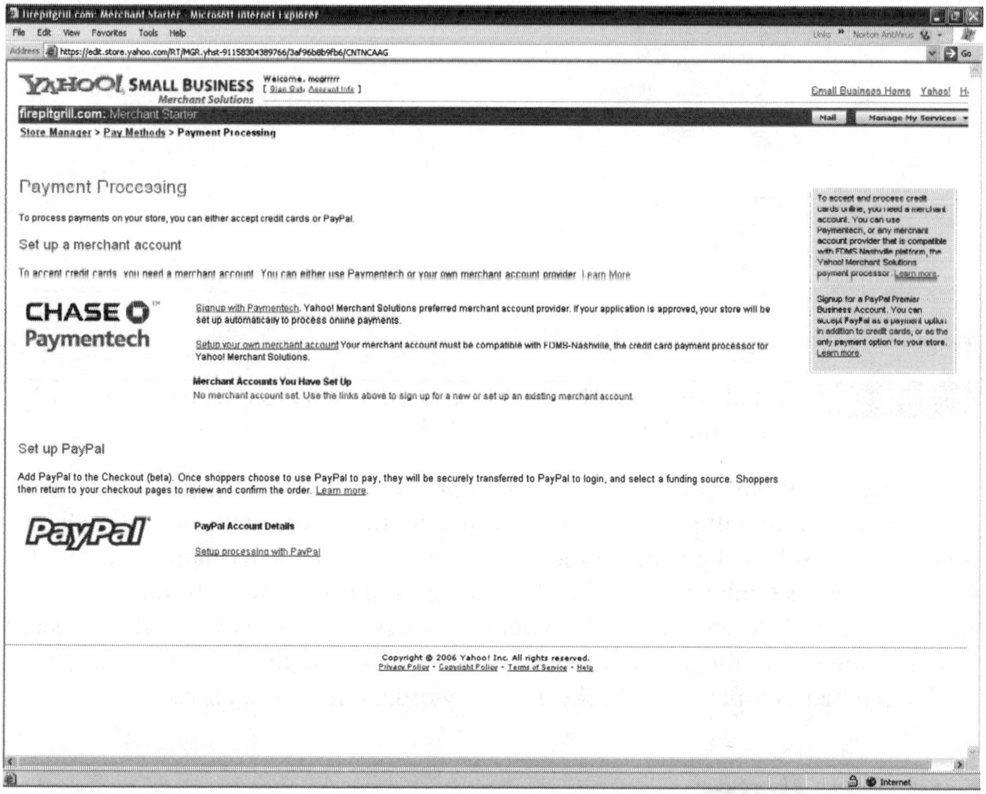

FIGURE 20-6   Use this page to navigate to Paymentech or PayPal to enable online credit card processing

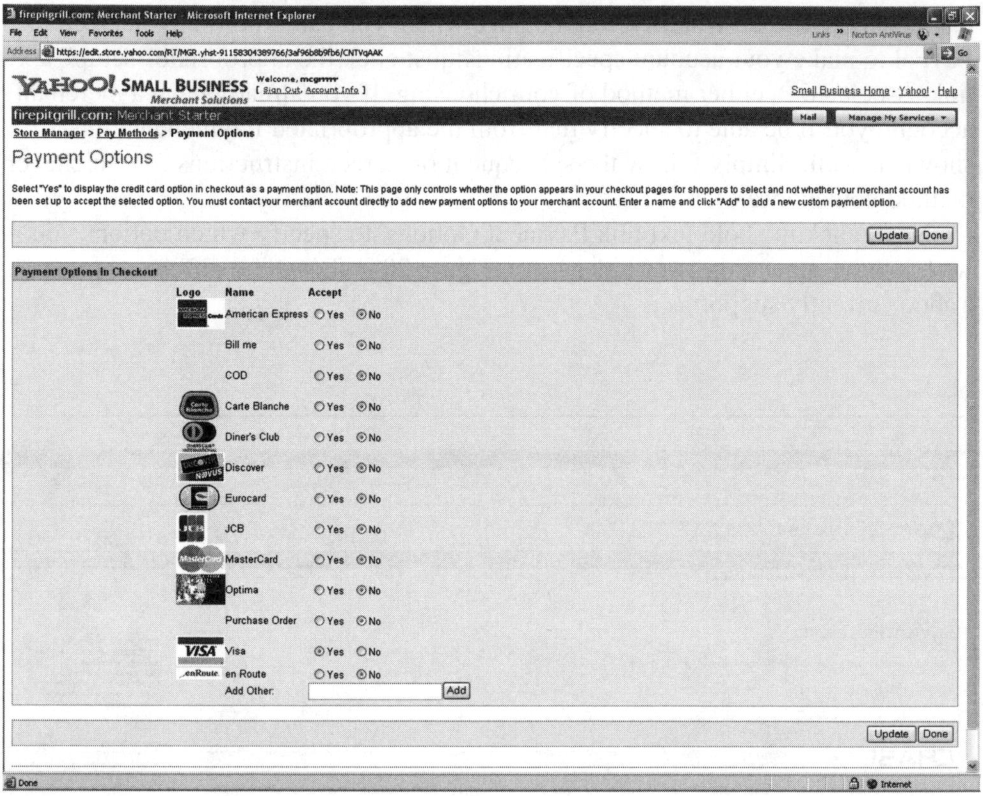

FIGURE 20-7   Use this page to select which payment options you want to appear on your order form

Select Yes or No options under the Accept column for each displayed payment method your store will process. Note that making these selections doesn't validate whether your selected payment processing method will actually manage a service (such as Diner's Club or Carte Blanche or others); this merely adds the enabled method to a pull-down selector that your customers can use to choose their desired payment method at the time of ordering. You can also use the Add Other field to enable payment by personal checks or money orders, if you so choose.

Setting Tax Rates

If the state you're operating your business from requires you to collect taxes on intrastate sales, Yahoo provides a place to establish this up front:

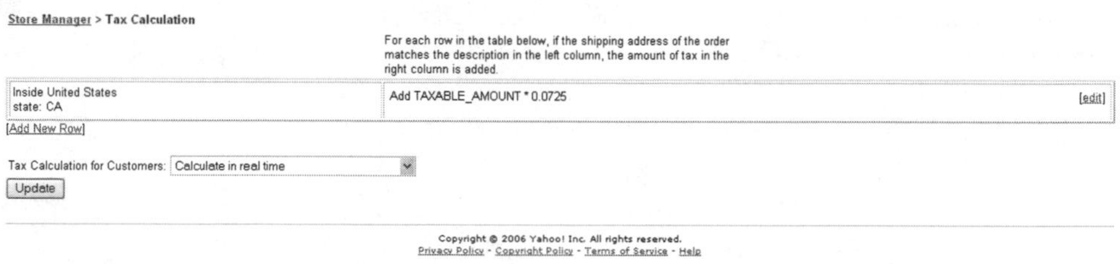

FIGURE 20-8   Setting up tax rates is simple through the Yahoo Store Manager

1. In Store Manager, click the Tax Rates text link.

2. On the subsequent page, click the Use the Auto Setup Wizard.

3. In the next page, the Where Are You based? element has United States preselected; click the button labeled Next.

4. On the next page is a table where you will select the state in which you need to collect sales tax (if you need to select more than one, hold down your keyboard's CTRL key to make multiple selections). Click the button labeled Done.

After completing those four simple steps, Yahoo will show you a table with the results of your selections, shown in Figure 20-8.

You'll notice that the Yahoo logic automatically captures the state tax rate for the states you have specified. Still, you may need to perform additional edits or add additional county tax rates to your settings. When you click the Update button as seen in Figure 20-8, you'll navigate to a new page, as shown in Figure 20-9, where you can make appropriate modifications to tax rate rules as they should be applied to purchases made from your online store.

When you're done, click the OK button.

Enabling Risk Settings

Finally, you'll wrap up the back-end configurations with a look at risk management. When customers visit your store, select items for purchase, and proceed through the checkout and order form process, you'll find it useful to apply certain validations prior to actually accepting an order. With the Merchant Solution risk toolset, you can screen for a variety of situations to prevent incomplete, incompatible, or even

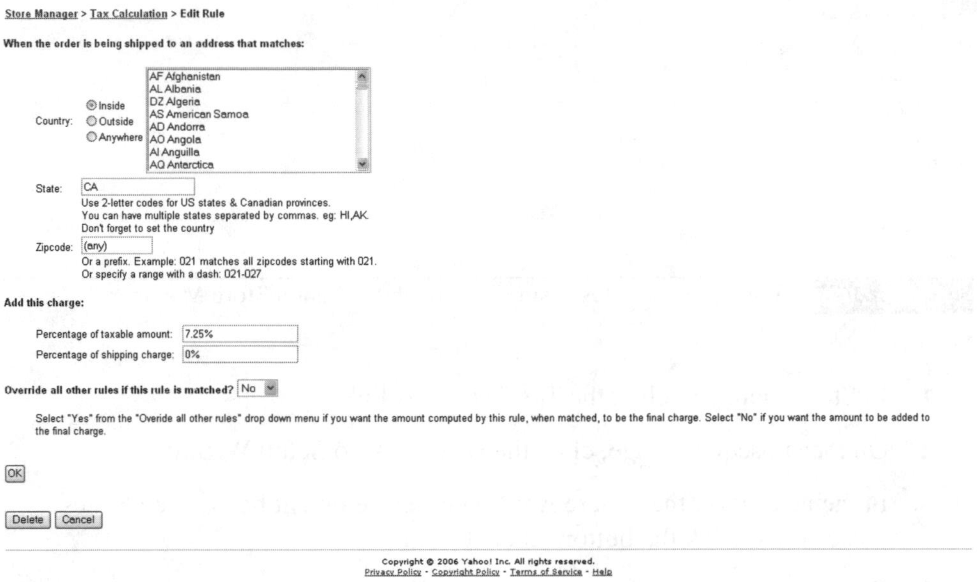

Store Manager > Tax Calculation > Edit Rule

When the order is being shipped to an address that matches:

Country:
- ◉ Inside
- ◯ Outside
- ◯ Anywhere

AF Afghanistan
AL Albania
DZ Algeria
AS American Samoa
AD Andorra
AO Angola
AI Anguilla
AQ Antarctica

State: CA
Use 2-letter codes for US states & Canadian provinces.
You can have multiple states separated by commas. eg: HI,AK.
Don't forget to set the country

Zipcode: (any)
Or a prefix. Example: 021 matches all zipcodes starting with 021.
Or specify a range with a dash: 021-027

Add this charge:

Percentage of taxable amount: 7.25%
Percentage of shipping charge: 0%

Override all other rules if this rule is matched? No

Select "Yes" from the "Override all other rules" drop down menu if you want the amount computed by this rule, when matched, to be the final charge. Select "No" if you want the amount to be added to the final charge.

[OK]

[Delete] [Cancel]

FIGURE 20-9 Merchant Solutions allows you to make appropriate adjustments to tax rate rules in your Yahoo Store

potentially fraudulent orders from being processed. Specifically, you can do the following:

- ■ Enable risk tools to mark transactions as approved, flagged, or rejected.
- ■ Set an order minimum dollar value point where risk verifications will be enacted.
- ■ Configure Address Verification System (AVS) settings.
- ■ Configure Card Verification Value (CVV) settings.

TIP

In order to utilize the Yahoo risk tools, you'll need to use the new checkout flow processing (mentioned earlier in this chapter during the discussion of order form settings). In addition, you'll need to have your merchant account setup completed (indicating which payment methods you'll accept and which tool you'll use for processing credit card payments) prior to enabling risk tools.

To begin configuring risk tools, click the Risk Tools text link under the Order Settings column on the Store Manager page. When you do, you'll see a new screen, as shown in Figure 20-10.

Next, click the Settings bold text link to navigate to another page (shown in Figure 20-11) where you'll establish the following:

- **Risk Tools**   Click the check box in this section to enable the risk checking options provided on this screen.

- **Order Minimum**   Enter an order value where, when reached on a customer's order, the risk tools checking will apply. For example, if you want to verify all orders $100.00 or over, enter 100.00 in the field.

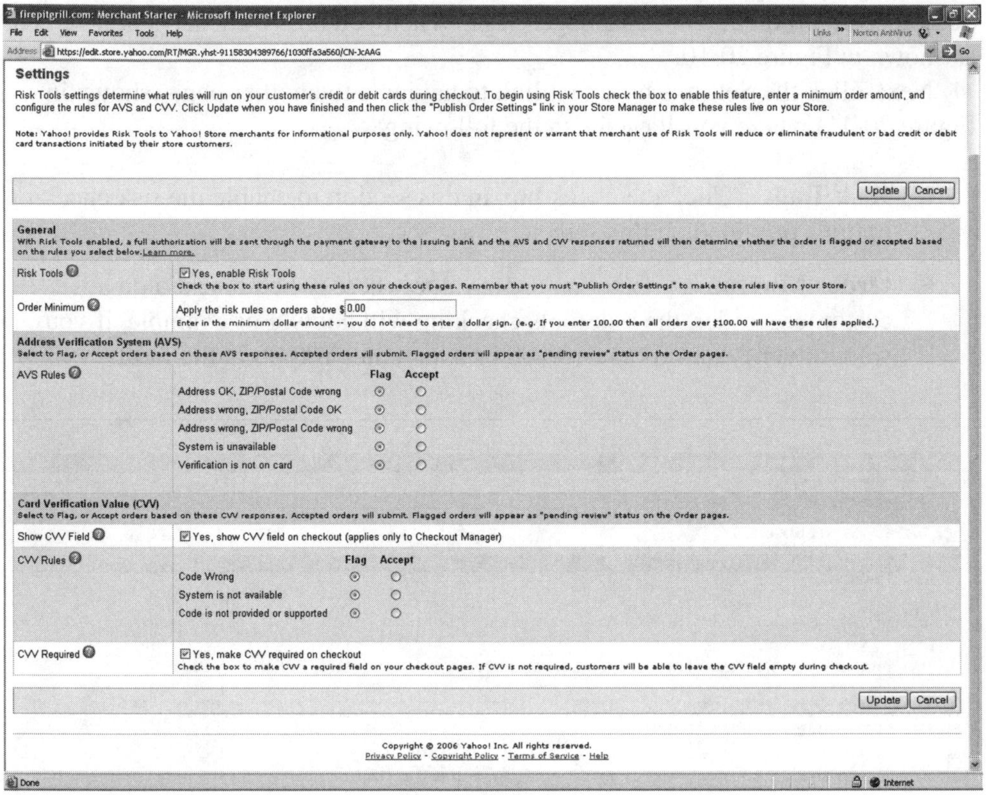

FIGURE 20-11 Use this page to establish your order risk tool settings

- **Address Verification System (AVS)** Select which AVS situations you want to check on customer orders.

- **Show CVV Field** Click the check box in this section to make the CVV field visible on your order form screen, allowing your credit card customers to enter the value when completing their order.

- **CVV Rules** Enable these rules for proper CVV verification.

- **CVV Required** Click this check box to make entry of a CVV value required. If left unchecked, your customers will not be required to provide the CVV code for their credit card.

With the risk tool settings enabled, click the Update button at the bottom of the screen. Note that, upon successful update of this screen's settings, you'll need to click the Publish Order Settings link on the Store Manager page.

With that, you're store setup is complete. Granted, there are many additional settings and options you can elect to also use, and I encourage you to continue exploring those within the Store Manager page and within the Store Editor page, too. But, for now, you've completed the minimum tasks to ready your store. In the next chapter, we'll take a final look at what you've done and run down a checklist of what you need to verify before your store goes live.

Chapter 21

Testing, Troubleshooting, and Checking Your Store's Readiness

With all that's been said and done in respect to setting up your Yahoo Store, congratulations are in order. Certainly there was much to learn, much to do, and many more options and additions still available to you to further enhance and enable your ability to make an online fortune. At this time, however, before getting too caught up in patting yourself on the back for a job well done, let's be sure that all you've accomplished truly does function in the way you want it to and, more importantly, in a way that your customers will expect it to. It's time to kick the tires, so to speak, to be sure your store will be able to deliver on its promises.

Testing the Front End

First off, return to the Store Editor and spend some time navigating around your store pages. Look very carefully at every aspect of your store content and design at this point to ensure it functions properly, doesn't lead into any dead ends (navigation pages from which there is no return), and clearly and completely conveys all your store has to offer.

> TIP
>
> *Sometimes, it's best to ask someone else to test your site for you. As the designer, it's very easy to miss glaring errors in your store content since you've been so close to its creation. And, as far as navigation goes, it's best to have someone else traverse your store to see if there are things a customer might do that you hadn't expected.*

To help you with your review of your store design, look for the following:

- **Inconsistencies in design**   Are the various page headers consistent or do they vary? If they vary, might they cause a customer to wonder if they've accidentally wandered out of your store during a visit? Aim for consistency and headers or logos or other such elements that will be present on every page, reminding the customers where they are and further promoting your store name throughout a customer's visit.

- **Misspellings**   The fastest way to undermine a customer's confidence is to have them encounter misspellings within your store. Scan for these very carefully and, when you're done, have someone else do the same. A misspelling will convey that you're not very thorough and may cause doubt in a customer's mind regarding how well you might (or might not) manage the intricacies of a secure and successful online sale.

■ **Dead ends**   As noted earlier, navigate the different buttons of your store and see if any lead you to a place from which you can't return (this shouldn't happen, thanks to the underlying design template provided by Yahoo, but you should double-check just the same). Try jumping from the Home page to section pages to product pages and back and forth. Then try creating an order and navigating out of it midway. Visit your Info and Policy pages and then try to navigate back to the home or section pages. Try to navigate in any way possible and then ask someone else to do the same. You'll be amazed at how customers will try to explore your store, often in ways you never intended or imagined.

■ **Missing content**   Check to be sure that all product information is available as you intended, where you intended.

I can't overstate the need to fully test the front end of your store before you open for business. When you're confident that you've poked into every possible nook and cranny and are satisfied with the results of your attempts to "break" your online store, be sure to click the Publish button on the Store Editor toolbar.

Testing the Back End

You'll recall all that you accomplished in Chapter 20 when you navigated and configured your order settings. If you followed the steps carefully (as laid out in that chapter and as prompted by the Yahoo site itself), you'll likely be in good shape. However, you still need to test your site to assure yourself that your customers will be able to easily and accurately initiate and submit a successful order. Yahoo has provided an excellent testing tool to help you troubleshoot the back end settings. Return to the Store Manager and click the text link Shipping & Tax Test located under the Order Settings column. This will initiate the test page, pictured in Figure 21-1.

On the Shipping & Tax Test page, you'll see you can act as the customer by entering order amounts, taxable and nontaxable, order quantities, and destination details. When you click the Calculate button, the entered values will be executed against the shipping and tax rate settings and rules you previously established, the

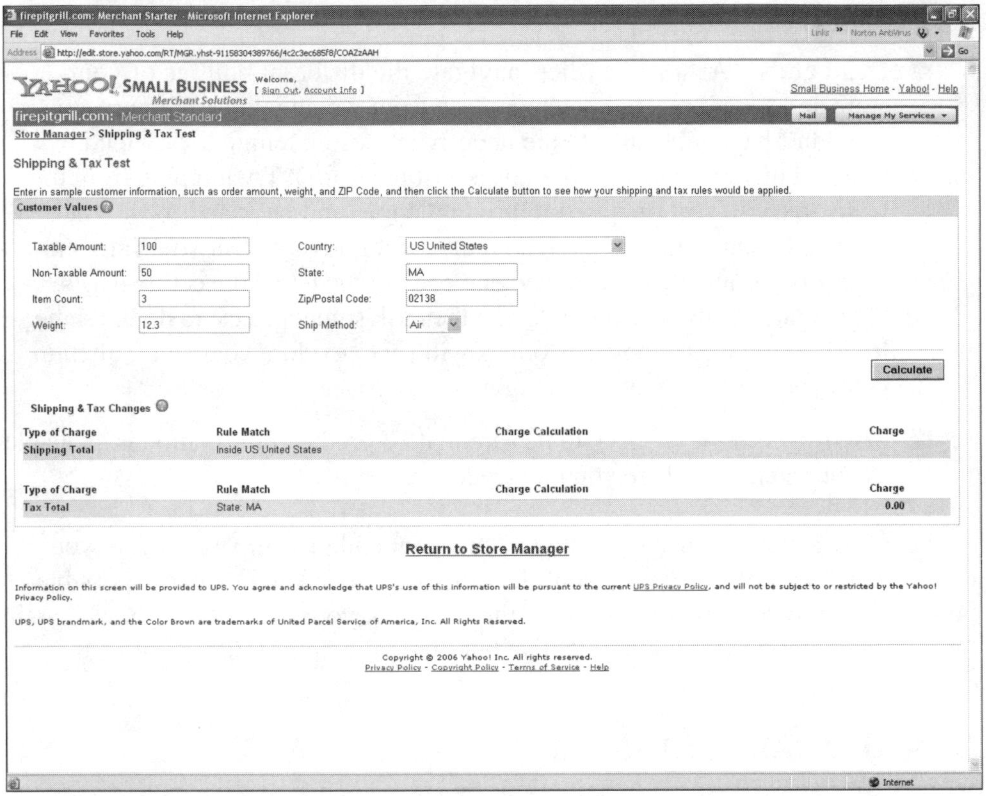

FIGURE 21-1 Use the Shipping & Tax Test page to confirm that your settings are functioning properly

results of which will appear in the lower area of the screen. Now you can review the results to ensure the final values are consistent with your intentions. If not, now's the time to return to the different areas of the order settings to make any necessary corrections before you open your store.

TIP *The Shipping & Tax Test page is one you'll likely use frequently as you manage and maintain your store. Any time you create a new shipping or tax rule, you should test it fully before republishing your order settings.*

When your testing is successful, be sure to return to the Store Manager main page and click the Publish Order Settings link to complete the process. You're ready to open your store!

One Last Check Before Opening Your Store

If you've been diligent in creating and testing the various elements of your Yahoo Store, you may feel quite confident that it's time to open your store. Well, Yahoo is eager for you to do just that, yet they'll ask you to perform one final check before you swing open your virtual doors. You may have noticed the yellow block of text at the top of the Store Manager page that indicates you need to complete and submit the Open for Business Form (see Figure 21-2).

Click the Open for Business Form text link within the yellow box and you'll navigate to the page shown in Figure 21-3.

Simply click the check boxes you see for each step noted on the Open for Business Form, provide your payment processing account specifications, and click the Save button. With that, you've done it—you're open for business! Take the time to test once more (yes, testing *is* good for your business) by processing an order or two just to be certain that all is well.

Congratulations on making it through this process. Read on to Part III of this book to discover ways to improve the visibility of your new store as you confidently march down the path to online fortune.

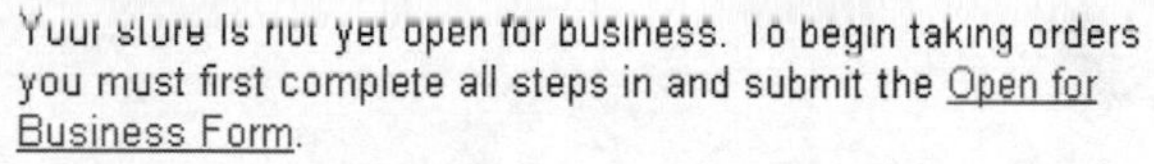

Your store is not yet open for business. To begin taking orders you must first complete all steps in and submit the Open for Business Form.

FIGURE 21-2   This block of text appears on the Store Manager page indicating you need to complete the Open for Business Form before your store can go live

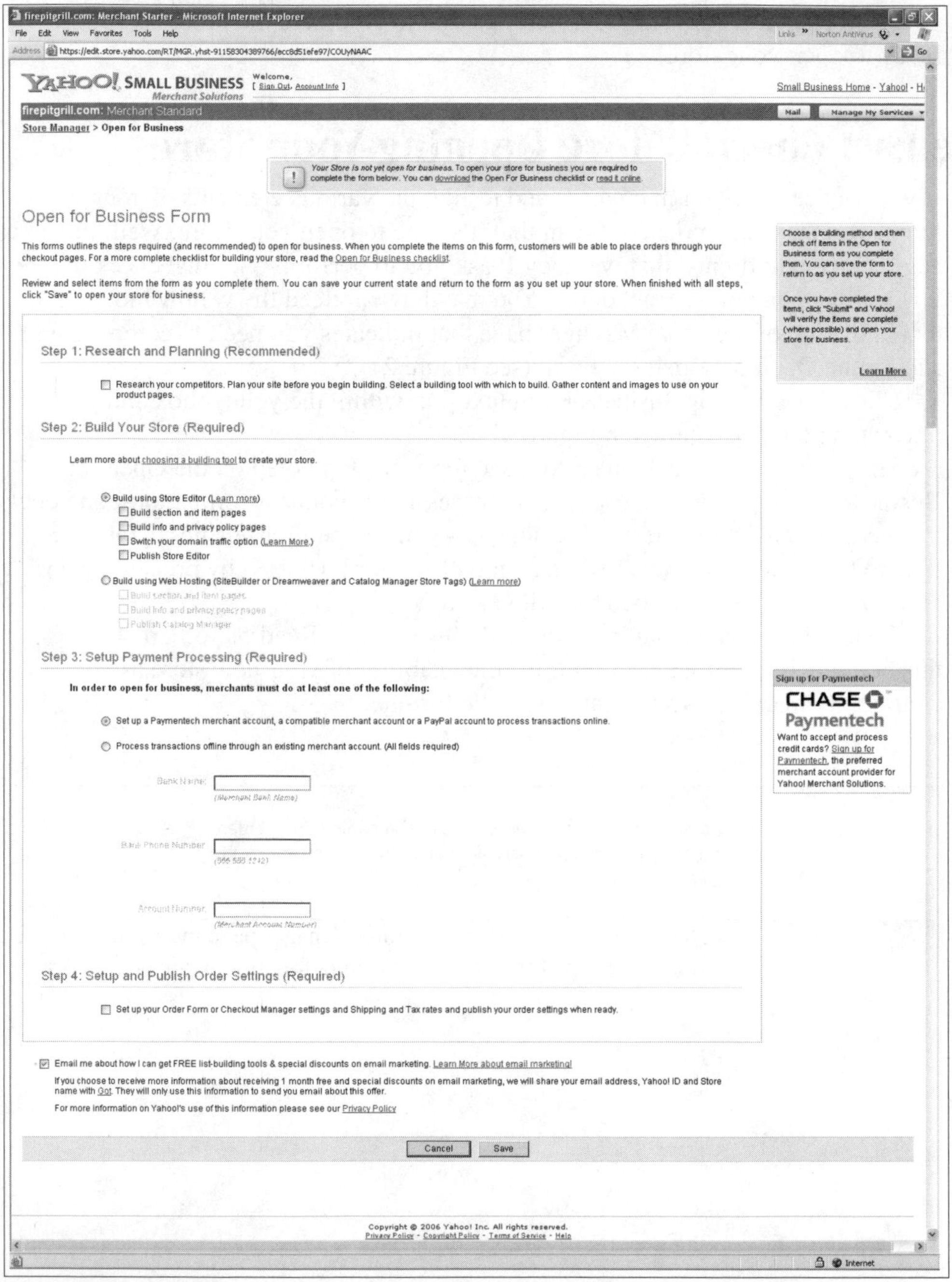

FIGURE 21-3　This block of text appears on the Store Manager page indicating you need to complete the Open for Business Form before your store can go live

Part III

Marketing Your Store

By Skip McGrath

Chapter 22

Getting Found in Search Results

You've set up your business, researched and sourced your products, built your store, uploaded your inventory and set up your payment and delivery systems. All you need now are customers.

The beauty of the World Wide Web is that you can market your products 24/7 in every time zone simultaneously—not only in the U.S. and Canada, but even around the world if you want. The problem, however, is that there are already millions of websites, with thousands of new websites coming online every day. Getting your website to appear on your customers' monitors is a daily challenge. The techniques to do this are constantly evolving. There are five basic ways to drive traffic to your site:

1. Submitting your site to search engines and making your site search engine-friendly so you come up in natural search results

2. Using pay-per-click advertising on major search engine sites

3. Using banner advertising on high traffic websites

4. Using paid e-mail campaigns

5. Receiving referrals and exchanges from other websites

We will discuss each of these techniques in the chapters in Part III.

Website Marketing Strategies

When someone sits down at their computer looking for something on the Web, they typically turn to one of the major search engines such as Yahoo, Google, MSN, or AOL (known as the Big 4 by webmasters). However, there are also dozens of other search engines used by millions of people, so you don't want to ignore these either. Getting your site found by search engines does take some work, but it is well worth it. If your website ranks high in the major search engines, it will drive tons of free traffic to your site.

This chapter will use some terminology that may be unfamiliar to you but that it helps to understand. A *search engine* is a web-based service that searches the entire web for matches to search queries. A lot of people confuse them with *directories*. A directory is a search engine that only searches through the list of sites that are indexed in that directory. Yahoo has a directory, and there are many others such as Froogle, Shop.com and so on. You can and should also submit your sites to directories.

The art (and it is an art) of getting your website found by search engines is called *Search Engine Optimization*, or SEO. People who do this for a living are called SEO experts or SEO companies.

Submit Your Site to Search Engines

The first step to getting your website (store) found by search engines is to submit your website to as many search engines as possible including the Big 4. You don't have to worry about Yahoo. When you launch your Yahoo store, Yahoo Merchant Solutions submits it to Yahoo's search engine automatically. Since Yahoo's search results feed other search engines such as AOL and Alta Vista, you are also automatically submitted to them.

To submit your site to Google, go to **www.google.com/addurl/?continue=/ addurl**. On this page, type the URL of your site and a comment such as what you sell into the appropriate boxes, and enter the unique security code to confirm you are a human doing this and not a robot (see Figure 22-1). Then click Add URL.

Notice that you only have to submit the main URL of your home page. When Google receives your submission it will crawl your site with its search robot, probably within a week or two of submitting the site, but it can take up to a month.

You can submit your site in a similar way to MSN at **http://submitit.bccntral .com/msnsubmit.htm**.

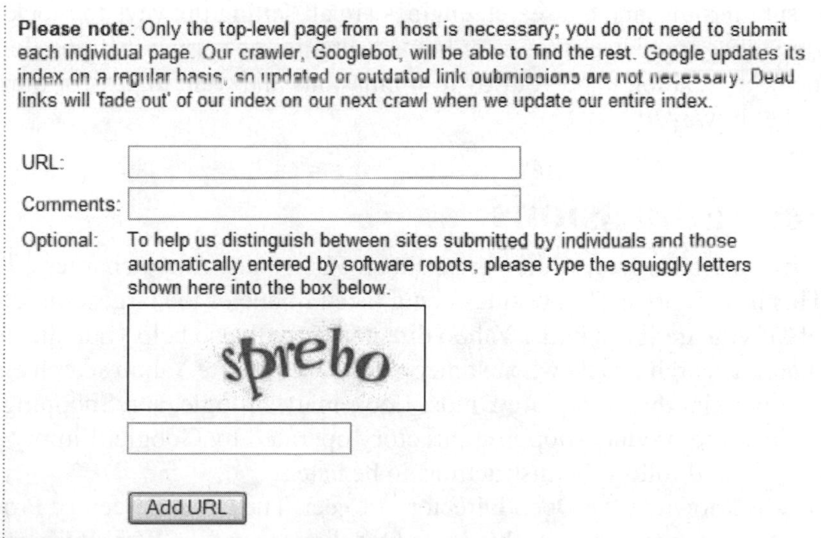

Please note: Only the top-level page from a host is necessary; you do not need to submit each individual page. Our crawler, Googlebot, will be able to find the rest. Google updates its index on a regular basis, so updated or outdated link submissions are not necessary. Dead links will 'fade out' of our index on our next crawl when we update our entire index.

URL:

Comments:

Optional: To help us distinguish between sites submitted by individuals and those automatically entered by software robots, please type the squiggly letters shown here into the box below.

sprebo

Add URL

FIGURE 22-1   Google URL Submit

Google, MSN, and Yahoo update their relevance algorithms from time to time to ensure that it finds the most relevant searches. Whenever you update your site in any significant way, it is always a good idea to resubmit your site. Don't worry about minor changes such as adding or deleting a product from your catalog. However, you might want to update your submission if you add a new product line, add or delete significant content, or make any significant changes to your site. Even if you don't make any significant changes, it pays to resubmit your site at least quarterly as Google and Yahoo do change how they look at sites.

After Google and Yahoo, you will want to make sure you submit to all of the larger search engines. These include:

AllTheWeb.com	AltaVista.com
Ask.com (Formerly Ask Jeeves)	Excite.com
Lycos.com	HotBot.com
Netscape.com	

Most of these sites have a link on their main page where you can submit your website URL. If they don't simply type **submit + site** in the search box on the main search page. For example, if you go to Excite.com, type **submit to excite** in the search box, and that will take you to a link where you will find instructions on how to submit your site.

When you do these types of searches, you will run across websites that offer to submit your website to hundreds of search engines for a fee. In general, these are robotic submissions and the search engines are all setting up ways to block them. There are other companies that offer human submission services. If you don't have the time or inclination to do your own submissions and want to pay for the service this is a better way to go.

Directory Submissions

Some directories are free, while others charge. Currently Yahoo charges $299 per year. This is a bit pricey, but besides being listed in one of the largest directories on the Web, if you are listed in the Yahoo directory it will also help your site come up in the natural search results when someone searches on the Yahoo search engine.

Other popular directories are Dmoz, Looksmart, Froogle, and Shopping.com. Froogle is a free product shopping directory operated by Google. Simply go to Froogle.com and follow the instructions to be listed.

Dmoz is known as the Open Directory Project. The Open Directory Project is the largest, most comprehensive human-edited directory of the Web. It is constructed and maintained by a vast, global community of volunteer editors. There is a link on the main page at dmoz.com to "suggest a site." Simply submit your URL and it will eventually end up being viewed by a Dmoz volunteer who will determine the proper category for your listing in the directory. This will help major search engines find your site.

Make Your Site Search Engine–Friendly

Ever since search engines became the most popular way for people to find websites, there has been a competition between the search engine companies who want to serve customers by delivering the most relevant results and webmasters who want to have their websites found. In the early days most results were based on keywords. They still are to some degree, but now other factors are also as important.

Other factors search engines use include size, content, the age of your site (older sites are ranked higher than brand new sites), how popular your site is, whether other websites link to it, how long your domain name has been registered for, and so on. Next, we will look at some of the strategies designed to take advantage of the search algorithms used by the major search engines.

Content

Most SEO experts will tell you that content is king. The top search engines look for websites that contain the relevant keywords you are searching for but rank them using other criteria as well. Rich, relevant content is probably the most important.

You may have a website where the keyword someone is searching for is repeated dozens of times, but unless you meet the other criteria; you will not come up very high in the results. Make sure your site is rich in content. In addition to your product descriptions and sales copy, create other pages with content related to your product. These can be in the form of "how to use" articles and instructions, Frequently Asked Questions (FAQs), customer testimonials, a newsletter, general informational articles, and so on. The other factor search engines look for related to content is how often your content changes. The major search engines send out robotic spiders to look at your website. If they see new content every time they visit your site, they will come back more often. This will tend to improve your position in the search results.

Use Targeted Keywords

The words a person most likely type into a search box are your target keywords. For example, say you have a page devoted to coin collecting. Anytime someone types **coin collecting,** you want your page to be in the top results. Then those are your target keywords for that page.

Each page in your website will have different target keywords that reflect the page's content. For example, say you have another page about the ancient history of coins. Then "coin history" or "ancient coin history" would be target keywords for that page.

Your target keywords should be at least two or more words long. On average, people tend to type in two- or three-word phrases more often than just a single word, because typing a single word such as coin will bring up too many results. Some search engines such as Ask.com actually favor questions. Users can type in questions such as **where can I buy ancient coins online?**

Search engines look first at the title of your page and the first few (10 to 20) words on the page. Then they look to see if the keywords are repeated in the content. This does not mean you can just create a page and repeat the keywords a number of times. The exact keyword count search engines look for is a heavily guarded secret, but most SEO experts (some of whom have actually worked for companies such as Google, Yahoo, and others) recommend a frequency of 2 to 3 percent. So, if your web page has 500 words on it, you want to repeat the keyword phrase at least 10 times on the page ($500 \times .02 = 10$). Don't stress out if you can't do this on every page, just try and work the keywords into your page's content as you create them. If you get to the end of the page, don't try any tricks such as just putting a list of keywords or putting keywords in white type on a white background, as the search engines are wise to this and may actually penalize you instead of ranking your site higher.

Create Keyword Targeted Landing Pages

As you create content, think in terms of creating special landing pages that are rich with the specific keywords you are targeting. For example, if you sell 1960s-era folk music, you might want to create a separate page for some of the more famous artists. You could create one page each for Joan Baez, Gordon Lightfoot, The Kingston Trio, Joe & Eddie, Bob Dylan, and The Brothers Four. This helps you receive more hits because people looking for folk music search for their favorite artists online.

For people searching for a place to buy a Joan Baez CD online, for example, you might want to have a page dedicated to Joan Baez with keywords such as:

Joan Baez
Joan Baez CD
Joan Baez online
Best of Joan Baez
Buy Joan Baez online

This page could have a short biography of Joan Baez, titles of all of her albums you have for sale, and other information that repeats the keywords above. That way, this page is more likely to come up when someone searches these terms than another page that lists Joan Baez along with dozens of other artists. If you were to create such a page, the list of albums that you have for sale should ideally link right to your shopping cart.

Use Research to Find Your Targeted Keywords

You may think you know the best keywords that people search, but when you perform an actual keyword research you will often be surprised. There are several keyword research tools, but Word Tracker at **www.wordtracker.com** and Keywords Analyzer at **www.keywordsanalyzer.com** are, in my opinion, the two best tools on the market.

Keywords Analyzer is a software program that you purchase for a one-time fee of $97. Word Tracker in an online service that you can purchase by the day, week, month, or year (for $7.36, $24.54, $49.08, or $245.38, respectively). You can try three searches for free at **www.wordtracker.com**. Both tools work about the same except that Word Tracker also gives you current pay-per-click pricing for your keywords.

When I did a keyword search for the term "firepit," Keywords Analyzer came back with over 90 related terms that people search for. The list is too long to put here, but here is a list of the top performing searches. The time period is one day:

Keyword phrase	Searches
firepit	2,016
California firepit	628
firepit outdoor	313
firepit table	234
copper firepit	187
firepit gas outdoor	170
firepit gas	150
build firepit outdoor	136
design firepit	109
firepit propane	109
firepit patio	108

Extend Your Domain Life

One of the things large search engines look at is the age and expected lifetime of your site. There is nothing you can do about the age, you will just have to stick around and earn your place. But you can do something about the expected life.

When you purchased your domain name you were given the option to purchase it for a specified period of time. Most people starting a new website opt for one or two years. If you purchase the name for five or even ten years, the search engines will figure that you plan to be around for a while and will give you greater points in their ranking algorithms.

Get Other Websites to Link to Your Site

One of the things search engines look for is how popular your website is in terms of how many other relevant websites link to you. The important word in that sentence is *relevant*. If you are selling kitchen gadgets and you have inbound links from gambling, dating, and real estate websites, this will actually hurt your positioning. A few years ago when webmasters learned that search engines rewarded you for inbound links, they set up or joined link farms where people traded links. This doesn't work any more.

The key is to reach out to other websites that have content related to yours and e-mail the webmaster and ask if they would like to trade links. Then simply create a page called Favorite Links where you post the link and a short message from the inbound website and ask the other webmaster to do the same for you.

Grow Your Website

Search engines reward size. A website with over 100 pages of content will be positioned in the results higher than one with 20 pages. It is not that hard to create content. Just think of subjects related to the product category you are selling and go out looking for content. For example, if you are selling kitchen gadgets, you can create pages of recipes or write little how-to articles about using your gadgets.

You can also place a review section on your website where customers can leave reviews. Another tactic is to create an online newsletter. As you build your customer list you can ask customers to subscribe to a monthly newsletter. Instead of sending the newsletter out in an e-mail, post the newsletter on a page in your website and send them an e-mail with a link to the page. After a few months your newsletter will result in pages and pages of content. Here's a tip: if your newsletter covers four topics, put each topic on a separate page. This will grow not only your total content, but the number of pages as well.

Getting Help

Optimizing your website for optimal results is a never-ending process. Eventually as you grow your business you may want to employ an SEO expert or consultant. If you take the steps I outlined in this chapter, the SEO's job will be easy and therefore inexpensive. If you don't, your expert will have a lot of work to do and these guys and gals don't come cheap.

If you do decide to seek help, this is a very competitive area and it pays to shop around. Just type **SEO** or **search engine optimization** in the search term field on Yahoo and it will come back with hundreds of results. Take your time and compare the offers, get references, and check several firms out before making a decision.

Chapter 23
Pay Per Click Advertising

In the last chapter you learned how to set up your website so search engines can find it. However, even if you do everything I recommended, it can still take several weeks or even months for the search engines to rank you high in the results. In the meantime you want to start making sales from your new store—so how do you get immediate traffic?

This is where pay per click (PPC for short) advertising comes in. Whenever you do a search in a major search engine, you will usually see either a list of sponsored results or a series of boxes down the left or right side of the search results page with small advertisements in them. On some search engines you will see both. If you look at the top of the search results in Figure 23-1, you will see three results preceded by bullets. These are not actual search results. These are sponsored results that the websites they link to paid for.

Now look at the list of results in the vertical box to the right of the page. These are also sponsored (paid) results. When a user clicks the results in bullets or the results in the table at the right of the page, they will be taken to the web page that advertiser paid for. Every time someone clicks one of these ads, the advertiser is charged for the click regardless of how long the person spends on the site or whether they buy something or not. This is called pay per click (PPC) advertising.

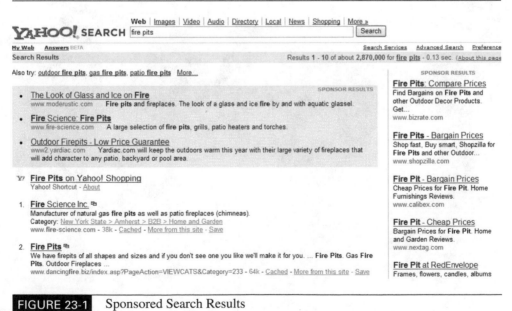

FIGURE 23-1   Sponsored Search Results

These ads are served up when someone types in a specific keyword that an advertiser has bid on. Depending on how competitive your desired keyword is, this can get very expensive, but there are some tricks to keeping your cost down. We will be discussing these as we go along in this chapter.

There are about a dozen companies who sell PPC advertising services, but the big three are:

Yahoo Search Marketing (Overture)   http://www.content.overture.com/d/

Google AdWords   https://adwords.google.com

Miva   http://miva.com/us/

Yahoo serves up advertising in two formats, both inline listings that look like search results and advertising boxes, as shown in Figure 23-1. Google and Miva both use the small advertising boxes shown in Figure 23-2.

> **NOTE**   *There is one more service I will talk about later called Shopping.com, which is a shopping comparison website owned by eBay. Merchants can list their store for prices that vary from 15 cents to a dollar per click. We will discuss Shopping.com when I cover the other shopping engines such as Froogle and Shop.com. eBay has also introduced a new shopping web site called eBay Express at www.ebay.express.com*

Sponsored Links

Santoku Knife at Amazon
Thousands of items from top brands.
Qualified orders over $25 ship free
Amazon.com/kitchen

Santoku Knives On Sale
A variety of Santoku knives, in
stock, free shipping.
www.chefsresource.com

Knife Santoku
Bargain Prices.
You want it, we got it!
BizRate.com

Santoku Knife
Save Up to 50% on Fine Knives.
Low Prices, No Tax - Free Shipping!
www.EverythingHome.com

FIGURE 23-2   Google and Miva Advertising Boxes

All three services differ in the way you select the keywords and create your ads. We will not be going through that in this chapter—it would be just too long. PPC is a subject that whole books have been written about. Each of the services, Yahoo, Google, and Miva, have excellent tutorials on their websites. As it is easy to spend a lot of money without getting good results if you don't know what you are doing, I strongly suggest you take the time to go through the tutorials before launching your campaign. What I will do in this chapter give you an overview of how PPC works, list some of the online tools that can help you, and discuss some of the strategies that make a PPC campaign successful.

Pay Per Click Pricing

Yahoo, Google, Miva, and other PPC services charge by the keyword. All three of the companies I will discuss use the auction format. The amount you bid determines your position. The highest bidder will be in the top position, the next highest bidder will be second, and so on. However you don't always pay the amount you bid. All of the major PPC services charge one cent more than the next highest bidder. For example, if you bid 50 cents for a certain keyword and the next competitor bid 40 cents, you would be charged 41 cents. If that competitor moved his bid up to 45 cents, then you would be charged 46 cents per click.

Finding Your Target Keywords

There are three major elements to a successful PPC campaign:

1. Finding the right keywords that people search for

2. Tracking conversions: optimizing your keyword budget for the best return on investment

3. Writing effective ads that get people to click

Let's look at number one first.

Finding the Keywords People Search For

Yahoo Search Marketing offers a free keyword research and pricing tool at **http://searchmarketing.yahoo.com/rc/srch/**.Figure 23-3 shows the main page where you select the various tools.

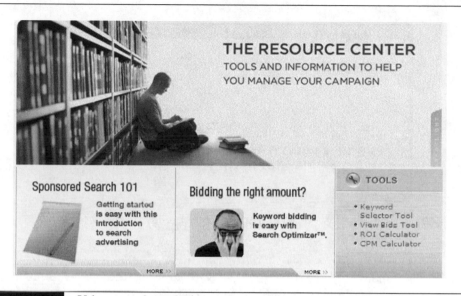

THE RESOURCE CENTER
TOOLS AND INFORMATION TO HELP
YOU MANAGE YOUR CAMPAIGN

Sponsored Search 101

Getting started
is easy with this
introduction
to search
advertising

Bidding the right amount?

Keyword bidding
is easy with
Search Optimizer™.

TOOLS

• Keyword
  Selector Tool
• View Bids Tool
• ROI Calculator
• CPM Calculator

MORE >>   MORE >>

FIGURE 23-3   Yahoo search marketing tools

If you look on the list of tools on this page you will see four options:

- Keyword Selector Tool
- View Bids Tool
- ROI Calculator
- CPM Calculator

When you click the link to the View Bids tool, you will get a page that looks like Figure 23-4. Simply type the main keyword for your product in the box and enter the security code. The results will come up in a new window as shown in Figure 23-5.

When I typed in the term "fire pit," Yahoo returned the results shown in Figure 23-5. Notice that the top bid is $0.90. (Note: These were the bid prices as of this writing. Keyword bid prices change rapidly, so you may get entirely different results if you perform the same search.) The top four results were:

1. $0.90
2. $0.63
3. $0.62
4. $0.57

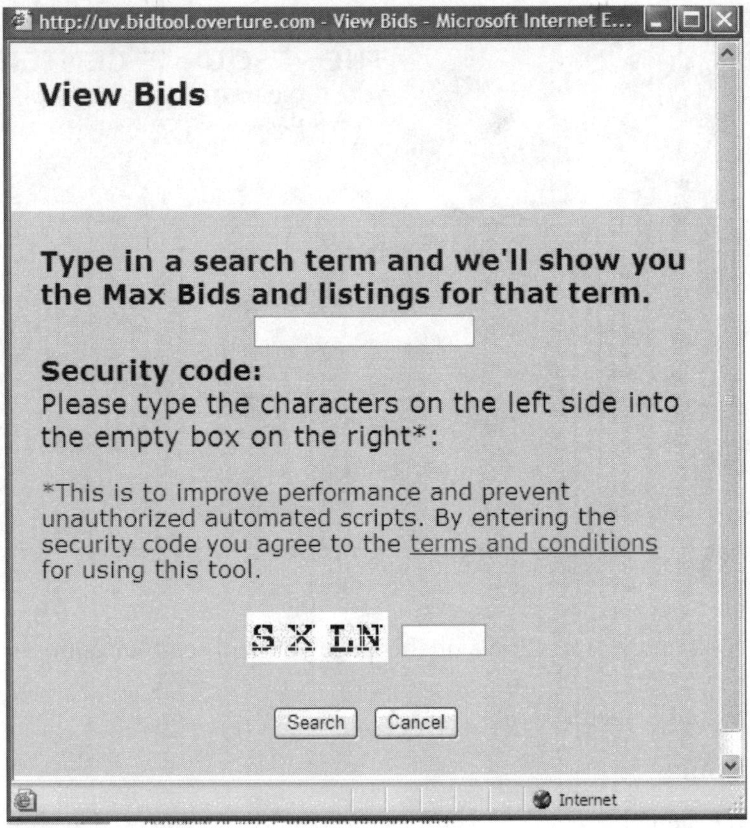

FIGURE 23-4   View Bids tool

It turns out that these are pretty expensive keywords. At almost one dollar a click for the top position you would need a pretty good conversion rate to make this profitable. For example, if your profit from each fire pit was $100 and it took 100 clicks at $0.90 to make a sale, it would cost me $90 to make $100.00.

Let's look at some other keywords that could also get us clicks but might cost less. If you go back to the Yahoo Tools page and click Keyword Selector Tool, it will bring up the window that's shown in Figure 23-6.

Type the word **fire pit** into the box and click the search arrow, and you get the results shown in Figure 23-7.

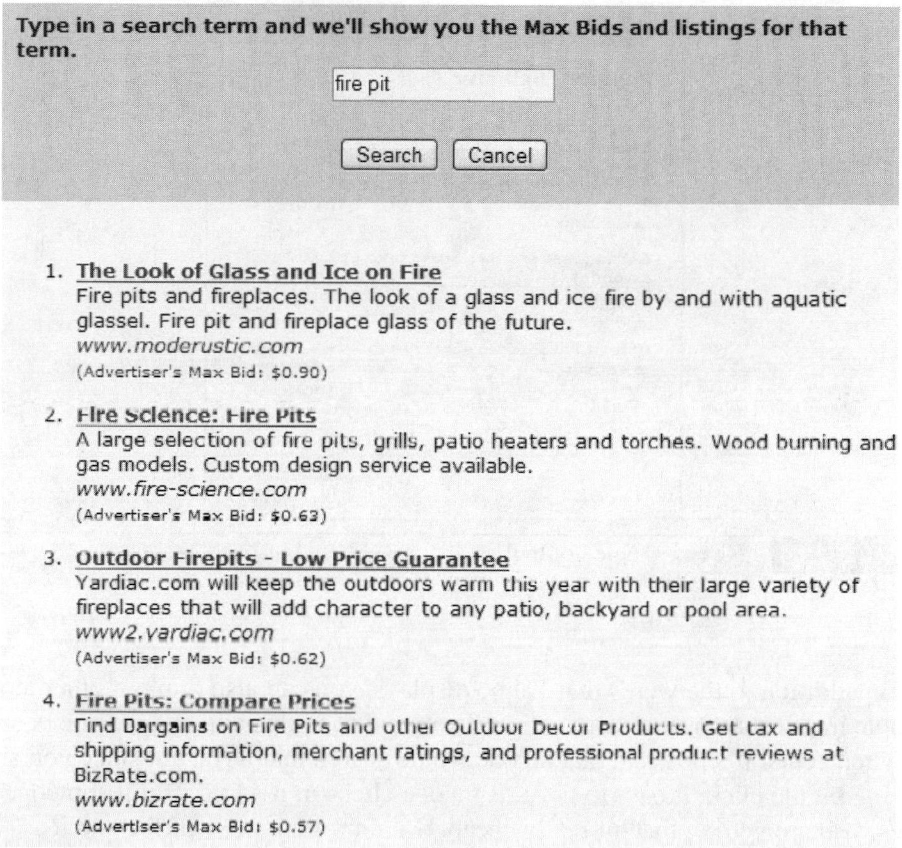

Type in a search term and we'll show you the Max Bids and listings for that term.

| fire pit |

[Search]   [Cancel]

1. **The Look of Glass and Ice on Fire**
   Fire pits and fireplaces. The look of a glass and ice fire by and with aquatic glassel. Fire pit and fireplace glass of the future.
   www.moderustic.com
   (Advertiser's Max Bid: $0.90)

2. **Fire Science: Fire Pits**
   A large selection of fire pits, grills, patio heaters and torches. Wood burning and gas models. Custom design service available.
   www.fire-science.com
   (Advertiser's Max Bid: $0.63)

3. **Outdoor Firepits - Low Price Guarantee**
   Yardiac.com will keep the outdoors warm this year with their large variety of fireplaces that will add character to any patio, backyard or pool area.
   www2.yardiac.com
   (Advertiser's Max Bid: $0.62)

4. **Fire Pits: Compare Prices**
   Find bargains on Fire Pits and other Outdoor Decor Products. Get tax and shipping information, merchant ratings, and professional product reviews at BizRate.com.
   www.bizrate.com
   (Advertiser's Max Bid: $0.57)

FIGURE 23-5   View Bids results

Figure 23-7 only shows a few results in the window, but if you scroll down in the actual window there are almost 100 different results for keywords that people type in when they are seeking information. Beside each keyword is the number of times that word is searched in a month. Some of them will not be relevant, such as *gas fire pit* (I am selling wood burning fire pits). If you look at some of the other words and terms and go back and run them through the keyword selector tool, you will see they come up with much lower bids. For example, I searched for the word *portable fire pit* and it came back at $0.57 for the top spot, with 372 hits a month. I also tried *portable firepit* and it came back at $0.43 for the number one position.

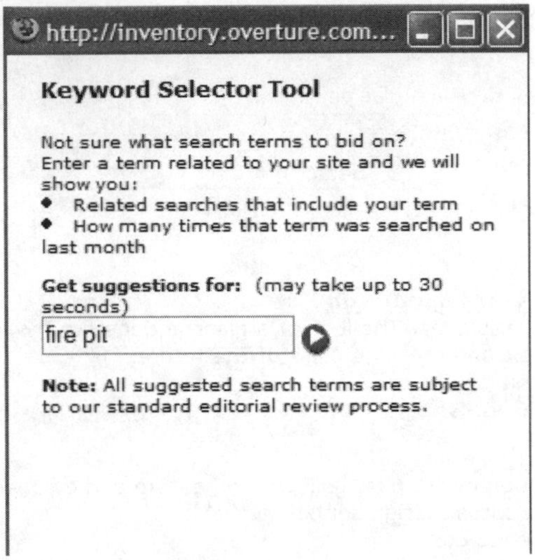

FIGURE 23-6   Keyword Selector tool

In addition to the words that Yahoo displays, you can also think of other terms people might search, such as *buy firepit online*. I tried this one and it came back at only ten cents. It's possible that no one would search that term, but since you are paying by the click, it pays to try it. If no one clicks it, it's free. But if someone does, you are getting that hit really cheap. (I did try it on my website and it returned 29 hits for the month, even though Yahoo said no one searches that term.)

Miva.com tends to be a lot cheaper than Yahoo. I can buy the base term *fire pit* or *firepit*, and most of the top variations for as little as $0.15 for the top position. I won't get as many clicks from Miva as I will from Yahoo, but I can test the various keywords there to determine which ones perform. If they are profitable, I can roll them out on Yahoo or Google with a larger budget.

Tracking Conversions

How do I know if a keyword is converting to a sale and how much that sale costs me? This is the most important question you need to ask before spending money on PPC advertising.

All three services offer conversion tracking. When you log onto your PPC service, look for a tab that says conversion tracking. Basically they all work the

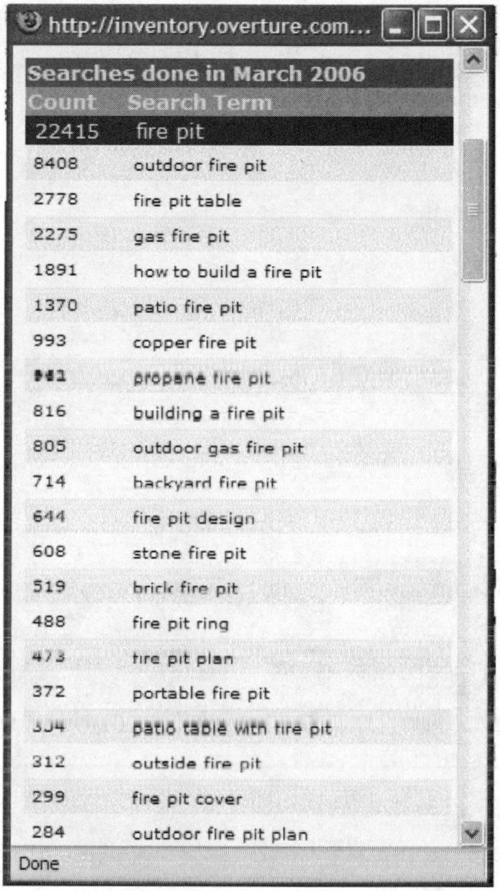

Count	Search Term
22415	fire pit
8408	outdoor fire pit
2778	fire pit table
2275	gas fire pit
1891	how to build a fire pit
1370	patio fire pit
993	copper fire pit
941	propane fire pit
816	building a fire pit
805	outdoor gas fire pit
714	backyard fire pit
644	fire pit design
608	stone fire pit
519	brick fire pit
488	fire pit ring
473	fire pit plan
372	portable fire pit
334	patio table with fire pit
312	outside fire pit
299	fire pit cover
284	outdoor fire pit plan

FIGURE 23-7   Keyword results

same way. Follow the instructions to generate a snippet of HTML code. You then paste the HTML code on the *thank you* or *order confirmation* page a customer sees when their order is complete.

This code is linked to each keyword and ad so you will be able to generate a report that shows the number of clicks on a specific ad by keyword and how many sales resulted from that action. You access this data from the Reports tab on Yahoo and directly on your campaign page in Google. Once you have your conversion data, you can really start targeting your keywords and ads.

ROI Calculator

If you go back to the Yahoo tools page, there is another link on that page to *ROI Calculator*. When you click that link a window opens like the one in Figure 23-8. I entered the following data into the window before calculating:

- 1200 clicks per month

- Average cost per click: $0.44

- Conversion rate 2% (the number of clicks that turned into a sale per my conversion tracking report)

- Average profit per sale: $80

The calculator returned the result of 263.64%. That means that I am making a profit of $2.63 for each dollar I spend on advertising. It is important that you monitor your conversions often and stay on top of them.

Guerrilla Keyword Tactics

Okay. You've got your keyword campaign running, but the big boys with the big budgets are keeping you in lower positions. Here are a few tricks you can use to level the playing field. A lot of big PPC users like to be in the top position. There is evidence that the top position performs better, but in reality anywhere in the top three is good. If you went to bid on a keyword and saw the following results on the bid selector tool, what would you do?

Position	Current Bid
1	$1.10
2	$0.55
3	$0.54
4	$0.22
5	$0.10

You could get into the number 5 position for only $0.11 or the number 4 position for only $0.23, but you really want to be in the top three. You can get into number 3 by bidding $0.55. You can't get number 2, because that other $0.55 bid predates yours.

You might think that it would be best to bid $0.56 and then to get into number 2, but that is not correct. Remember what I said earlier: Yahoo charges one penny more than the next lowest bidder even though you bid more. The first position bid of $1.10 represents that person's maximum bid, but she is only paying one penny more or $0.56 right now. We will assume this person is your competitor since she is bidding on the same keyword, so let's make her pay her maximum bid. If you place your bid at $1.09, you will actually only pay $0.56 per click, but her cost per click now goes up to $1.10—almost double what she was paying before.

Now you want to be careful with this strategy and monitor your clicks and costs closely—every day! If the other bidder is sharp and paying attention, she will go in and move her bid down to $1.08 and then who is the bigger fool? This can be like playing chicken. Basically, what you are trying to do is challenge a bully. Sometimes it works and sometimes it doesn't. I have done this in situations where the other person is not paying attention and doesn't realize what happened until the end of the month when they get their bill. Others simply give up right away, leaving you the number one spot at a good price. I have also encountered advertisers who will fiercely defend their position. So remember, if you are using this strategy, check your keyword bids and positions daily.

The inverse of this strategy is to be the PPC bully yourself. When you find a good performing keyword, even if the top bid is only 10 or 20 cents, go ahead and bid a dollar or more. New people coming in and seeing this will usually be frightened of challenging your top bid. Once again, check your bids and positions daily if you are doing this as it can really cost you a lot of money if one of the other bidders is a bully too.

Writing Great Ads

All three services give you a headline and a certain amount of text. Think of each character as a valuable piece of real estate. You have to make each character count. Your headline has to attract the attention and your text has to convince the person to click your ad so they visit your website. Remember: you are paying by the click, so you only want qualified buyers. Lookers waste your money. When I buy PPC advertising to sell a physical product, I like to qualify my clickers by telling them specifically what I am offering. Here is an example related to my firepits:

Hot Deals on Firepits

We have the lowest prices on the
web for top quality patio firepits
www.firepitgrills.com

Now what is wrong with this ad? First of all, I only sell wood burning firepits. If someone was looking for a gas firepit and clicked this ad, they would realize I don't have what they are looking for and click away. But I would still have paid for that click.

Hot Deals on Firepits

Lowest prices on the web for the best
wood burning firepit made in America.
www.firepitgrills.com

By telling the consumer exactly what we are offering, we stand a better chance of getting clicks from actual shoppers who are looking for exactly what we sell. Think like you were writing a classified ad for your local newspaper. You have to capture the buyer's attention and you want to cram as much information into the space that you have. Using power words in headlines such as *hot, new, sale, sexy,* and *stunning* will help you capture attention. Now tell them what you have or give them a reason to click your ad. And, always be as specific as you can.

Staying on Top of the Pack

Pay per click (PPC) advertising and Search Engine Optimization (SEO) are Internet technologies that are constantly changing and evolving. If this is going to be a significant portion of your marketing budget, then you will need to stay on top of the changes and keep up to date on new features and techniques as they evolve. There are several blog sites run by PPC and SEO professionals. This can be a good way to keep up to date and even post questions on the blogs to get answers to specific. You can search for the blogs on Yahoo, but here are a few well-known ones to get you started:

Duncan Perry's Blog on PPC marketing   www.payperclickanalyst.com/

Brad Fallon covers both PPC and SEO   www.bradfallon.com/

Pandia covers all aspects of SEO   www.pandia.com/sew/index.php (Search Engine News)

Even blogs come and go, so as you read this I suggest you perform a search for the latest blogs and news on these very important topics.

Chapter 24

Cross Marketing and Promotion

Optimizing your web store for search engines and using PPC advertising are probably the two main ways to promote your website, however there are other ways as well. In this chapter we will take a look at some other techniques.

Target Returning Customers

There is an old saying in the marketing game that it is easier and less costly to sell something to an existing customer than to capture a new customer. Therefore, one of the first things you want to do is capture the name and e-mail address of each customer in a database file.

There are several ways to do this. You can offer a box on your order confirmation page where people opt in (subscribe) to your e-mail or newsletter list or, once someone purchases from you, you can send them an e-mail offering them to opt in to your list.

There are several services that provide e-mail management and auto-responders. I have used an online service called Topica at **www.topica.com** for over five years and am very pleased with their service. Other large providers are Constant Contact at **www.constantcontact.com** and Aweber at **www.aweber.com**. These services provide list maintenance and management, opt-in and unsubscribe services, auto-responders, double confirmation, and landing pages where your customers go once they have opted in. Most importantly they also have the ability to manage bounces and track the number of clicks and opens.

TIP *Whichever method you use, you can build your list a lot faster if you give the customer a good reason for opting in, such as a coupon for a discount on their next purchase or a free e-book. All of the services just mentioned have the capability of delivering electronic attachments. You'll also want to capture the customer's first and last name in addition to their e-mail address to help get your future mailings through spam filters.*

Once you have a database of customers, you will need to come up with a marketing plan. If your business specializes in an area such as photography, music, fashion, sports, or hobbies, you can create a monthly newsletter on your topic. Each month, send out an informative newsletter with ads and promotions embedded in them. For example, if you sell photographic equipment, you could send out monthly digital photo tips.

If you have the kind of business that appeals to return customers, it can also be helpful to set up your shopping cart whereby the customer creates a login name and password. When they do this, their information can autofill into the shopping cart to keep them from having to re-enter their name and address each time they shop.

Link and Banner Exchanges

As we mentioned in Chapter 22 on search engine optimization techniques, relevant inbound links can help the popularity of your website with search engines. The key is relevancy. Search engines may actually penalize you for large numbers of nonrelevant links, especially those from gambling, shopping, and dating sites. If you are selling shoes online, you don't want mortgage sites linking to your website.

The best way to get relevant links is to offer to exchange links with websites that have related content. For example, if you sell shoes, you can trade links with other fashion resellers (who do not offer shoes) such as sites that sell dresses, jewelry, or handbags.

Some webmasters create a special links page that you find in the navigation bar called favorite links or recommended links. You might want to consider doing this if you get a large number of links.

In addition to links, some websites will even agree to exchange banners. If this appeals to you, you will need to design several banner sizes so a webmaster can select the one that fits the site. Some popular banner sizes are

- Horizontal banner: 468 × 60 pixels

- Horizontal ½ banner: 234 × 60 pixels

- Skyscraper: 120 × 600 pixels

- Square: 125 × 125 pixels

When you design your banners, stick with basic designs in common or neutral colors such as gray and beige so they will easily fit with other website color schemes. Stick with static banners and avoid animation because a lot of webmasters don't like that.

You might wonder why I haven't mentioned paid banner advertising. You can purchase banner impressions from several online advertising agencies. When banners first started this was a pretty good way to advertise, but so many large companies are doing this that banner advertising has lost its effectiveness and the cost per thousand impressions (cpm) is quite high compared with other targeted types of advertising. Additionally, the traffic is not very targeted. You pay for every impression regardless of where it appears. By exchanging banners, you can control where they appear. If you sell kitchen gadgets, a banner on a recipe site is far more effective than a banner that appears on a political wonk website. When it comes to paying for advertising, I would much rather pay for a click than an impression any day.

Permission-Based Marketing Campaigns

A lot of website owners are reluctant to use mass e-mail marketing because they confuse it with spam. Spam is the sending of unsolicited e-mails to mass lists. E-mail marketing is sending advertising e-mails to potential customers who have agreed to receive them. The current name for this type of marketing is *permission-based marketing*. In a sense, when you collect the name of a customer who agrees to receive e-mail, that is permission-based marketing. This is fine for selling to your customers, but what about finding new customers? You either have to rent lists from a broker (very dangerous in my opinion), or employ the services of a permission-based marketing company.

The marketing company gets more than a name and e-mail address. Each prospect fills out an online form that lists their personal demographics and areas of interest. The customer is then sent another form that asks their permission to send them marketing messages. There is usually an incentive for doing this such as prizes, coupons, or other offers.

There are a number of permission-based marketing companies that provide this service. These companies don't sell or rent the names. Instead, you construct the e-mail and they e-mail the offer for you.

In my experience, this type of campaign works best if you have a highly targeted list that is directly relevant to your marketing message.

Be careful when selecting a company to work with. I worked with one company, Estrela Marketing. They billed themselves as one of the largest permission-based email marketing companies in the country. It turned out it was just a scam. I spent $2,000 with them and they never produced a single email. The best advice I can give you about picking a company is to make sure they have a list that meets your target audience and to get their references and check them.

Affiliate Marketing

Affiliate marketing programs are hot; they are the most used and fastest-growing marketing technique on the web today. Even large companies such as Wal-Mart and The Sharper Image use affiliate marketing. Before getting into website marketing, I spent many years as a commission-based sales person and later managing commission-only sales forces. Affiliate marketing is the web version of hiring an army of commission-based sales people. The way it works is very simple. An affiliate is someone with a website or a large mailing list. The affiliate signs an agreement with you to market your products in return for a commission on the sale.

Obviously, you are thinking that this sounds like a lot of work. How would you track all the sales and pay the affiliates? Fortunately, there are a number of companies that do all of this for you. Here is a list of some of the largest affiliate management companies and their websites:

Adzoogle	**www.adzoogle.com**
Campaign Street	**www.campaignstreet.com**
Commission Junction	**www.cj.com**
Kolimbo	**www.kolimbo.com**
Link Share	**www.linkshare.com**
Partner Weekly	**www.partnerweekly.com**

Commission Junction is the largest of the affiliate management companies listed here, but it's also the most disliked by affiliates due to their complex and nonuser-friendly site. They are also the most expensive: their fee schedule is steep and the cost to start a program can easily go over $5000. Kolimbo is one of the fastest-growing services, is well-loved by affiliate advertisers, and has very reasonable startup fees.

How Does an Affiliate Program Work?

Let's get some terminology out of the way first. As someone who pays affiliate commissions you are known as a *publisher*. The affiliate who promotes your programs is called an *affiliate* or an *advertiser*. Companies like Adzoogle and Kolimbo are called *affiliate management companies (AMCs)*.

Once you sign up with an AMC, you go into their system and set up your products and commission levels. If you sell a wide variety of products at different prices, you set up a commission percentage, such as a flat 5 percent commission on all sales made to customers who were sent to your site by an affiliate. If you are selling just a few products, you can set up specific commissions on each product. For example at my Auction Seller's Resource website, **www.skipmcgrath.com**, I sell two products. One is The Wholesale Buying System that sells for $77, and the other is The Complete eBay Marketing System for $127. I pay a $13 commission on The Wholesale Buying System and a $24 commission on The Complete eBay Marketing System.

Once you set up your system, you are ready to start recruiting affiliates. You do this in two ways. The large AMCs listed previously all have thousands of affiliates. Part of their service is to help you recruit affiliates from their existing networks. The other way is to create a link on your website to a page that describes your affiliate program and lists the commissions it pays. This page should then have a link to your join page at your AMC.

When an affiliate signs up, they get access to a management page where they can grab the HTML code for prewritten text ads, e-mail ads, and banners. This code has an action that embeds a tracking cookie on the computer of anyone who clicks one of the ads. So, if I visit an affiliate's website and she has a banner advertising your website and I click on the banner, my computer will download a small cookie. If I purchase anything from your website, that cookie will tell your AMC that I made a purchase. At the end of the month, your AMC will send you a bill for all of the commissions that you own, plus their monthly fee or handling fee. When you pay that bill, the AMC will turn around and pay your affiliates.

Some affiliate programs pay two or three levels down. That is if I am one of your affiliates and I recruit another affiliate under me, I will earn an override commission on each sale that affiliate makes. People who can recruit affiliates are called *super-affiliates* and are much sought after by publishers. Super-affiliates are people with a lot of traffic to their websites and/or a large mailing list. It is not uncommon for super-affiliates to earn over $100,000 a month. At this point you might be thinking: "Forget my kitchen gadgets, I'm going to become an affiliate." It turns out you don't have to forget selling your products—you can do both. In fact, we are going to cover affiliate marketing and other ways to monetize your website in the next chapter.

Blogging for Dollars

Blogs is short for *web logs*, a sort of personal website that is more like a journal than an e-commerce website. People are hungry for information. If your product area relates to an art, collectible, sports, hobbies, or anything with a following, you can start a blog on the subject. Blogs are very simple to set up—much simpler than the Yahoo Store you just built. You can buy blogging software and host the blog on your website, or you can set up a blog for free at **www.blogger.com**, which is run by Yahoo's rival, Google. Frankly, I am surprised that Yahoo hasn't started a competitive blogging service. Blogger is free and you can create a blog and publish your first post in about 30 minutes.

Blog posts come up in search engines. The more frequently you post, the higher your blog will rank. There is also a technology called Really Simple Syndication (RSS for short), where people can subscribe to your blog and get a notice whenever you publish a new post.

A blog can help your website in several ways. First of all, you can place links in your blog to your site. This will help you win position with the search engines. Some webmasters also have a page on their website where they post their daily blog. If you update your blog frequently, you'll get additional free content that is updated when the search engines spider your site. This will give you additional points with the search engines.

So the value of your blog is that it will help your search engine position, and you can place links and ads on your blog that will (I hope) drive readers to your website where they can become customers. The other value of a blog is that it helps your credibility. This way when people visit your website they will already know you and will not be hesitant to purchase from you.

Driving Traffic from Offline Sources

The final way to drive traffic to your website is to advertise and promote your store with offline sources. This can be as simple as a business card or flyers you hand out to people you meet, to taking out newspaper, radio, and TV advertising designed to get people to visit your website.

If your Yahoo Store is an adjunct to a physical retail store, you probably have customer lists or a way to capture customer's names for mailing and promotions. Since it costs less overhead to sell online, why not try promoting your web store to your retail customers? Once again, here is where a coupon can help. When someone buys something in your store, just throw a coupon in the bag with the receipt that gives the customer the address of your web store and a coupon code for a discount on their first purchase.

The advantage of advertising a website offline is that you don't have to "sell" in the ad. Instead of expensive display ads with product photos and coupons, I find I can drive a lot of traffic to my website with a small classified ad. At my other online store, **www.ezauctiontools.com**, I sell a line of digital photo light tents. I can take out a small classified ad in photography magazines for under $50 instead of a $4 \times 4"$ display ad that might cost as much as $2,000 and get nearly the same results.

The final way to promote your store offline is word of mouth. Always carry business cards with you that contain your web address. I like to call this the *three-foot rule*. Everyone who gets within three feet of me learns what I do for a living. If they show any interest, I give them a business card and invite them to visit my website.

Index